More Than a Plea for a Declaration of Rights

More Than a Plea for a Declaration of Rights

The Constitutional and Political Thought of George Mason of Virginia

John R. Vile

TALBOT PUBLISHING
Clark, New Jersey

ISBN 978-1-61619-631-8

TALBOT PUBLISHING
AN IMPRINT OF
THE LAWBOOK EXCHANGE, LTD.
33 Terminal Avenue
Clark, New Jersey 07066-1321

Please see our website for a selection of our other publications and fine facsimile reprints of classic works of legal history:
www.lawbookexchange.com

Library of Congress Cataloging-in-Publication Data

Names: Vile, John R., author.
Title: More than a plea for a Declaration of Rights : the constitutional and political thought of George Mason of Virginia / John R. Vile.
Description: Clark, NJ : Talbot Publishing, 2019. | Includes bibliographical references and index. | Summary: "Analysis of Founding Father George Mason's political writings and thought by a leading Constitutional history scholar, John R. Vile. Mason is primarily known for his refusal to sign the Constitution. His writings examined here, including substantial portions of the Fairfax Resolves of 1774, the Virginia Declaration of Rights of 1776, and his Objections to this Constitution of Government (1787) in opposition to ratification, have exercised a significant influence on American political thought and events. The Virginia Declaration of Rights, which Mason principally authored, served as a basis for the United States Bill of Rights, of which he has been deemed the father"-- Provided by publisher.
Identifiers: LCCN 2019028012 | ISBN 9781616196318 (hardcover)
Subjects: LCSH: Civil rights--United States. | Civil rights--Virginia. | Mason, George, 1725-1792 | Virginia. Declaration of Rights. | Constitutional law--United States--History. | Constitutional law--Virginia--History.
Classification: LCC KF4749 .V55 2019 | DDC 342.7308--dc23
LC record available at https://lccn.loc.gov/2019028012

Printed in the United States of America on acid-free paper

TABLE OF CONTENTS

Preface

George Mason's Life and Thought and this Book's Approach to It

Although George Mason was an important figure in revolutionary Virginia and in the years of transition from the Continental Congresses to the new Constitution, one of his biographers calls him the "Forgotten Founder" (Broadwater 2006) and so he largely is. What fame he has achieved is largely the result of his influence either on the Declaration of Independence, for which Thomas Jefferson rightfully receives most of the credit, or the federal Bill of Rights, which James Madison largely compiled and shepherded through the first Congress. Moreover, although some biographers have lauded Mason as an opponent of slavery who proclaimed the equality of all men in the Virginia Declaration of Rights, his record on slavery was complicated by his role as a slave owner and by his willingness to argue against the Constitution of 1787 both for permitting the continuing importation of slaves *and* for not adequately protecting southern interests in slaves.

Mason did not attend the Second Continental Congress, whose delegates signed the Declaration of Independence and have been subsequently immortalized in many books, and he refused to support the adoption of the U.S. Constitution without prior amendments, despite having spent an entire summer in Philadelphia helping to craft a substitute for the Articles of Confederation. Mason died in 1792 thus depriving him of the opportunity, which he initially refused and which it is unlikely that he would later have taken, of serving in the new government in which the generation that followed him would serve as presidents, judges, and cabinet officers.

BRIEF BIOGRAPHY

George Mason, IV, was born on December 11 (Old Calendar, November 30), 1725 probably in Fairfax County in Tidewater, Virginia, where he spent most of his early life. Mason was a fourth-generation Virginian, whose original forbear with the same name had supported the King in the British Civil War, and whose other namesakes had come to occupy positions of increasing influence. After moving to Virginia, George Mason I had begun in 1651 clearing the forests that would develop into an estate of thousands of acres and hundreds of slaves by the birth of George Mason IV who was, along with the Lees and Randolphs, a member of the celebrated First Families of Virginia.

Mason's grandfather, George Mason II had been the first to move to Fairfax County. George Mason III, the father of the Virginia statesman, drowned in a boating accident when his namesake, the oldest of three children, was only 9 years old. His education fell to his mother Ann Stevens Thomson, who appears to have relied chiefly upon private tutors. Mason also took advantage of his access to the well-stocked library of John Mercer, an uncle who was a well-respected, if somewhat opinionated lawyer (Brown 2017). Probably because he was expected to assume the responsibilities of tending to his plantation when he turned 21, George Mason did not attend William and Mary or the College of New Jersey or study abroad, as some sons of Virginia gentry did, including Mason's younger brother Thomson, who became an important figure (a lawyer and revolutionary advocate) in his own right (McGill 2017). Mason's writings show that the education he had received familiarized him with the Bible, classical writings, and contemporary political theory.

Mason married sixteen-year old Sarah Eilbeck from a wealthy family in Charles County Maryland on April 4, 1750, and they spent their first years together building Gunston Hall, a well-proportioned Georgian style brick house close to the Potomac River in Virginia that has, since 1949, been opened to the public by the Colonial Dames of America. The Mason house was surrounded by outbuildings (including slave quarters) and gardens and two rows of cherry trees on each side, which, when viewed from the road, appeared to be four solitary trees. For the inside of the house, the Masons had the help of craftsmen from England, William Buckland and William Bernard Sears, whose detailed work remains an architectural masterpiece. Mason paid close attention to his plantations, which continued to grow and prosper, and he had a strong interest in western lands, furthered by his long-time role as treasurer of the Ohio Company to which George II had given an initial 200,000 acres of land, with promises of half a million if the Company succeeded in settling 100 families within 7 years and constructing a fort to protect them (Rowland 1893, 197).

As was typical of men of his wealth and station, Mason began serving as a Justice of the Peace in 1747, became a trustee for the town of Alexandria, and was a vestryman and sometimes church warden of the Truro Parish Church. He even ran, initially unsuccessfully, for the Virginia House of Burgesses, where he served from 1758-1761 and later in the House of Delegates from 1776-1780. Although he never engaged in combat, he was also a militiaman, who rose in 1756 to the rank of Colonel, by which title he was frequently addressed.

Mason had a happy home life, fathering nine children who would live into adulthood before his wife's untimely death in 1773 after an extended illness that also brought about the premature delivery and early deaths of twin boys. Writing in his family Bible after his wife's death, Mason observed that "in the Beauty of her Person and the Sweetness of her Disposition, she was equaled by few, and excelled by none of her Sex" (*PGM,* I: 481). He further observed that "Tho' an only Child, she was a remarkably dutiful One; an easy & agreeable Companion; a kind Neighbour; a steadfast Friend; an humane Mistress; a prudent & a tender Mother; a faithful, affectionate, & most obliging Wife; charitable to the Poor, and pious to her Maker; her Virtue & Religion were unmixed with hypocrisy or Ostentation" (*PGM,* I: 482). Although Mason established close relationships with his children, they learned to keep their distance when he was in his study or absorbed in a book (Mason 2004).

As conflicts between the colonies and Britain grew, Mason shared the sentiments of neighbors like George Washington and others who believed that it was necessary to stand up for American rights. This is reflected in the draft of a letter that he penned in 1766 for publication in response to British merchants. They had urged the colonists to accept the bitter pill of the Declaratory Act, which asserted parliamentary authority to tax the colonies, along with the happy news of the repeal of the Stamp Act, but Mason was insistent that it was important that the colonists register their dissent. Similarly, in July 1774, Mason helped draft the Fairfax Resolves, which reiterated his support of the principle of no taxation without representation.

Often known as the "reluctant statesman" (Rutland 1961), Mason, who suffered debilitating attacks of hereditary gout, which is connected to rheumatism, was not inclined by physique or disposition to enjoy legislative service or to spend time away from his home and family. He spent much of his life trying to ensure his family's financial security by increasing his own land holdings and paying close attention to his farms. Although his oldest daughter took on many household tasks, his responsibility for nine surviving children after his wife's death in 1773 provided further rationale, if he needed it, for him to evade such public service.

In a letter to his neighbor, Martin Cockburn, dated August 22, 1775, Mason described how members of Virginia's convention (its revolutionary government after the Governor's dissolution of the House of Burgesses, whose members had included Thomas Jefferson and Patrick Henry) had begged him to serve in the Continental Congress. He had even observed "Tears run down the President's check" when he refused (*PGM,* I: 250). Mason did serve in the Third and Fifth Virginia Conventions, the first of which saw his appointment to the Committee of Safety and the Committee of Correspondence, and the latter of which was responsible for drafting both the Virginia Declaration of Rights and the state constitution, which Mason orchestrated, and which remain among his most signal accomplishments.

After the death of his wife, Mason wrote a will in which he included his thoughts of public service, which both cautioned against its trials but held up a high standard for those who chose to serve. Suggesting that his sons treat liberty itself as an inheritance, he thus wrote that:

> I recommend it to my sons, from my own Experience in Life, to prefer the happiness of independance & a private Station to the troubles and Vexations of Public Business; but if either their own inclination or the Necessaty of the times shou'd engage them in Public Affairs, I charge them, on a Fathers Blessing, never to let the motives of private Interest or ambition to induce them to betray, nor the terrors of Poverty and disgrace, or the fear of danger or of death deter them from Asserting the liberty of their County, and endeavouring to transmit to their posterity those Sacred rights to which themselves were born (*PGM*, I: 159).

On February 5, 1780, Mason wrote a letter to James Mercer in which he observed that: "This cold weather has set all the young Folks to providing Bedfellows. I have signed two or three Licences every Day since I have been at Home. I wish I knew where to get a good one myself; for I find cold Sheets extreamly disagreeable" (*PGM*, II, 618). On February 26, of that same year, he wrote to a cousin about how marriage had suited Mason's brother well and saying that "I wish you cou'd recommend some Widow or old maid to me; she must be tolerably Handsome tho' goodnatured & Sensible" (Quoted in Copeland and MacMaster, 1975, 208). By April 11, Mason, who was 54, succeeded in his quest by marrying Sarah Brent (1730-1806), a previously unmarried neighbor who was about 50 years old and thus perhaps qualifying as the "old maid" he had desired. Sarah's family had moved, like Mason's own ancestors, to Virginia from Maryland. The couple signed a marriage agreement that served to protect both their properties. Although Sarah came from a family of Roman Catholics, they were married by the Rev. James Scott, who was an Anglican minister.

In 1786 Mason was one of two official Virginia representatives who met at Mt. Vernon to discuss trade relations between Virginia and Maryland, in a prelude to the Annapolis Convention. In 1787, in the longest trip that he took in his entire life, Mason attended the Constitutional Convention in Philadelphia. He attended in the sincere conviction that the current government needed to be strengthened and that the Convention was the proper way to do it, and he participated actively in convention debates. Toward the end of the session, however, he was disappointed over a number of decisions including those related to slave importation, to congressional control over tariffs, to the convention's failure to set up a privy council to advise the president, and to the lack of a declaration of rights. He ultimately joined fellow Virginia delegate Edmund Randolph and Elbridge Gerry of Massachusetts in deciding not to sign the final document. The following year he went to Richmond as a delegate from a neighboring county to oppose ratification of the document unless and until amendments, including a declaration of rights, were added and other adjustments were made.

Although he professed some satisfaction with the bill of rights that James Madison introduced in the first Congress and which the requisite number of states ratified in 1791, Mason resigned his seat on the Fairfax Court (on which he had never been a very faithful member) rather than pledge to support the new constitution. He also rejected a proffered seat to the U.S. Senate in 1790, a decision that was probably influenced by his poor health.

His opposition to the Constitution broke the cordial relationship that he had retained through much of his life with his neighbor George Washington, which pained Mason.

He noted in a letter to his son John that he authored on March 13, 1789, that "I am truly conscious of having acted from the purest motives of honesty, and love to my country, according to that measure of judgment which God has bestowed on me, and I would not forfeit the approbation of my own mind for the approbation of any man, or all the men upon earth" (*PGM*, III, 1142). He remained active in Virginia affairs until his death at Gunston Hall on October 7, 1792, a year in which Thomas Jefferson visited him at his home. Mason was buried beside his first wife (the burial site of his second wife remains unknown).

Seemingly far less concerned with personal fame than many of his contemporaries, what is left of Mason's collected letters and papers fill a mere three volumes. Today, he is primarily remembered for his opening critique of the Constitution —"There is no Declaration of Rights."—and, at times, not altogether accurately, for his opposition to slavery.[1] Now honored by having a major university in northern Virginia named after him and frequently lauded for his influence on the First Amendment to the U.S. Constitution, or the Bill of Rights in general (Senese, 1989), few know Mason for much more. Fortunately, his house, which is located not far from Mount Vernon, provides tourists lucky enough to go there with further context for his

---

[1] Wallenstein (1994) correctly observes that Mason's opposition to the slave trade is sometimes interpreted as opposition to slavery in general. As Chapter 7 of this book documents, although he actively opposed future slave importation, he actually critiqued the Constitution in part because it failed to protect slavery. Ironically, one of Mason's slaves whom he listed when drafting his will on March 20, 1773, was named Liberty (PGM, I: 151), presumably a name bestowed by his parents rather than by Mason himself.

life and work. The National Park Service has also dedicated a memorial to Mason which portrays him in bronze sitting on a marble bench within the Pansy Garden near the Jefferson Memorial and surrounded by a number of his more memorable quotations.

As this book seeks to demonstrate, however, not only did Mason's conceptions of a Declaration of Rights differ fairly significantly from modern conceptions of a bill of rights, but his other contributions are also important in their own right. This book proceeds through Mason's life by examining the key documents that he wrote or to which he contributed. Although I have designed each chapter so that it can be read individually or consulted for reference, the book as a whole is designed both to highlight the central themes and the development of Mason's thought. It thus examines these documents in chronological order.

ORGANIZATION OF THIS BOOK

The first chapter that follows this preface focuses on three documents, most of which illustrate Mason's rising concern over parliamentary claims of sovereignty. The first was a plan for replevying [recovering] goods and distress for rent, in which he expressed a preference for cultivating Virginia lands with white tenants rather than black slaves. The second is a letter that Mason wrote in 1766 for publication in London's *Public Ledger* in response to merchants from that city who had essentially counseled colonists to abandon their opposition to parliamentary sovereignty in the aftermath of the repeal of the Stamp Act and the adoption of the Declaratory Act. The third consists of an analysis of Virginia charters that Mason authored in

1773 with the intention of highlighting colonial rights, undoubtedly including his own interests in the Ohio Company.

The second chapter focuses on three additional writings leading up to Mason's authorship of the Virginia Declaration of Rights. The first is an analysis of the Fairfax County Resolves of 1774, which expressed opposition to British policies. In addition to presenting what the Resolves said, this chapter also provides evidence that Mason was their primary author. The second document consists of Mason's defense of a general test oath, which he drafted in 1775, as part of his efforts on the Committee of Safety to protect Virginia. The third, which does more to illuminate his budding republicanism than his opposition to British claims of power, consisted of remarks that he made in 1775 before the Fairfax Independent Company defending annual election of militia leaders by their companies.

The third chapter examines Mason's authorship of the Virginia Declaration of Rights, which emerged from Virginia's Fifth Convention, which, with its predecessors, had replaced the state legislature, which Governor Dunmore had dismissed. This chapter highlights the manner in which this Declaration both differed from, and helped prepare the way for, later declarations and bills of rights including the first ten amendments to the U.S. Constitution. It further details how Mason, who consistently supported religious liberty, willingly accepted changing its provision providing for the toleration of religion to one, suggested by James Madison, more affirmatively granting its free exercise.

Chapter Four moves from the Declaration of Rights to the Virginia Constitution of 1776, which was also a product of Virginia's Fifth Convention. Although it cannot currently be established with absolute certainty who authored each section of this document, it is clear that Mason's hand seemed to have been its general guide. Moreover, his known beliefs are in accord with its central premises, which included the importance of separation of powers, bicameralism, and civilian control of the military, all of which are considered to be important principles of modern American constitutionalism.

Chapter Five examines Mason's major writings during the Articles of Confederation. His letters, a petition that he authored for the freeholders of Prince William County that was extremely critical of wartime measures, and an Address and Instruction that he authored for Fairfax County freeholders all demonstrate that he was highly critical of both state and congressional actions that he thought were tending either toward tyranny or aristocracy. Although these reflect his concerns over the government during this period, they also give insight to his criticism of the Constitution that followed.

The sixth chapter of this book moves from Virginia to Philadelphia where Mason served as one of only three delegates who attended the Constitutional Convention during the entire summer of 1787 and then refused to sign the proposed document. This chapter demonstrates how Mason's initial enthusiasm for a new document waned after compromises made during the last two weeks, including the Convention's decision to drop the requirement for two-thirds majorities of Congress on navigation issues, to permit the importation of slaves for another 20 years, and to reject his proposal to add a declaration of rights. This chapter further delineates the objections that Mason made during the last days of the convention and the criticisms that a number of Federalists launched against those objections.

The seventh chapter follows Mason's arguments at the Virginia Ratifying Convention in Richmond where he took a middle course between Federalists who wanted to ratify the document and Anti-federalists who opposed ratification. He showed himself willing to adopt the document but only after certain changes were made. This chapter shows how Mason's critique of the proposed U.S. Constitution expanded during the debates sometimes raising arguments that he had not advanced at the Convention and showing increased concern that the new government might lean in a monarchical or aristocratic direction.

Chapter eight examines three local issues that engaged Mason in his later years. These were Mason's concern over placement of a poorhouse within the town of Alexandria, his proposal to move the courthouse from the town of Alexandria to a more centrally located place in the county, and his opposition to a redistricting plan for his congressional district that he thought might undercut his county's representation. These works all suggest that, for all the documents he authored, Mason recognized that politics in practice did not always live up to the intentions of those who drafted them. His reservations about drawing boundaries of congressional districts show that, at a time when there are increasing concerns over partisan gerrymandering, Mason might ally with those who question whether Madison's Federalist No. 10 sufficiently addressed issues of district size and with those who believe that the principle of "one person, one vote" may not always be adequate to guarantee democratic republican government.

As the title of this book suggests, Mason has been too long remembered, and then not altogether accurately, as the primary Anti-federalist proponent of a bill of rights. He was, in truth, a principled republican thinker and constitutionalist who, despite contradictory views on slavery, was devoted to human rights and limited government. Although some of his concerns may, in retrospect, seem exaggerated, many of them would re-emerge among Democratic-Republicans during America's first party system. Others remain at the forefront of modern democratic theory.

AUDIENCE FOR THIS BOOK

There are two current primary ways to access Mason's thought. One is by reading one of his biographies, and the other is to read through three volumes of his letters and papers. Although I have found both to be highly rewarding, I have sought in this book to put less emphasis on Mason's life than his biographers and less emphasis than the editor of his papers on his correspondence. I have instead focused on his major political writings, and especially the documents that he wrote or to which he contributed.

As a student of American political theory and constitutional law, I am most interested in Mason's political and philosophical stances and on the arguments that he made for them. I have accordingly designed this book for historians, political scientists, and law professors who are interested in these topics, but I have purposely kept the writing accessible and the length reasonably short for lay readers (especially those who visit Gunston Hall and other early American historic sites) who are chiefly interested in accessing the thought of one of America's lesser-known Founding Fathers. There are numerous books, appropriate for courses on American political thought, that outline the political philosophies of James Madison, Thomas Jefferson, and Alexander Hamilton, but none that do the same for Mason. I believe that this book will help meet this need.

By clearly identifying the subjects of each chapter, I further hope that this volume will be of use to reference librarians and to others who may be seeking commentary on specific works that Mason authored. I have sought to make their task easier through the use of descriptive chapter titles and by including an index to the book.

ACKNOWLEDGEMENTS

I continue to be grateful to the support that I receive from Middle Tennessee State University and especially from my staff and from librarians, who have been particularly helpful with interlibrary loan requests. Three anonymous reviewers contributed comments that helped as I revised this book, and I am particularly grateful to them. I am also indebted to my editors at Talbot Publishing.

REFERENCES

Broadwater, Jeff. 2006. *George Mason: Forgotten Founder.* Chapel Hill: The University of North Carolina Press.

Broadwater, J. March 6, 2014. "George Mason (1725-1792)." Encyclopedia Virginia. Retrieved from http://www.EncyclopediaVirginia.org/Mason_George_1724-1792.

Brown, Bennie. 2017. "John Mercer: Merchant, Lawyer, Author, Book Collector," in *"Esteemed Bookes of Law" and the Legal Culture of early Virginia*, ed. Warren M. Billings, and Brent Tarter. Charlottesville: University of Virginia Press.

Copeland, Pamela C. and Richard K. MacMaster. 2016. *The Five George Masons.* Charlottesville: University of Virginia Press.

McGill, Kathy O. 2017. "A Meteor and a Generous Mind: The Revolutionary Political Thought of Thomson Mason," *The Virginia Magazine of History and Biography* 125: 98-137.

Mason, George. *The Papers of George Mason, 1725-1792,* ed. Robert A. Rutland. 3 vols. Chapel Hill: The University of North Carolina Press, 1970), pp. 65-72. [Cited throughout this book as *PGM*].

Mason, John. 2004, *The Recollections of John Mason: George Mason's Son Remembers His Father and Life at Gunston Hall.* Ed. Terry K. Dunn. Epm Publishers.

Rowland, Kate Mason. 1892. *The Life of George Mason, 1725-1792.* 2 vols. New York: Russell & Russell, Inc.

Rowland, Kate Mason. 1893. "The Ohio Company." *The William and Mary Quarterly* 2 (April): 197-203.

Rutland, Robert A. 1961. *George Mason: Reluctant Statesman.* Williamsburg, VA: Colonial Williamsburg.

_____. 1976. *George Mason and the War for Independence.* Williamsburg, VA: Virginia Independence Bicentennial Commission.

Senese, Donald J. 1989. *George Mason and the Legacy of Constitutional Liberty: An Examination of The Influence of George Mason on the American Bill of Rights.* Fairfax, County, VA: Fairfax County Historical Commission.

Wallenstein, Peter. 1994. "Flawed Keepers of the Flame: The Interpreters of George Mason," *The Virginia Magazine of History and Biography* 102 (April): 229-260.

More Than a Plea for a Declaration of Rights

1

George Mason's Earliest Political Writings

Although Mason successfully managed a large plantation and had accepted a number of local posts, including service in the militia, apart from his bookish reputation, there was little in his first 40 years that would have indicated that Mason would have an important influence on American political thought. This changed as the colonies confronted the Stamp Act and a series of assertions of parliamentary authority, especially in the area of taxation.

PLAN FOR REPLEVYING GOODS AND DISTRESS FOR RENT (1765)

Mason's first foray into political writing appears to have been a letter that he penned to George William Fairfax and George Washington, who were representing his district in the House of Burgesses. The document combined Mason's fairly deep knowledge of legal terminology (especially considering that he was not a member of the bar) with a concern over the institution of slavery that he would retain throughout most of his adult life—during all of which he was a major slave owner. Despite his own status as a wealthy planter, it also showed concern for members of the lower classes.

The document, which Mason wrote on December 23, 1765, was precipitated by the Stamp Act, which had led to the closure of a number of courts, who had refused to use the stamps required to certify legal proceedings. Mason feared that, in such circumstances, plantation owners would be able to foreclose on the property of tenants in temporary distress, who might otherwise have been able to go to court to get a three-month delay. He accordingly proposed a workaround whereby such tenants would be able to get a restraining order from a single magistrate to avoid such seizures.

The most fascinating part of the document is in the first two paragraphs, found in *The Papers of George Mason,* edited by Robert Rutland (hereafter cited as *PGM*), where Mason argued for the utility "of encouraging the Importation of free People & discouraging that of Slaves, which "Policy" he did not think had ever "been duly considered in this Colony" (*PGM,* I: 61). Mason believed that such an approach would have led to wider settlement and cultivation and would have been less detrimental to "the Morals & Manners of our People" (*PGM,* I: 61). He explained that "one of the first Signs of the Decay, & perhaps the primary Cause of the Destruction of the most flourishing Government that ever existed was the Introduction of great Numbers of Slaves" in ancient Rome (*PGM,* I: 61-62). Perhaps recognizing that the widespread presence of slaves in the colonies might undermine colonial arguments against British policies or remind the British of the colonial fear of slave revolts, he further observed that "tis not the present Intention to expose our Weakness by examining this Subject too freely" (*PGM,* I: 62).

Noting that leasing lands was more beneficial than working them with slaves, Mason observed that the common-law practice of allowing a landlord the right to "distrain," or seize, goods on the land of a tenant who owed him money had been moderated by statutes that allowed the tenant to "replevy," or recover, such goods for a three-month period on bond after which they would repay their debts with interest. Mason further observed that this right "has not only been exercised in this Colony from it's first Settlement, but has obtained in our Mother-Country from Time immemorial," and that "Uninterrupted life & long Experience carry with them a Conviction of general Utility" (*PGM*, I: 62). Showing Mason's knowledge of contemporary political economy, he observed that this exception had been necessitated by "the fluctuating State of our Trade, the Uncertainty of our Markets & the Scarcity of Money" (*PGM*, I: 62).

Fearing that officers might refuse "to take a Bond for Want of Stamp'd Paper" (*PGM*, I: 62), Mason offered his alternative for action on the part of a single magistrate. Arguing that his alternative "will protect the Tenant from Oppression by confirming the Indulgence the Act of Assembly formerly gave him, at the same Time that it secures the Land-lord in the Payment of his Rent" (*PGM*, I: 64), Mason proceeded to defend his alternative against charges that it vested undue power in judges (a concern that he later expressed in his criticism of the U.S. Constitution) by observing that such an action would be a "mere Matter of Form, in which the Court cou'd exercise no judicial Power" made at "the Tenant's own Request" (*PGM*, I: 64).

The repeal of the Stamp Act made introduction of such legislation unnecessary. Mason's letter shows that he never considered slave labor to be on par with that of free labor, and that he feared that the institution had a corrupting influence on political life. Although he never seemed to identify fully with slaves as persons, he was able to look beyond his own class interests in recognizing the problems of white tenants as well as fellow plantation owners. In contrast to some of his later expositions on the subject, Mason opposed what he believed to be the corrupting influence of slavery on republican government in general rather than slavery by African-American slaves in particular, and though arguably undercut by his own status as a slave owner, he did not explicitly tie his argument to the idea of white superiority.

MASON'S REPLY TO THE COMMITTEE OF MERCHANTS IN LONDON (1766)

Just as Mason's first political work was an attempt to find a workaround the Stamp Act, he wrote the second as a letter to a newspaper in the aftermath of its repeal. He dated the letter June 6, 1766 "To the Committee of Merchants in London" for publication in the London *Public Ledger.* Mason labeled the document, in his own handwriting, as a "copy" of a letter that he had "published in the Public Ledger." However, Robert Rutland, the editor of Mason's papers, has been unable to find copies of the article and thus justifiably doubts that the *Ledger* actually published it, probably because the paper considered Mason's letter to be intemperate (*PGM,* I: 72-73). Moreover, after Parliament adopted the Declaratory Act of 1766, a number of British newspapers, including the *Gazetteer and the* New Daily Advertiser, had refused to print any letters arguing for a contrary view (Chaffin 1974, 16)[1]

---

[1] Historians remain divided about whether Mason also wrote an article later published under the title of "Atticus" that appeared in May, 1769. It essentially urged the colonies to cease many of their imports including the purchase of slaves, to put pressure on the British for their acts of oppression. See PGM, I, 106-109. Even if Mason did not author the piece,

Whether it was published or not, Mason was apparently under the impression that it had been, and the letter remains significant in presenting insight into the state of his mind a full ten years before his authorship of the Virginia Declaration of Rights. It shows that he shared the sentiments of other Americans that the British were treating them like second-class citizens (Breen 1997, 29-30). Moreover it places him both among those who had already contemplated the possibility of armed conflict even before the Revolution, and among those who had continued to hope to perpetuate the existing ties to Britain.

THE MERCHANTS' LETTER

Mason wrote his letter in response to "*A Letter from the Committee of Merchants in* London, *trading* to North America, *directed to the merchants in* New York, *dated Feb.* 28, 1766." Although their names were not included in the copy that Mason read, thirty leading London merchants, many of whom would have had substantial ties to the colonies, had signed the letter. One of two publications called the *Virginia Gazette* (the one edited by Alexander Purdie), which appears to have evaded the Stamp Act (Schlesinger 1935, 78), had published the letter on May 16, 1766, likely copying it, consistent with the practice of the times, from a paper in New York. Mason sought to protect his own anonymity by signing his response as "A VIRGINIA PLANTER" and by further identifying himself as being on the "Virginia Potomack [sic.] River," rather than as the master of Gunston Hall.

---

it is possible that it expressed sentiments that he had written to Dr. David Ross of Maryland or Richard Henry Lee of Virginia (PGM, I: 109).

The letter to which Mason was responding was relatively short, constituting a mere seven paragraphs ("Letter from Committee of Merchants," 1766). Its initial tone was conciliatory. Indeed, it began with heartening news that Parliament was in the process of repealing the Stamp Act and with the anticipation of "some beneficial regulations and extensions of the trade of America, which we hope may be obtained in the course of this session of Parliament" [f's changed where appropriate here, and elsewhere, to s's; other Mason's spellings retained]. By the time that he wrote, Mason would almost surely have known that on March 18, 1766, Parliament had, indeed, repealed the Stamp Act while simultaneously adopting the Declaratory Act. This second act, which did much to mitigate the good will that the repeal of the Stamp Act might otherwise have engendered, continued to assert Parliament's continuing right to tax the colonies. Colonial leaders, citing the principle of "no taxation without representation," which they traced back both to the Magna Carta (1215) and to the English Declaration of Rights (1689), had consistently denied this power.

The London merchants had anticipated both acts of Parliament. They observed that one of the objections they had faced in seeking repeal of the Stamp Act was that if such an appeal were effected, its corresponding assertion of authority to tax would be "waste paper, and that the colonies will understand very well that what is pretended to be adopted on mere commercial principles of expedience is really yielded through fear, and amounts to a tacit, but effectual surrender, of its rights, or at least a tacit compact that it will never use it." The merchants, who were likely far more concerned with the commercial implications of the tax repeal than with what they thought were abstract philosophical quarrels about parliamentary power in the colonies, undoubtedly also thought that they had their finger on the pulse of British thinking and chose therefore to offer practical advice to their New York counterparts.[2]

The merchants accordingly advised the colonists to refrain from making the arguments that their opponents were already attributing to them. They should not "triumph on the repeal, and affect to seize the yielding of Parliament as a point gained over Parliament," lest this send the signal that its measures had been "*too weak and timid.*" If the colonies responded instead with "duty, submission, and gratitude," this would vindicate the "moderation" the London merchants had advocated and result in the regaining of "*their loyalty, their affection, and their trade.*"

Observing that the colonists had "friends . . . in the present Ministry," the merchants proceeded to explain that "the intemperate proceedings of various ranks of people on your side of the water" had made the work of such friends

---

[2] Alison G. Olson's study of the London mercantile lobby has recognized that "The merchants as a group did not concern themselves with 'politics'—the constitution and functioning of the British government were matters beyond their expertise—and they did not take up 'general issues of humanity.' It followed that they did not take up colonial matters as questions of principle, nor did they espouse colonial causes. Their job was simply to inform the government what their interests were because they were in the best position to know them" (1982, 25). Where Olson thereby emphasized the role the British merchants played in informing the British government of colonial concerns, the letter of the London merchants to their New York counterparts emphasizes the manner in which they also sought to inform the colonists of British sentiments and interests.

In time, American political movements would become more closely aligned with similar movements, especially those involving John Wilkes, within Britain. See Sainsbury 1978.

difficult. Although the colonists might have taken pride in the convening of the Stamp Act Congress in New York, the British merchants were undoubtedly thinking of rioting in Boston and other cities, the forced resignation of customs officials, and the burning of the home of the Massachusetts Lieutenant Governor, Thomas Hutchinson (Taylor 2016, 94-104). The merchants thought that by "their violence, in word and action," the colonists had "awakened the honour of Parliament, and thereby involved every friend of the repeal in the imputation of betraying the dignity of Parliament." This had effectively forced Parliament to adopt the Declaratory Act along with the repeal of the Stamp Act.

Undoubtedly with a view firmly fixed on the financial bottom line, the London merchants therefore advised their New York counterparts that "If . . . you would make the proper returns to your country, if you have a mind to do credit to your friends, and strengthen the hands of your advocates, hasten, we beseech you, to express filial duty and gratitude to your parent country." Should the colonists interpret the repeal of the Stamp Act as a capitulation to the principle of parliamentary taxation, "then indeed your enemies here will have a complete triumph; your friends must certainly lose all power to serve you; your taxmasters probably [will be] restored, and such a train of ill consequences follow as are easier for you to imagine than for us to describe." Expressing confidence that the colonial merchants would exert their influence to facilitate such filial duty, they declared themselves to be "your affectionate humble servants."

MASON'S CRITIQUE

As a leading planter whose livelihood depended on exporting tobacco and other agricultural products and whose quality of life was enhanced by the goods that he was able to purchase from Britain, Mason might well have ignored this letter. After all, the London merchants had not addressed it to Virginia planters but to New York merchants. Moreover, its authors were arguably less interested in debating arguments over Parliament's power to tax the colonies than in offering practical, if somewhat condescending, advice as to how the colonies could continue to stay on the good side of the present ministry.

However, Mason understood that the letter "tho' addressed to a particular Set of men," was "intended for the Colonys in general" (*PGM*, I: 65). Moreover, Mason was likely insulted by what he considered to be the letter's clear subordination of political principles to business considerations. Exercising "the Right of a Freeman," Mason immediately indicated his irritation over how the British so often considered themselves as parents of colonial children, with the prerogative to exercise "the authoritative Style of a Master to a School-Boy" (*PGM*, I: 65). Mason paraphrased the London letter in a long paragraph mimicking words of parents or a schoolmaster seeking to shame such a youngster. In arguments that presaged Thomas Paine's observation in *Common Sense* that "there is something very absurd in supposing a continent to be perpetually governed by an island" (1953, 26), Mason further identified such an approach as "ridiculous, when applied to three Millions of us loyal & useful Subject as any in the British Dominions, who have been only contending for their Birth-right, and have now only gained, or rather kept, what cou'd not, with common Justice, or even Policy, be denyed [sic.] them." (*PGM*, I: 66).

By referencing his own status as a "freeman," and referring to a "Birth-right," Mason was indicating that he and his fellow colonists had the same rights as other Englishmen. If the Declaratory Act asserted "unjust, oppressive, or unconstitutional Principles," then it deserved to be treated as "waste paper" (*PGM*, I: 66). Noting that "the greatest & wisest Men in the Nation" had made "a just & necessary Distinction between Legislation & Taxation" (*PGM*, I: 66), Mason thought that it was possible to accept the former without conceding power over the latter. Claiming therefore to recognize "the supreme Authority of Great Britain over her Colonys [sic.],"[3] Mason himself seemed to take on the role of a school master by counseling the London merchants that "it is a Power which a wise Legislature will exercise with extreme Tenderness & Caution, and carefully avoid the least Imputation or Suspicion of Partiality" (*PGM*, I: 67).

Indicating that colonial grievances extended far beyond questioning the right of Parliament to tax them, Mason accused the British of denying colonists "the Ancient Tryal [sic.], by a Jury of our Equals" (*PGM*, I: 67). In accusations that Jefferson later echoed in the Declaration of Independence, Mason further noted that British laws permitted American Freemen to be transported a thousand miles away to be tried by a civil court created by the Ministry and therefore lacking

---

[3] I cannot ascertain with certainty whether Mason had arrived at the point, which the colonists would take fairly consistently up to the Declaration of Independence, where he is consciously distinguishing "the supreme Authority of Great Britain," arguably exercised by the King with respect to external matters, rather than by the Parliament, or not, but the language is certainly consistent with such a view.

independence, on mere "*probable* Cause of Complaint,"[4] potentially reducing them "from Opulence to Indigence" in the process (*PGM*, I: 67).

Questioning whether "the Foundations of the State" can "be saped, & the Body of the People remain unaffected," Mason warned that "Incroachments" against the colonies could become "Precedents" against themselves" (*PGM*, I: 67). Further moving from issues of taxation to issues of trade, Mason questioned the wisdom of British commercial regulations that prohibited the colonies from exporting goods that "she does not want" and from importing goods that "she does not produce or manufacture" (*PGM*, I: 67). Perhaps seeking to emphasize common Protestant ties with Britain, Mason likened such laws to an Italian regulation requiring people to sour their wine in order to promote the sale of sweeter wine by Roman Catholic Convents.

In writing the Declaration of Independence, Thomas Jefferson later noted that the colonists had previously appealed to their common "sanguinity" with Englishmen. In similar fashion and even more intimate language, Mason observed that the colonists were "fellow-Subjects." They were "nurtured in the same Principles of Freedom; which we have both suck'd in with our Mother's Milk: that in crossing the Atlantic Ocean, we have only changed our Climate, not our Minds, our Natures & Dispositions remain unaltered; that We are still the same People with them"

[4] Note that Mason is not thereby insisting on probable cause for search warrants (a subject of today's Fourth Amendment), but on the insufficiency of such probable cause as a reason for transporting Americans to foreign shores for trial.

(*PGM*, I: 68).[5] As if reversing British condescension toward the colonists, Mason noted, consistent with his enduring reputation for republicanism, that, unlike the British, the colonists were "not yet debauched by Wealth, Luxury, Venality, & Corruption" (*PGM*, I: 68), and that the colonists' less than grateful response to the repeal of the Stamp Act was thus justified.

Demonstrating the depth of his sentiments with respect to the evils of parliamentary taxation, Mason thought that slavery would be no better if the British Parliament inflicted it on the colonies than if "a Turkish Divan" (*PGM*, I: 68) were to do so.[6] In reference to the warning that, if the colonists did not prove to be obsequious enough, "our Task-Masters will probably be restored,"[7] Mason minced no words. If the reference were to "Stamp-Officers," those who learned their lessons about the depth of colonial opposition would hardly want to return, whereas if the reference were to the "Stamp-

---

[5] Rutland, the editor of Mason's papers (PGM, I: 72), noted that the first part of this sentence appears to be a paraphrase of Horace's thoughts in his *Epistles*, (I, xi) that "Not their own passions, but the climate changed." With due deference to Horace's reputation, in my judgment, Mason's sentiments on this topic are more elegantly expressed than Horace's, at least in translation.

[6] In his Extracts from the Virginia Charters, Rush later said that an action by the British Ministry was more typical of "the Divan at Constantinople" (PGM, I: 178, n. 13).

[7] The letter from London merchants printed in the *Virginia Gazette*, while not easily read, at least not on-line, used the word "taxmaster." I do not know whether this was itself an error, which Mason sought to correct in his re-quotation, or whether Mason consciously substituted the word "Task-Masters," which better fit the parallel that he was drawing between British policies and slavery, and perhaps to the treatment of the Israelites by the Pharaohs.

Ministry," then "we despise them too much to fear them" and their "Clovenfoot" (*PGM*, I: 68).

As the passion of his language increased, Mason speculated as to whether the British would have followed the ministry in enforcing the Stamp Act through military force. As if to deter such a move, he pointed out that it would take many troops to enforce British will 2000 miles away. As he phrased it, "Three Millions of People driven to Desperation are not an Object of Contempt" (*PGM*, I: 68).[8]

Almost as if answering the choice between gratefulness and stubbornness that the British merchants had posed, Mason observed that "America, however weak in herself, adds greatly to the Strength of Great Britain, which wou'd be diminished in Proportion by her Loss" (*PGM*, I: 68). Mason offered his own caution and prospects of grandeur to the London merchants: "with prudent Management, she [America] might become an impenetrable Bulwark to the British Nation, and almost enable it to stand before the Stroke of Time" (*PGM*, I: 68).

Further pressing the possibility that conflict over the Stamp Act could have broken out into full-scale war, Mason asked "Cou'd you have destroyed us without ruining yourselves?" (*PGM*, I: 69). Pointing to the debts that Americans owed to the British, Mason observed that "there is no determinate End to this Commercial Chain; break but one

---

[8] In essay No. 106 "Of Plantations and Colonies," dated December 8, 1722, John Trenchard and Thomas Gordon, whose *Cato's Letters* were widely read in the colonies, had observed that "Force can never be used effectually to answer the end, without destroying the colonies themselves. Liberty and encouragement are necessary to carry people thither, and to keep them together when they are there; and violence will hinder both" (II, 750). The editor of Mason's Papers (PGM, I: 73), labels this essay as No. 67.

Link of it, and the whole is destroyed" (*PGM,* I: 69). He reinforced this image with analogies to "a Set of Nine Pins" and a bursting bubble (*PGM,* I: 69).

Praising God that such evils had, at least for the moment, passed, Mason expressed additional thanks to "our most gracious Sovereign," to "the present & prudent Temper of Parliament," to "the wise & honest Conduct of the present Administration," to "the unwearied Diligence of our Friends the British Merchants, & Manufacturers," to "the Unanimity of the Colonys [sic.] themselves," and to Prime Minister Pitt (*PGM,* I: 69). Comparing the policies of Prime Minister George Grenville, who had advocated the Stamp Act, to the foolishness of Pericles in engaging Athens in the disastrous Peloponnesian War, Mason sought to reassure British merchants by portraying America as an agricultural partner rather than as a commercial competitor: "Our Land is cheap and fresh, we have more of it than we are able to employ; while we can live in Ease & Plenty upon our Farms, Tillage, & not Arts, will engage our Attention" (*PGM,* I: 69). In such circumstances, trade between America and Britain would continue to flourish: "Until you lay Us under a necessity of shifting for ourselves, You need not be afraid of the Manufactures of America" (*PGM,* I: 70). Mason further observed that "It is by Invitations & Indulgence, not by Compulsion, that the Market for British Manufactures is to be kept up, & increased in America" (*PGM,* I: 70).

For Mason freedom was of one cloth. Foreshadowing his later defense of religious liberty, he thus seamlessly observed that seeking the British effort to control the market was "as ineffectual, as destructive of the End it aims at, as Persecution in Matters of Religion, which serves not to extinguish, but to confirm the Heresy" (*PGM,* I: 70). Pointing out that "there is a

Passion natural to the Mind of Man, especially a free Man, which renders him impatient of Restraint," Mason predicted that having tasted liberty, Americans would never submit to "Oppression," and that "Such another Experiment as the Stamp-Act wou'd produce a general Revolt in America" (*PGM,* I: 70). Citing developments elsewhere, Mason sagely doubted that other European powers would stand by as Britain crushed the colonies, while hoping that "the Union, Liberty, and mutual Happiness of Great Britain, & her Colonys [sic.] may continue, uninterrupted, to the latest Ages!" (*PGM,* I: 70).

Recognizing that "America has always acknowledged her Dependence upon Great Britain," which was sustained by both "Interest" and "inclination," Mason drew some careful distinctions. These would become even more familiar in the years ahead as the gulf between the colonies and Britain widened. He thus asserted that America had been settled, "not at the Expence, but under the Protection of the English Government," while acknowledging "that Protection & Allegiance are reciprocal Dutys" (*PGM,* I: 70).

In 1776, the colonists would declare their independence on the basis of natural rights, but in his letter, Mason sought to "claim Nothing but the Liberty & Privileges of Englishmen, in the same Degree, as if we had still continued among our Brethren in Great Britain" (*PGM,* I: 71). In words that the Constitution would later echo, Mason further hoped to "transmit" such rights "unimpaired to our Posterity" (*PGM,* I: 71). After asking whether America's friends could expect concessions that would lead to loss of liberty, he quoted five lines of verse:

—If I cou'd find Example
Of thousands, that by base Submission had
Preserv'd their Freedom, I'd not do't; but since
Nor Brass, nor Stone, nor Parchment bears not one;
    Let Cowardice itself forswear it.—[9]

Pointing out that "Our Laws, our Language, our Principles of Government, our Inter-marriages, & other Connections, our constant Intercourse, and above all our Interest, are so many Bands which hold us to Great Britain," Mason opined that they could only be broken "by Tyranny and Oppression" (*PGM,* I: 71). Rather than "open the wounds," Mason hoped for healing (*PGM,* I: 71).

MASON'S SELF-DESCRIPTION

Having delivered himself of his sentiments, Mason illumined his own station in life as he attempted to establish his own bona fides. Noting that he spent "most of his Time in

---

[9] The editor of Mason's papers was unable to identify this quotation, but with the help of my colleague, Dr. Philip Phillips, I have been able to find that it comes close to the lines from William Shakespeare's *Winter's Tale,* Act I, Scene 2, lines 357-363, p. 1247 in *The Complete Works,* ed. by Stanley Wells and Gary Taylor. Oxford: Clarendon Press, 1986:

> . . . If I could find example
> Of thousands that had struck anointed kings
> And flourished after, I'd not do't. But since
> Nor brass, nor stone, nor parchment bears not one,
> Let villainy itself forswear't.

I cannot tell if Mason purposely altered the lines, to redirect them from the evil consequences likely to come from challenging kings to the consequences of seeking to preserve freedom through "submission," or whether he simply quoted the lines somewhat incorrectly from memory.

Retirement," rarely "meddled in public Affairs," enjoyed "a moderate but independent Fortune," and was "content with the Blessings of a private Station," Mason identified himself as an American-born Englishman and as a supporter of the British throne who abhorred Jacobitism—those who had supported restoration of the Roman Catholic Stuart line of James II (*PGM*, I: 71).

Just as Thomas Jefferson would later claim in a letter of May 8, 1825 to Henry Lee that, while not copied from previous works, he intended the Declaration of Independence to be "an expression of the American mind," so too, Mason denied that he was "singular in this my Political Creed" (*PGM*, I: 72). Instead, he said that his sentiments were "the general Principles of his Majesty's Subjects in America," which he attributed to "more than nine-tenths of the People who have been so basely misrepresented to you" (*PGM*, I: 72).[10]

Eschewing any desire to answer anyone who might wish to respond, Mason said that he was disinclined "to turn Author" (*PGM*, I: 72). He was content to let the chips fall where they might, either in vindication or in correction as to any errors, and listed himself as "Your most obdt. Sevt, A VIRGINIA PLANTER." This term arguably emphasized a class dimension that might have distinguished Mason from other Virginia freemen, but would likely evoke greater notice from London merchant than if it had originated from a small farmer.

---

[10] I know of no way of ascertaining whether Mason was correct, but he may well have either overestimated the degree to which his views were representative or overstated his case. Alison G. Olson thus notes that in 1766, "only fifteen of the thirty politically involved Virginia merchants signed a petition to the House of Lords for repeal of the Stamp Act" (1983, 383).

Analysis

Mason's letter demonstrates the manner in which he and fellow planters (Breen 1997) thought that British elites were treating them condescendingly and violating the rights that they had brought with them to the New World. Although Mason professed that he and his compatriots remained loyal to the British King, he already had contemplated the possibility that continuing oppression could lead to revolution. Although they were bound by strong ties of language and consanguinity, the colonists had their pride, and the ties to the mother country could be cut by continuing acts of oppression.

Mason's Extracts from Virginia Charters (1773)

Mason was not a lawyer, but he was considered to be a good legal draftsman for constitutional provisions. One credential that would have furthered this reputation would have been his knowledge of colonial charters, which were arguably among the closest predecessors to the written constitutions that the states would later formulate (Lutz 1988). Sometime in 1773, probably in or near the month of July, Mason copied and annotated extracts from Virginia Charters, which he seems largely to have borrowed from William Stith's *History of the First Discovery and Settlement of Virginia,* which was first published in 1747, and from *Acts of Assembly,* which were published in 1733, 1752, and 1769 (*PGM,* I: 183-884).

Mason's manuscript was titled "Extracts from the Virginia Charters with some Remarks on them made in the year 1773" from the handwriting of a copyist found in the Bancroft Collection. The editor of Mason's papers suggests that "It was probably written for the perusal of certain members of the General Assembly in the hope that a Petition would sent to the Crown" based on its arguments (*PGM*, I: 182). The Privy Council had recently limited the power of colonial governors to grant lands, but Mason, who had a life-long interest in expanding his property holdings, had continued to buy headright certificates for such properties.

Although Mason's editor suggests that Mason's primary concern was that of "headrights and the territorial limits of Virginia" (*PGM*, I: 182), the manuscript also casts light on the widening gap between British and American interpretations of the Constitution. Mason approached the work not as a theoretician but as a patriot who believed that Great Britain was encroaching on traditional American rights as guaranteed in their charters. As a Virginian and as the Treasurer of the Ohio Company, he was especially interested in vindicating his colony's claims to western lands.

ORGANIZATION OF THE EXTRACTS

Mason opened with two paragraphs. The first summarized a charter that Charles II issued in 1676, confirming the right of 50 acres to everyone coming to the colonies. The second referred to Section 4 of the third charter that James I issued (Mason did not include a date for it) confirming the rights of the people to harbors and fishing rights.

Mason then proceeded by examining four other charters in chronological order and—although he omitted some—section by section. He began with a charter from April 10, 1606, and then proceeded to charters of 1609, 1612, and 1621 before circling back to the Charter of 1676, thus ending his analysis just as James II was attempting to transfer most of the propriety colonies into royal colonies (Haffenden 1958).

The period that he covered was one during which the monarchy was more powerful than the parliament, thus providing support for colonial assertions that they could owe allegiance to the former without therefore recognizing the taxing power of the latter (Varga 1954).

CHARTER OF 1606

Mason observed that in 1606, James I commissioned the London Company and the Plymouth Company to create two colonies "in Virginia, & other Parts and Territories of America, along the Sea Coasts, between 34 Degrees & 45 Degrees of North Latitude" (*PGM,* I: 163). The London Company had the right to plant the first colony, which included 50 miles north and south of the coast where its explorers had settled and 100 miles inland. It also prohibited others from settling in the lands behind them. The Plymouth Company had a similar grant.

The charter indicated that settlers came to America with rights. Section VII thus provided that each colony "shall have a Council which shall govern & direct all Matters & Causes which shall arise or happen within the same several Colonies" (*PGM,* I: 164). Perhaps as important as this representative mechanism was the guarantee that the colonists would take their "privileges & immunities" with them (*PGM,* I: 164). Section XV had elaborated further:

> That all & every the persons being his Majesty's subjects, which shall dwell & inhabit within every or any of the said Colonies or Plantations & every of their Children which shall happen to be born within any of the Limits and precincts of the said several Colonies & plantations, shall have & enjoy all Liberties, Franchises & Immunities, to all

> Intents and Purposes, as if they had been abiding & born within the Realm of England, or any other of his Majesty's Dominions. (*PGM*, I: 165)

In his annotations, Mason observed that this was the charter under which Christopher Newport had sailed three ships from England to Virginia, where they had founded Jamestown, which for many years was "the Seat of Government" (*PGM*, I: 165).

CHARTER OF 1609

Mason further observed that James I had granted an enlarged charter to the "Colony & Dominion of Virginia," which had "been joined by a great Number of the Nobility & principal Gentry in England," in 1609 (*PGM*, I: 165). This had extended the boundaries to 200 miles up and down the coast. The charter had also awarded lands to those who settled there. In his annotations, Mason observed that this included 50 acres of land for each settler. He further noted that in 1621, the King had granted 50,000 acres to a Captain Newce, who had agreed to import 1,000 persons, and that 50 acres was also given to each of those who helped transport sixty "Young Maids" to the colony. Drawing from William Stith, Mason observed that that "Ancient Right & Privilege" was continued in an Acts of Assembly of 1662 and in a Charter of 1676 (*PGM*, I: 166, n. 2).

The 1609 Charter had provided for a Council that remained in England to help govern and administer the colony. Section XXII of the charter, however, had reaffirmed:

> That all & every the persons, being the subjects of his Majesty, his Heirs & Successors, which shall go & inhabit

> within the said Colony & Plantation & every of their Children and posterity which shall happen to be born within any of the Limits thereof, shall have & enjoy all Liberties, Franchises, & Immunities of free Denizens & natural Subjects, within any of their other Dominions, to all Intents & purposes, as if they had been abiding & born within the Realm of England, or any other of the Dominions of his Majesty, his Heirs & Successors. (*PGM*, I: 168).

Mason's commentary on this section was particularly pointed. He observed that this document had made it clear that such rights would continue to the posterity of the settlers, "for ever; notwithstanding the Dissolution of the Virginia Company, had such Dissolution been ever so legal" (*PGM*, I: 168, n. 3). By contrast, he observed "a new doctrine" by "Writers against America," who claimed that the King, never had power to grant such rights. Noting that, in colonizing America, the British had faced a situation, not known since the time of the Greeks and Romans, he observed that although the colonists could have expected that "by the Laws of Nature & Nations" they would have "carried with them the Constitution of the Country they came from, & consequently been entitled to all its advantages" (*PGM*, I: 168, n. 3), they had further secured their rights by entering into compacts with the King to this end. Even had these charters been defective, "their posterity have enjoyed these Rights & privileges from Time immemorial" and have therefore "acquired a legal Title" (*PGM*, I: 168, n. 3).

Although the king had granted colonial charters, the colonists themselves had come "at their own private Expence & Hazard, amidst a thousand Difficulties & Dangers" (*PGM*, I: 168, n. 3). In a line that he would repeat in the Fairfax Resolves, Mason observed that "Equally false and absurd is the Idea of Great Britain's Right to govern these Colonies as conquered Provinces, for we are the Descendants, not of the conquered, but of the conquerors" (*PGM*, I: 168, n. 3).[11]

Mason argued that although "Kings Lords and Commons compose the British Legislature . . . the Constitution has lodged the executive power in the Crown. The Disposition of foreign or newly acquired Territory hath ever belonged to the Executive. This power has been constantly exercised by our Kings in numberless instances" (*PGM*, I: 168, n. 3). Mason further reasoned that "If the Crown can make an absolute & unlimited Alienation to Foreigners; a fortiori, can it make a modulated Grant to Subjects" (*PGM*, I: 168, n.3).

CHARTER OF 1612

The Charter of 1612, which James I also issued, had enlarged former grants. Mason noted that Section IV of this charter was especially important because its grants of fishing rights might be helpful in any future disputes with Maryland

---

[11] In Calvin's Case, 7 Coke Reports 1a, 77 ER 377 (1608), the King's Bench issued a decision that established that the King had exclusive authority over conquered territories and that he alone governed until he promulgated English laws there (Varga 1954, 282). As Mason was pointing out, the situation was complicated in America by the fact that the colonists themselves, and not forces of the king, had done most of the "conquering" of Native-American tribes. In *A Summary View of the Rights of British America,* Thomas Jefferson would make a similar point: "American was conquered, and her settlements made and firmly established, at the expense of individuals, and not of the British public. Their own blood was split in acquiring lands for their settlement, their own fortunes expended in making that settlement effectual" (Jefferson, 1950, I, 122). "Tom Long" had made a similar point in published correspondence in Massachusetts (Martin 1986 105).

over the subject (*PGM*, I: 170, n.4). Reaffirming the rights of the London Company Council to make general policies for the colony, this Charter has also provided "for the ordering & disposing of Matters, & Affairs of greater weight & Importance, & such as concern the public weal," the latter being a term that Mason would later use with frequency, by "one great & general Assembly" and general courts (*PGM*, I: 170-171).

CHARTER OF 1621

Mason noted that what he called the Charter of 1621, actually a commission that the King had issued constituting Sir Francis Wyatt and His counsellors of state as officers, "is generally presumed to have been the Original plan, & first Draught of our Constitution, from which the Assembly of Virginia took its rise" but that "it was in fact rather a Confirmation of that Form of Government, which the people here, in imitation of their Mother Country, had before adopted" (*PGM*, I: 172, n. 6). Mason observed that two years earlier Sir George Yeardley had held "an assembly of the representatives of the people," later called the House of Burgesses, although most members represented counties rather than burroughs," the word from which Burgesses was derived (*PGM*, I: 172).

This document from 1621 had provided for two "supreme Councils" in Virginia, the Council of State and the General Assembly, which would assist the governor. Mason believed that the jurisdiction of the Council had subsequently reached "an alarming & enormous height" (*PGM*, I, 173, n. 7). This was at least partially mitigated by the facts that the office was not hereditary, the emoluments of the office were relatively modest, and "because Luxury, Venality, and a general Corruption of Manners have not yet thoroughly taken Root among us," as they presumably had in Britain (*PGM* 1970: I, 173, n. 7).

Mason did have one concern, which would occupy him to the end of his life (See his speech at the Constitutional Convention of 1787 at Farrand, II: 370). Mason acknowledged that his comments might appear "Foreign to the design of the annexed Extracts" and might have been motivated by "An Enthusiastick Impulse," which some might find offensive. He explained that "slow Poison . . . is daily contaminating the Minds & Morals of our People":

> Every Gentlemen here is born a petty Tyrant. Practiced in acts of Despotism & Cruelty, we become callous to the Dictates of Humanity, & all the finer feelings of the Soul. Taught to regard a part of our own Species in the most abject & contemptible Degree below us, we lose that Idea of the Dignity of Man, which the Hand of Nature had implanted in us, for great & useful purposes. Habituated from our Infancy to trample upon the Rights of Human Nature, every generous, every liberal Sentiment, if not extinguished, is enfeebled in our Minds. And in such an infernal School are to be educated our future Legislators & Rulers. The Laws of impartial Providence may even by such Means as these, avenge upon our Posterity the Injury done a set of Wretches, whom our Injustice hath debased almost to a Level with the Brute Creation. (*PGM,* I: 173, n. 7).

The most fascinating aspects of these comments was they that not only failed to address the charter he was analyzing but that they also managed neither to mention the word slavery nor his own role as a slave owner.

In examining provisions whereby the governor would have a veto over laws adopted by the General Assembly, Mason provided further commentary. He noted that the

Council remained even after a royal governor replaced a governor from the London Company. Moreover, in the early years of the colony, members of the Council outnumbered members of the House of Burgesses, but as the more democratic house grew in numbers, members of the Council came to be considered a separate branch, rather than a group who would simply walk upstairs from the lower chamber. Admitting the necessity of a "separate Branch, such an intermediate Power between the People and the Crown" to combat "the tumultuary Nature of Public Assemblies," Mason suggested that this branch should be for life, or at the very least be "equally independent of the Crown and of the People; and that neither the Administration nor the common Judicative powers of the State can be safely lodged in their hands" (*PGM,* I: 174, n. 8).

Further extending his criticism to the courts, Mason said that in order "to secure the property of Individuals" it was necessary to have an appeal from any judgment. He therefore considered it a "Capital Error in the Constitution of our supreme Courts" that, because they handled cases of original jurisdiction, this left those against whom they ruled in such cases without redress (*PGM,* I: 174-175, n. 8).

Mason proceeded through a provision of the charter, which gave power to the Treasurer, the Council and the Company of England until such time as the colony could enact its own laws. He observed that the London Company, having thus created "This Ordinance or Charter for settling a Form of Government in Virginia," under authority of the King's charters when its powers were in full force and its authority was unquestioned, "it gave the People of Virginia as good a Title to chuse their own Representatives to enact laws, as if it had been made & granted by the King itself" (*PGM,* I:

175). Mason hazarded that an ordinance of such long standing "could be shaken only by Violence & Injustice, aided by our own Folly, or by Force of Arms" (*PGM*, I: 175, n. 9).

Mason did acknowledge that in 1624, the King suppressed meetings of the Virginia Company within London and that members of his Privy Council appointed a new governor, which the Company resisted before finally growing weary and allowing the transformation of the colony from a propriety colony to a crown colony. Although Mason considered this action to be illegal, he welcomed the fact that it brought the colony under the king's protection. Mason noted that Charles I's grant to Lord Baltimore, as well as the creation of Pennsylvania and Carolina had encroached on the original boundaries of Virginia, and that a subsequent grant with similar potential had led to the adoption of another Charter in 1676, which was designed "to confirm their Liberties, Privileges, Immunities, Rights & Properties" (*PGM*, I: 177, n. 9).

CHARTER OF 1676

Moving to a discussion of that charter, issued by Charles II and dated October 10, Mason believed that it prevented the establishment "of any new Government or Proprietary in any part of Virginia" (*PGM*, I: 177, n. 10). The charter also provided that the governor would reside in Virginia, except on such occasions when he was called back to England, and it affirmed existing property rights, including the right to receive fifty acres upon immigrating. Showing that Mason was already coming to equate the rights of charters with those of written constitutions, he believed that "being thereby made a part of the Constitution of Virginia," this provision "cannot be avoided or invalidated by any Proclamation,

Instruction or other Act of Government" (*PGM,* I: 178, n. 12). After recording another provision providing that the Governor and Council had full power to hear all felonies, Mason further noted that this provision was "very inconsistent with the extraordinary Measure lately adopted by the British ministry" providing for trials out of the colony, which action, he said, was "much better become the Divan at Constantinople, than the Cabinet of London" (*PGM,* I: 178, n. 13). Mason also expressed opposition to an attempt, which ultimately proved unsuccessful, to merge Virginia's claims to Ohio with claims authored in 1772 to a group of speculators supported by Robert Walpole (Marshall 1965).

As he ended his review, Mason again summarized his thoughts, which were consistent with other Virginia patriots who attempted to deny parliamentary taxing power while acknowledging continuing allegiance to the king: "By this Charter the subjects of Virginia are for ever to remain under the immediate protection of the British Crown & be subject only to its Government here" (*PGM,* I: 179, n.14). He further stated that it would be inconsistent with the goal of encouraging its growth to have confined the colony to its original geographical limits. He specifically noted that several thousand Virginians had settled west of the Blue Ridge Mountains and that the sale of land to them had been used to support William and Mary College.

ANALYSIS OF CHARTER SUMMARIES

Mason's abstract of colonial charters was aimed in part at defending the claims of Virginia against those of other colonies and the claims of the Ohio Company (in which he had interests) against those of rivals, but it was also part of a much larger colonial narrative. This narrative was designed to show that Americans and brought the rights and privileges of British citizenship with them, including self-government, which included the right not to be taxed without their consent.

Michael Kammen has thus noted that such narratives gave similar answers to five questions. As to why settlers had come to America, they had done so to enjoy their liberties and secure their prosperity. As to their circumstances, they had emigrated at their own expense. As to their relationship with England, they were retain English rights in perpetuity. As to the constitutional and social consequences, they retained a bond with the King without being in subject to parliament. As to the significance of their founding, they were not mere pawns but freemen (Kammen 1970, 341-341).

Mason would soon be drawing up a declaration of the rights for Virginia, but before he did so, he would go on to take the lead in drafting the Fairfax County Resolves, and attempt to formulate policies in regard both to test oaths and annual elections.

REFERENCES

Billings, Warren M. 2004. *A Little Parliament: The Virginia General Assembly in the Seventeenth Century.* Richmond: Library of Virginia.

Breen, T.H. 1997. "Ideology and Nationalism on the Eve of the American Revolution: Revisions Once More in Need of Revising." *The Journal of American History* 84 (June): 13-39.

Chaffin, Robert J. 1974. "The Declaration Act of 1766: A Reappraisal." *The Historian* 37 (November): 5-25.

Farrand, Max, ed. 1966. *The Records of the Federal Convention of 1787.* 4 vols. New Haven, CT: Yale University Press.

Haffenden, Philip S. 1958. "The Crown and the Colonial Charters, 1675-1788: Part I." *The William and Mary Quarterly* 15 (July): 297-311.

_____. 1958. "The Crown and the Colonial Charters, 1675-1688: Part II." *The William and Mary Quarterly* 15 (October): 452-466.

Jefferson, Thomas. "From Thomas Jefferson to Henry Lee, 8 May 1825." Founders Online. https://founders.archives.gov/documents/Jefferson/98-01-02-5212.

Jefferson, Thomas. 1950. *The Papers of Thomas Jefferson,* Vol. I, 1760-1776. Ed. Julian P. Boyd. Princeton, NJ: Princeton University Press.

Kammen, Michael. 1970. "The Meaning of Colonization in American Revolutionary Thought." *Journal of the History of Ideas* 31 (July-September): 337-358.

"*A Letter from the Committee of Merchants in* London, *trading* to North America, *directed to the merchants in* New York, *dated Feb.* 28, 1766." *Virginia Gazette* (Purdie) 16 May 1766, p. 2 of 4. Found at http://research.history/org/CWDLImages/VA_GAZETImages/PD/1766/0043hi.jpg.

Lutz, Donald S. 1988. *The Origins of American Constitutionalism.* Baton Rouge: Louisiana State University Press.

McCarthy, Finbarr. 1995. "Participatory Government and Community Property: Two Radical Concepts in the Virginia Charter of 1606." *University of Richmond Law Review* 29 (March): 327-380.

Marshall, Peter. 1965. "Lord Hillsborough, Samuel Wharton and the Ohio Grant, 1769-1775." *The English Historical Review* 80 (October): 717-739.

Martin, Thomas S. 1986. "The Long and the Short of It: A Newspaper Exchange on the Massachusetts Charters, 1772." *The William and Mary Quarterly* 43 (January): 99-110.

Mason, George. 1970. *The Papers of George Mason, 1725-1792,* ed. Robert A. Rutland. 3 vols. Chapel Hill: The University of North Carolina Press), pp. 65-72. [Cited throughout this book as *PGM*].

Olson, Alison G. 1982. "The London Mercantile Lobby and the Coming of the American Revolution." *The Journal of American History* 69 (June): 21-41.

_____. 1983. "The Virginia Merchants of London: A Study in Eighteenth-Century Interest-Group Politics." *The William and Mary Quarterly* 40 (July): 363-388.

Paine, Thomas. 1958. *Common Sense and Other Political Writings.* New York: The Liberal Arts Press.

Sainsbury, John. 1978. "The Pro-Americans of London. 1769 to 1782." *The William and Mary Quarterly* 35 (July): 423-454.

Schlesinger, Arthur M. 1935. "The Colonial Newspapers and the Stamp Act." *The New England Quarterly* 8 (March): 63-83.

Shakespeare, William. 1986. *The Complete Works.* Ed. Stanley Wells and Gary Taylor. Oxford: Clarendon Press.

Trenchard, John and Thomas Gordon. *Cato's Letters: or, Essays on Liberty Civil and Religious, and other Important Subjects.* Four volumes in two. Ed. Ronald Hamowy. Indianapolis: Liberty Fund. 1995.

Taylor, Alan. 2016. *American Revolutions: A Continental History, 1750-1804.* New York: W.W. Norton & Company.

Varga, Nicholas. 1954. "The English Parliament's Authority over Virginia before the Restoration." *The Virginia Magazine of History and Biography* 62 (July): 281-288.

2

GEORGE MASON, THE FAIRFAX RESOLVES, AND OTHER EARLY WRITINGS

As he began commenting on public affairs, Mason largely went it alone, but as the controversy between the colonies and Britain continued over constitutional rights, Mason found himself not only voicing his own sentiments but serving as the spokesman for others. As localities began to articulate their grievances, Mason stepped in to orchestrate the Fairfax County Resolves. He went on to make remarks to the local militia company and to formulate Virginia's policies with regard to test oaths. These three documents are the primary subject of this chapter.

FAIRFAX COUNTY RESOLVES (JULY 18, 1774)

On July 18, 1774, a meeting of Freeholders meeting at the Fairfax County Courthouse, over which George Washington presided, issued a document known as the Fairfax County Resolves. One of many such documents that would rise to a crescendo in the months leading up to the Declaration of Independence (Maier 1997), the Fairfax Resolves were among the most articulate. Although they were especially directed to responding to the Coercive, or Intolerable, Acts that Great Britain had adopted in the wake of the Boston Tea Party (Ammerman 1974), they articulated a broader view of British/American relations.

AUTHORSHIP

As is the case with many such documents, it has thus far proven to be impossible to establish its source with complete certainty. The copy of the Resolutions in George Washington's papers is written in Mason's hand, and the editor of Mason's papers points to a number of stylistic similarities between the wording of the Resolutions and Mason's other works (*PGM*, I: 200). He does, however, note that, "The style of the resolves is Mason's, but as is often the case, the resolves represent a consensus rather than an individual opinion" (*PGM*, I: 200). An article by Donald M. Sweig, which relies on a letter that George Washington published on July 11, 1774, indicates that a draft of the Resolves had been in existence before George Washington and George Mason were believed to have compiled them (which goes as much to timing as to authorship) and that the resolves were more likely the result of a committee effort (1983).

In my experience, committees, as committees, rarely compile documents with the coherence of the Fairfax County Resolves. Committees or Congresses may—as in the case of the Declaration of Independence—amend, refine, or delete portions of a proposed document, but, if they retain the coherence of the Declaration of Independence or the sophistication of the Fairfax Resolves, they almost always have a central author or authors.

As his later refusal to sign the Constitution and his fight against ratification of the document in Virginia demonstrates,

Mason was not reticent about expressing opposition, when he thought the occasion called for it. Even absent absolute proof that Mason was the primary author, or one of the primary authors of, the Fairfax Resolves, there is no indication that he expressed any dissatisfaction with its sentiments. At the very least, the Document opens a window into what Mason and his contemporary Virginia freemen were thinking. Given the parallels between the Resolves and Mason's known sentiments, which I will note throughout the examination of the document, I believe there is convincing evidence that he drafted them and that they therefore provide an open window into his thinking at the time.

ANALYSIS OF THE DOCUMENT

The Fairfax Resolves were divided into 24 separately numbered resolves, each of which began with the term "RESOLVED that." After identifying the word "resolve" with "a firm intention," "a resolution," and "firmness or steadfastness of purpose," the *Oxford English Dictionary* (*OED*) defines a resolve as "A formal decision, determination, or expression of opinion made by or submitted to a deliberative assembly, meeting, etc." It adds that the usage is "Now chiefly U.S." In this vein, the *OED* cites a letter of Benjamin Franklin in 1774 in which he noted to Edmund Burke that "I hear your proposed resolves were negative by a great majority." On October 14, 1774, the First Continental Congress adopted its "Declaration and Resolves," outlining opposition to British taxation. Virginia and Kentucky would later adopt resolutions opposing the Alien and Sedition Acts. The first paragraph of the Fairfax Resolves observes that it was the product of "a general Meeting of the Freeholders and inhabitants of the County of Fairfax."

THE ASSERTION OF EQUALITY OF RIGHTS

Consistent with their status as "freeholders," the first paragraph began with a bold statement, indicating that "this Colony and Dominion of Virginia can not be considered as a conquered Country; and if it was, that the present Inhabitants are the Descendants not of the Conquered, but of the Conquerors."[1] John Locke was among contemporary philosophers who, although not necessarily consistent on the point, argued that a nation might choose to enslave a conquered people in a just war rather than killing them (Farr 2008). Virginia freemen were pointing out that they had never been so conquered. Indeed, they, rather than the British, had triumphed over Native-American inhabitants.

Moreover, in further explaining their status, the Resolves observed that their ancestors had settled the land not "at the national Expence of England, but at the private Expence of the Adventurers" under authority of a "solemn Compact with, and under the auspices and Protection of the British Crown." This resolution was consistent with the larger colonial attempt to distinguish due loyalty to the English King without accepting the legislative authority of Parliament, especially with respect to taxes. The resolution further observed "That our Ancestors, when they left their native Land, and settled in America, brought with them (even if the same had not been confirmed by Charters) the Civil-

---

[1] Broadwater (2006, 269) points out that in his "Extracts from Virginia Charters" (*PGM*, I: 168, n. 3), Mason had labeled as "false and absurd . . . the Idea of Great Britain's Right to govern these Colonies as conquered Provinces, for we are the Descendants, not of the Conquered, but of the conquerors." This parallelism certainly suggests that Mason authored both documents.

Constitution and Form of Government of the County they came from; and were by the Laws of Nature and Nations, entitled to all it's Privileges, Immunities and Advantages; which have descended to us their Posterity, and ought of Right to be as fully enjoyed, as if we had still continued within the Realm of England." This argument was, of course, quite similar to the argument that Mason had made in his response to the merchants of London.

Mason would long be known as an opponent of hereditary succession, but he and his fellow Virginians clearly believed that under both the laws of nature and of nations, they were entitled to the same legal rights as if they had stayed in Britain. Notably, the language "ought of Right to be" was in direct contradiction to the British Declaratory Act of 1766, which had asserted that the colonies "have been, are, and of right ought to be subordinate unto, and dependent upon the imperial crown and parliament of Great Britain" (Quoted in Munves 1978, 9). This language was later echoed in Richard Henry Lee's Resolution for Independence that the Second Continental Congress incorporated within the final paragraph of the Declaration of Independence. Likewise, the language of "Privileges" and "Immunities" was later incorporated both within the text of Article IV, Section 2, of the U.S. Constitution, which guaranteed state citizens the "Privileges and Immunities of Citizens of the several States," and in Section 1 of the Fourteenth Amendment, which prohibited states from making or enforcing laws abridging such privileges or immunities.

PARLIAMENTARY AUTHORITY

Scholars have noted that the accusations that constitute the backbone of the Declaration of Independence focus on abuses of the king, never directly mentioning Parliament, but simply identifying its members as among "the others" with whom he had consorted. The Declaration could focus on the King because earlier documents, including the Fairfax Resolves, had explained why the colonies had already rejected parliamentary authority in America. Resolutions two through ten were among the provisions that laid such a framework, thus providing some of the unstated context behind this later Declaration.

The Second Resolve cut to the very heart of recent British/American controversies by evoking a principle that the colonists frequently attributed either to the Magna Carta or the British Declaration of rights. This Resolve thus identified "the most important and valuable Part of the British Constitution," as "the Fundamental Principle of the People's being governed by no Laws, to which they have not given their Consent, by Representatives freely chosen by themselves, who are affected by the Laws they enact equally with their Constituents; to whom they are accountable, and whose Burthens they share." The resolve further connected this principle to "the Safety and Happiness of the Community," and its absence to either a "despotic Monarchy, or a tyrannical Aristocracy."

One possible response to the principle of "no taxation without representation" would have been for the British to offer representation to the colonists within the Parliament, but the third Resolve, presumably with a view toward the distance involved, denied that such representation was possible "from their Situation." It accordingly proclaimed that "the legislative Power here can of Right be exercised only by [our] Provincial Assemblys or Parliaments, subject to the Assent or Negative of the British Crown."

This resolution did accept limited parliamentary control over "our Trade and Commerce," namely laws restraining "our importing from foreign Countrys, such Articles as they cou'd furnish us with." However, it did so more as a matter of colonial acceptance in repayment for British defense than as a matter of constitutional right. Again drawing from wider currents of colonial thought, the Resolve distinguished colonial power over its own "internal Policy" from such trade regulations.

A strong impetus for the taxes that Britain attempted to impose on the colonists in the wake of the French and Indian War stemmed from the huge debts that it had incurred in fighting this War. Given that the first resolve had acknowledged the role of Britain in defending the early colonists, what about parliamentary requisitions for such defense? Granting "the Duty of these Colonies, on all Emergencies, to contribute, in Proportion to their Abilities, Situation and Circumstances, to the Necessary Charge of supporting and defending the British Empire, of which they are Part," the resolution argued that if "treated upon an equal Footing. . . the Motives of Self-Interest and Preservation will be a sufficient Obligation; as was evident thro' the Course of the last War." Indeed, this resolution argued that it would be no less improper to dun the colonies for supplies than it would be to tax Englishmen in the event that their representatives failed to provide adequate funds for defense.[2]

---

[2] One characteristic feature of Mason that is missing from the Fairfax Resolves, albeit which may be implied by this part of them, is his tendency to emphasize the role of citizen militia and to decry the use of standing armies.

Resolution 5 continued in this same vein and may well have provided some of the foundation for the Declaration and Resolves that the Continental Congress adopted on October 14, 1774. Whereas the Declaration of Independence grounded its arguments clearly on natural rights, the earlier Declaration and Resolves had cited three sources, namely "the immutable laws of nature, the principles of the English Constitution, and the several charters or compacts" (Vile 2015, 77). So too, the fifth resolve asserted that parliamentary claims to legislate on behalf of the colonies were inconsistent with "the first Principles of the constitution," "the original Compacts," "the Privileges of a free People, and the natural Rights of Mankind." Such laws were designed to reduce the colonies "from a State of Freedom and Happiness to Slavery and Misery."

Resolution 6 further pointed to the "inseparable" nature of "taxation and Representation." It described this tie as "the only effectual Security to a free People, against the Incroachments of Despotism and Tyranny." After reiterating the reasons that the British Parliament could not possibly legislate fairly on behalf of such a distant people, Resolution 7 predicted that the continuing exercise of such power would "establish the most grievous and intolerable species of Tyranny and Oppression, that ever was inflicted upon Mankind."

CONTINUING CONNECTIONS TO BRITAIN

Although within two years the Declaration of Independence would proclaim a severing of colonial ties to the mother country, the Fairfax Resolves announced no such intention. Resolve 8 thus stated "that it is our greatest Wish and Inclination, as well as Interest, to continue our Connection with, and Dependance upon the British

Government" albeit as "Subjects" rather than as "Slaves." As ironic as such language might have seemed coming from a slaveholder, or from a colony with so many slaves, such terminology was consistent with other contemporary documents from slave-holding framers (Breen 1997, 32-33).

WIDENING THE FIELD OF OPPRESSORS AND EXPRESSING SOLIDARITY WITH BOSTONIANS

Resolve 9 widened the charges against the British Parliament to include the King's ministers, thus still technically excluding the King from direct blame.[3] It did so by focusing on "a premeditated Design and System, formed and pursued by the British Ministry, to introduce an arbitrary Government into his Majesty's American Dominions." This resolve sought to show such an intention by mustering evidence of British attempts falsely to charge Americans with seeking independence and by citing acts that the Declaration of Independence later condemned. These included "various Acts of Violence and Oppression," the dissolution of colonial assemblies, and abolishing or altering ancient charters, which could "end in the Ruin both of Great Britain and her Colonies."

Resolve 10 reminded readers that Fairfax County was responding to the Boston Port Bill and other Coercive, or Intolerable, Acts of Congress, some of which the Declaration of Independence later referenced. In addition to questioning parliamentary taxation of the colonies, this resolve mentioned "creating new and dangerous Jurisdictions here,"

---

[3] Liddle notes that even after Washington's forces began fighting the British after Lexington and Concord, he typically referred to British troops as "the Ministerial Troops" rather than directly associating them with the King (1969, 967).

taking away trial by jury, allowing prosecutions within another country, "the Act inflicting ministerial Vengeance upon the Town of Boston," and attempts to abrogate the charter of Massachusetts Bay. As if to show that the colonists could come to the aid of their own, this resolution opened a "subscription" to take care of the needs that the ministry had inflicted on that city.

Resolve 11 further elaborated on responses to British actions against Boston. Suggesting that Virginians might be willing to contribute toward paying the East India Company for the destruction of its tea in the so-called Boston Tea Party (thus honoring property rights), it made it clear that because it considered members of this company to be "the Tools and Instrument of Oppression in the Hands of Government and the Cause of our present Distress," it recommended against further purchases of its property. It even suggested burning any remaining stores of the product once restitution had been made.

THE NEED FOR UNION AND SACRIFICE

Recognizing the need for colonial unity in the face of British provocations, Resolve 12 said that colonists "ought to regard every Act of Violence or Oppression inflicted upon any One of them, as aimed at all." Perhaps more importantly, it called for a Congress of deputies from through the colonies "to concert a general and uniform Plan for the Defence and Preservation of our common Rights, and continuing the Connection and Dependance of the said Colonies upon Great Britain under a just, lenient, permanent, and constitutional Form of Government." Action on this and similar resolutions would lead to the calling of the Continental Congresses. By thanking those within Britain who were siding with

Americans, Resolve 13 arguably demonstrated that the American view of the British Constitution was not unique.

Early Americans generally looked unfavorably at partisan disputes. Resolve 14 accordingly "RESOLVED that every little jarring Interest and Dispute, which has ever happened between these Colonies, shou'd be buried in eternal Oblivion." The Resolve went on to touch on sentiments that Mason advocated throughout most of his life. It thus argued "that all Manner of Luxury and Extravagance ought immediately to be laid aside," and that "it is the indispensable Duty of all the Gentlemen and Men of Fortune to set Examples of Temperance, Fortitude, Frugality and Industry" as well as to improve "Arts and Manufactures in America" by cultivating "Flax, Cotton, and other Materials for Manufacturers" and selling sheep to neighbors who could increase the production of wool.

Resolve 15 further proposed that the colonies should boycott British goods until Britain provided for the "Restoration of our just Rights and Privileges." It also sought to prevent merchants from taking advantage of this projected boycott by attempting to raise prices in the interim and proposed that colonists should refuse to employ such individuals as agents.

The next two resolves both addressed issues on which Mason had taken the lead. Resolve 16 thus proposed that merchants and venders be subject to a nonimportation oath, that the names of those who refused to do so should be publicized, and that those who adopted the oath should be certified. Resolve 17 further proposed not only to prohibit further importation of slaves into the colonies but to declare "our most earnest Wishes to see an entire Stop for ever put to such a wicked cruel and unnatural Trade."

Resolve 18 proposed banning the export of lumber to the West Indies, Resolve 19 further proposed that the colonies collectively stop the production and export of tobacco, "provided the same Measure shall be adopted by the other Colonies on this Continent," taking care also to suspend any debts due after this time. Resolve 20 proposed "a solemn Covenant and Association" by all the colonies affirming the boycott, and publishing the names of any individuals who refused to sign as "Traitors to the Country," while Resolve 21 suggested further breaking off trade with any "Colony Province or Town" refusing to agree to the plan. Resolve 22 proposed to exempt colonies from adhering to any measures designed to punish Boston, and to "inviolably adhere to such Measures as shall be concerted by the general Congress, for the preservation of our Lives Liberties and Fortunes."

A SUITABLE PETITION

Having begun by asserting that Americans had the same rights as residents of Britain, the penultimate resolve (No. 23) recommended that deputies to the Congress, for which the Resolves had called, should "draw up and transmit an humble and dutiful Petition and Remonstrance to his Majesty, asserting with decent Firmness our just and constitutional Rights and Privileg[es,]" and "lamenting the fatal Necessity of being compelled to enter into Measur[es] disgusting to his Majesty and his Parliament, or injurious to our fellow Subjects in Great Britain." Moving from near obsequiousness to the threat of war, the resolution called for reaffirming "ou[r] Duty and Affection to his Majesty's Person, Family, [an]d Government, and our Desire to continue our Dependance upon Great Bri[tai]n; and most humbly conjuring and beseeching his Majesty, not to reduce his faithful Subjects of America to a State of desperation, and to reflect, that from our Sovereign there can be but one Appeal," presumably a resort to arms.

The final resolution was directed to George Washington and George Broadwater, the Fairfax delegates. It directed them to present these resolutions to the convention to begin in Williamsburg in August as it considered "the Measures proper to be taken in the present alarming and dangerous Situation of America."

A REEXAMINATION OF AUTHORSHIP

One of the reasons the Resolves proved so effective in stimulating a call for a continental congress was that they reflected wider colonial sentiments, few of which were peculiar to any single patriot. The Document clearly opposed the authority of Parliament to enact taxes for the New World while seeking continuing connection to Britain through attachment to a common king, whom it did not directly criticize. Because the Resolves were claiming the rights of Englishmen, most rights were therefore framed in terms of such rights rather than in terms of natural rights.

I cannot identify any sentiments within the Resolves, which may well have involved compromises, that went directly against Mason's own views, and I can identify many opinions that align with those he was known to have and some language that was identical with that which he used elsewhere. Mason believed that the colonists had brought their rights as Englishmen with them to the New World. He opposed the authority of Parliament to tax the colonies. He emphasized the importance of colonial charters. He opposed the Coercive Acts. He led in the movement to seek leverage by boycotting British goods and limiting exports. He opposed party politics and thought that excessive luxury could corrupt republican governments. He opposed continuing slave importation. He hoped to avoid war but recognized that such war was preferable to slavery. In summary, there is good reason to believe not only that the Resolves reflected Mason's sentiments but that he was also their primary author.

REMARKS ON ANNUAL ELECTIONS FOR THE FAIRFAX INDEPENDENT COMPANY (APRIL 1775)

Historians and political scientists are constantly seeking to tease out the relationship between classical liberal political theory, which is often associated with individualism as exemplified in John Locke (Hartz, 1955), and republicanism, which has roots in Machiavelli (Gould 1993). These ideologies often overlapped, but whereas liberalism tended to stress individual self-preservation and self-interests with respect to the preservation of their rights, republicans tended to emphasize civic participation and patriotism. Both were wary of entrenched power. One republican solution was to vest defense of the nation in the hands of its citizens, who like their Roman forbears (as Garry Wills showed in his 1984 book, the Roman general Cincinnatus was an especially lauded Roman, whom citizens often identified with George Washington) would melt back into the local population once military dangers had passed, rather than constituting a separate interest that might seek its own power. Republicans further tied this notion to the idea of keeping elected officials on a tight electoral lease, where they would have to return to resume their place among their fellows and feel the consequences of their own actions.

BACKGROUND

Both of these sentiments, and many more, are embodied in George Mason's "Remarks on Annual Elections for the Fairfax Independent Company," which he authored sometime in April of 1775, the same month that the battles of Lexington (after which Mason enthusiastically named one of his plantations) and Concord broke out in Massachusetts.[4] At the time, Mason was chair of the local Committee of Safety, which was responsible for taking charge of local militia. Although regular British troops had participated in the French and Indian War and subsequently remained behind, especially in Boston and New York, to enforce British policies, the British had expected the colonists to take care of their own defense, particularly with respect to Native-Americans. To this end, colonial governors had appointed militia leaders, whom they drew from local elites.

Within a month after Mason was writing, militiamen had resisted attempts by Virginia Governor John Murray, the Fourth Earl of Dunmore, to take colonial gunpowder supplies from Williamsburg. He subsequently took refuge aboard a ship and sought to enlist slaves to oppose the colonists. Meanwhile, former state legislatures met in a series of

---

[4] In a letter to William Lee dated June 1, 1775, Mason summarized his feelings: "The Americans were pretty unanimous before, but the acts of the present session of Parliament, and the blood lately shed at Boston have fixed every wavering mind, and there are no difficulties or hardships which they are not determined to encounter with firmness and perseverance. God only knows the event, and in His hands, confiding in the justice of our cause, we cheerfully trust it!" (*PGM*, I: 237).

"conventions," described in the next chapter, to transact the people's business.

Contemporary scholars have been unable to find the original of Mason's speech, but Kate Mason Rowland included the text in the biography of Mason that she wrote in 1892, which has since been reprinted (1964, I: 430-433). The first sentence of the remarks indicate that Mason prepared or delivered his comments in response to a motion by a fellow "gentleman" to provide for annual elections of militia leaders. This would appear to have been a double departure from prior experience because it would have left the power of such elevation with the troops themselves (rather than with the governor) and because it would have kept militia leaders on a relatively short lease. Read as such, Mason's remarks appear extremely democratic.

There is, however, another side to the story, which Michael A McDonnell has illuminated in a wider study of colonial militia and minute men. He points out that the Fairfax County Militia Association, which Mason was addressing, was not a broad collection of patriots from all ranks of society, but an association of gentlemen planters (1998). Indeed, in a manuscript that he composed on September 21, 1774, apparently for the association, Mason noted that its membership was limited to 100 men, each of whom would supply their own uniforms, lead, and gun-flints (*PGM*, I: 211), which was likely well beyond the means of small farmers. Ignoring Parliament, this agreement bound its members to "hold ourselves in Readiness, in Case of Necessity, hostile Invasion, or real Danger of the Community of which we are Members, to defend to the utmost of our Power, the legal prerogatives of our Sovereign King George the third, and the just Rights & Privileges of our Country, our

Posterity & ourselves upon the Principles of the British Constitution" (*PGM*, I: 211).

Resolutions that scholars believe George Mason and George Washington drafted for the Fairfax County Committee of Safety on January 17, 1775 (and likely influenced by similar resolutions in Maryland that it cited), which levied a poll tax to raise money for ammunition, further identified the theory behind the militia. It observed "that a well regulated Militia, composed of gentlemen freeholders, and other freemen, is the natural strength and only stable security of a free Government, and that such Militia will relieve our mother country from any expense in our protection and defence, will obviate the pretence of a necessity for taxing us on that account, and render it unnecessary to keep Standing Armies among us—ever dangerous to liberty" (*PGM*, I: 212).[5]

---

[5] Yet another Document, the Fairfax County Militia Plan "for Embodying the People," which was contained in a Mason letter dated February 6, 1775, but which cannot definitely be attributed to Mason (and may have been copied or patterned after a similar document in Maryland), although somewhat redundant with the January 17 resolutions, casts further light on the thinking of Mason and his contemporaries.

It begins as follows: "Threatened with the Destruction of our antient Laws & Liberty, and the Loss of all that is dear to British subjects & Freemen, justly alarmed with the Prospect of impending Ruin,--firmly determined, at the hazard of our Lives, to transmit to our Children & Posterity those sacred rights to which ourselves were born; and thoroughly convinced that a well regulated Militia, composed of the gentlemen, Freeholders, and other Freemen, is the natural Strength and only safe & stable security of a Free Government, & that such Militia will relieve our Mother Country from any Expense in our Protection and Defence, will obviate the Pretence of a necessity for taxing us on that account, and render it unnecessary to keep any standing Army (ever dangerous to liberty) in this Colony, WE the Subscribers, Inhabitants of

These resolutions further complicate McDonnell's analysis because they contemplate service not only by "gentleman," but also by "freeholders, and other freemen." Moreover, Mason favored defending Virginia through a wider system of minutemen, who, like members of his own company, would be allowed to choose their own officers (Copeland and McMaster 1975, 189-190) [6]

SURVEY OF MASON'S REMARKS

Mason began his Remarks on Annual Elections for the Fairfax Independent Company by reflecting on "the principles on which this company was first instituted, and the purposes for which it was formed." Citing words from "the deepest politician who ever put pen to paper," which is a clear reference to Machiavelli, one of the founders of civil republicanism (Ganter 1937), Mason observed "that no institution can be long preserved, but by frequent recurrence to those maxims on which it was formed."

A year later, one of the charges that the Declaration of Independence leveled against George III was that he was "transporting large armies of foreign mercenaries, to compleat the works of death, desolution & tyranny, already begun." Ironically, John Lind, who defended the King against this and other charges in the Declaration, attributed the King's use of mercenaries to the fact that the "ordinary

---

Fairfax County, have freely & voluntarily agreed, & hereby do agree & solemnly promise, to enroll & embody ourselves into a Militia for this County, intended to consist of all the able-bodied Freemen from eighteen to fifty Years of age." (*PGM*, I: 215).

[6] McDonnell, 1998, large attributes the collapse of the minute men in Virginia and the state's eventual reliance on regular troops as the result of the state's failure to give members control over their own leaders.

establishment of the British army" in Britain which was chiefly a naval power, was "so small" that the British used them in all their wars (1776, 96).

If mercenaries might have served the republican goal of minimizing the threat of a regular army within Britain, the practice of hiring foreign forces to squelch colonial grievances was otherwise contrary to notions of republican citizenship. In continuing his remarks, Mason thus observed that "This company is essentially different from a common collection of mercenary soldiers." Whereas mercenaries would presumably work for the highest bidder and be willing to participate in aggressive actions abroad, Mason's company "was formed upon the liberal sentiments of public good, for the great and useful purposes of defending our country, and preserving those inestimable rights which we inherit from our ancestors." Arguably appealing to feelings of noblesse oblige among his gentlemen colleagues, Mason anticipated that his company would "influence a martial spirit of emulation, and [serve] to provide a fund of officers, that in case of absolute necessity, the people might be the better enable to act in defence of their invaded liberty." To this end, "gentlemen of the first fortune and character among us . . . have submitted to stand in the ranks as common soldiers, and to pay due obedience to the officers of their own choice." The company could not afford to "tarnish" its example "by any little dirty views of party, of mean self-interest or of low ambition."

In sentiments that the Virginia Declaration of Rights would later repeat, Mason observed that "We came equals into this world, and equals shall we go out of it. All men are by nature born equally free and independent." Like classical liberal thinkers, Mason observed that men created society in order "[t]o protect the weaker from the injuries and insults of the stronger" by entering into "compacts" through which they gave up "some of their natural rights, that by union and mutual assistance they might secure the rest."

Such civil compacts were "calculated for the general good and safety of the community," and every power vested by men in men should be directed to this end. Power vested for periods that were longer might be called "government," but they in fact constituted "oppression."

In later justifying separation of powers in the proposed Constitution in Federalist No. 51, James Madison observed that "If men were angels, no government would be necessary" (Hamilton, Madison, and Jay, 322). In his Remarks, Mason showed that he has a similar view of human nature. Seeking to account for the origins of "arbitrary and despotic powers" upon such foundations, Mason pointed to "the insidious arts of wicked and designing men, the various and plausible pretenses for continuing and increasing authority, the incautious nature of the many, and the inordinate lust of power in the few." As though a kid had been boiled in its own mother's milk (the striking Biblical analogy that Mason employed), thus were the means of human preservation "perverted to his ruin."

Lauding those, whom Mason described as "some of the best men that this world ever produced," who had sought "to restore mankind to its native rights," Mason observed that "the most effectual means that human wisdom hath ever been able to devise is frequently appealing to the body of the people, to those constituent members from whom authority originated, for their approbation or dissent." He quoted two lines of poetry from Dryden to indicate that whenever "the free voice of the people is suppressed or corrupted" or the military is not "dissolved into and blended with that mass from which it was taken, inevitable destruction to the state follows."

Although the idea of subjecting elected political leaders, one of whose primary goals is that of reflecting the wishes of their constituents, to periodic elections is widely accepted, one might well question whether the same principle should apply in military affairs, where expertise about tactics and logistics might be at a premium and where incompetent leadership might lead to disaster. Mason anticipated this objection but made no such distinction. Indeed, he observed that "whenever any military establishment or authority is not, by some certain mode of rotation, dissolved into and blended with that mass from which it was taken, inevitable destruction to the state follows." In a clear indication of Mason's assessment of England, Mason warned that rotation of offices was necessary to avoid allowing the corruption of the British constitution to take hold in America.[7]

The Roman Republic was a frequent source of inspiration for advocates of republicanism, and Mason was no exception. He attributed the vigor of the Roman Commonwealth to the fact that "new consuls were annually elected, new levies made, and new officers appointed." He observed that this practice had provided "an inexhaustible fund of experienced officers, upon every emergency, untainted with the dangerous impressions which continued command naturally makes," thus adding an additional element to the argument by suggesting that long exercise of command itself works against the notions of equality on which Mason thought legitimate government is

---

[7] Mason's later works will more explicitly blame many of these problems on hereditary appointments, which, by their very nature, are unaccountable to voters.

founded. Mason thought that Roman abandonment of rotation of commanding officers within the military had led people to consider themselves not as "the soldiers of the Republic, but as the troops of Marius or of Sylla, of Pompey or of Ceasar, of Marc Antony or of Octavius."

Referring to North America as "the only great nursery of freemen now left upon the face of the earth,"[8] Mason urged his audience to "cherish the sacred deposit," to "strive to merit this greatest encomium that ever was bestowed upon any country," and to keep sight of the maxim "that all power was originally lodged in, and consequently derived from, the people." Resorting again to Biblical language, which was particularly appropriate for a military audience, Mason said that "We should wear it as a breastplate, and buckle it on as our armour."

As he got to his penultimate paragraph, Mason observed that "By investing our officers with a power for life, or for an unlimited time, we are acting diametrically contrary to the principles of that liberty for which we profess to contend, and establishing a precedent which may prove fatal." Almost as though he were making a U-Turn, however, Mason introduced two arguably discordant elements.

The first suggested that allowing individuals to be "rechosen" for later nonconsecutive terms, opened the door to the return of officers of approved merit." The second was an exception for the gentleman (presumably George

---

[8] Mason quoted "a learned and revered writer," who was undoubtedly Jonathan Shipley, Bishop of St. Asaph, who published *A Speech Intended to Have Been Spoken by the Bishop of St. Asaph, on the Bill for Altering the Charters of the Colony of Massachusetts Bay*. See Paul H. Smith, com., *English Defenders of American Freedoms, 1774-1778*. Washington, 1971, 31-48. The quotation is from page. 41.

Washington), who had been unanimously selected because of "his public merit and experience." It is difficult to know whether to charge Mason with inconsistency or to praise him for recognizing that theoretical principles sometimes require exceptions. Subsequent experience, including Washington's return to civilian life after the Revolution as well as his decision not to seek a third presidential term, suggest that Washington may have been among those individuals who was not corrupted by the blandishments of power.

In Book III of *The Politics,* Aristotle associated citizenship with an individual's right to share in "the administration of justice and in the holding of office" (1974, 93). Consciously or otherwise, Mason ended his remarks with similar sentiments, observing that "no young man will think himself degraded by doing duty in the ranks, which he may in his turn command, or has commanded." Citizens will rally to the cause when they consider themselves included among decision makers.

ANALYSIS

Apart from his final concessions, Mason's speech combined liberalism's emphasis on egalitarianism with the republican emphasis on the duties of citizenship and the principle of popular accountability. Mason's emphasis on the darker side of human nature might further reflect a Christian emphasis (Mason was an Anglican) on the corrupting power of original sin and the need for constant vigilance in constructing political structures to cabin its influences.

GENERAL TEST OATH (AUGUST 1775)

If members of the Convention could not get him to attend out-of-state meetings, its members were not going to let him completely off the hook. They appointed him head of the local Committee of Safety, and he took these duties seriously. They also asked Mason and Josiah Parker to draft a general test oath, although it is unclear whether the Convention chose them, because they thought they favored such a resolution, because they hoped that they might draw up a more liberal oath than others, or for some other reason. The Convention postponed action on this resolution on August 22, 1775 but apparently adopted it, or one similar to it, in 1777 (*PGM*, I: 249).

Test oaths have a long history, often tied to religious bigotry, as in the neighboring colony of Maryland, where they had been used to persecute Roman Catholics (Asper 1969). Fortunately, Virginia was not attempting to ascertain loyalty or disloyalty through use of religious tests. However, it had an obvious problem, at a time before it had formally declared independence from Britain and during which many Patriots were still professing loyalty to King George III, namely, that of avoiding outright civil war. Moreover, it was common for English merchants, who would rightfully be expected to maintain their loyalty to their country, to set up offices in Virginia cities, which they would have to abandon if forced to profess loyalty to the colony. Mason thus observed in his previously cited letter to Martin Cockburn that:

> A very sensible petition from the merchants who are Natives of great Britain has been put into my Hands, & will be presented to-day or tomorrow praying that some certain Line of Conduct may be prescribed to them, & a recommendation to the people from the Convention respecting them. As I drew the ordinance for a general Test, I have endeavour'd to make it such as no good Man

> wou'd object to the Merchants here declare themselves well pleased with it (*PGM*, I: 251).

The circumstances that had led Governor Dunmore to dissolve the state legislature, and attempt to govern from a ship from which he encouraged slaves to revolt against their masters had created a virtual state of war. Tensions were further heightened by news that conflict had already commenced between American Minutemen and British Regulars in Massachusetts. The Continental Congress did not declare formal independence until July of 1776, but it had adopted its Declaration of the Causes and Necessity of Taking up Arms more than a month prior to Virginia's general oath.

Although it did not, like the Declaration of Independence or Virginia's later Declaration of Rights, outline general principles of government, Mason's opening paragraph laid out the stakes as many Virginia Patriots must have viewed them. Just as the Declaration of Independence would argue that British actions evinced a plan to reduce the colonies under an absolute tyranny, so too, Mason's Ordinance for the General Test Oath referenced the "long premeditated and now avowed Design of the British Ministry to force Loyal Colonists into an abject surrender of their Rights and Privileges as Freemen." (*PGM*, I: 246) The Document specifically cited Dunmore's actions "by an unexampled & wanton suspension of the Law of the Land & Institution of that horrid Supporter of Tyranny, Law Martial, by seising, and imprisoning and transporting the persons of our peaceable Citizens, by declaring our Servants and Slaves free and inviting & arming them to assassinate their Masters, our innocent Wifes and helpless children" (*PGM*, I: 246-247). As would be expected, even planters who might have wished for an end to further importation of slaves, regarded Dunmore's encouragement of slave revolts as one of his most shocking and barbarous acts (Parkinson 2016, 141ff).

The document further observed that some of these "cruel and horrid Measures have been countenanced & supported by some wicked Persons among ourselves in wanton violation of their plighted Faith voluntarily offered in support of our late happy Constitution" (*PGM*, I: 247). This had led "by an Appeal to Heaven, to enter into a more firm Union for our common defense, and to distinguish those deserving our Protection from such as are enemies to our just Cause" (*PGM*, I: 247).

The oath, which was to apply to all freemen over the age of 16, was as follows:

> I _____ _____ of the Parish of _____ in the Country of _____ in the Colony of Virginia do solemnly & sincerely promise & declare that I will not directly or indirectly violate the Association now in force in this Colony but that I will conform thereto so long as the same shall continue in force; that I will not take up Arms against the good People Freemen Inhabitants of this Colony or any other part of America acting under & in support of the Ordinances of general Convention during the unhappy differences now subsist between Great Britain and America, nor will I directly or indirectly by correspondence, Signs or Tokens or by any ways or means aid, assist, or support any Power that shall or may be employed against the good People of America: and I do declare that I will defend and support this Colony against all Invasions & Insurrections whatsoever that shall or may be made against the Rights & Liberties of America according to my abilities & pursuant to ordinances of General Convention—So help me God— (*PGM*, I: 247).

There are a number of notable aspects of this oath. First, and this is characteristic of Mason's life-long approach, although adopted by a state convention, the oath was to be administered at the parish and county level. Second, it continued to refer to Virginia as a colony (no complete legal separation had as yet been effected), while seeking to insure not only that office takers would not fight against it but also that they would not fight against "any other part of America" or "against the good People of America." Third, Mason designed the oath chiefly as a means of self defense. It did not pledge anyone to support a fight against Britain but simply to protect against any possible invasion by British authorities or against "the Rights & Liberties of America." Fourth, the reference to "the unhappy differences now subsisting between Great Britain and America" seemed to express hope that sentiment might yet turn in a happier, even pacific, direction.

The oath did seek to suppress freedom of the press by limiting "correspondence, Signs or Tokens" of support for the British, but even modern American law recognizes the possibility of such restraints during times of "clear and present danger," or when faced with threats of "imminent lawless actions." Moreover, correspondence could easily have been used to pass on secret information or communicate plans for attack.

Although the Document ended, as did most contemporary oaths, by invoking God's help, it did not require the affirmation of any theological doctrines. Anglicans were, of course, expected to pray for the British King, but the oath, would not have proscribed this. Moreover, immediately after the oath, the Convention had "Provided always that the people called Quakers shall affirm to the same effect & also subscribe the same." Like a comparable provision that the U.S. Constitution later embodied with respect to the oath of the president, this was designed to overcome the Quakers' belief that any form of swearing was ungodly.

Any oath that neighbors seek to enforce against neighbors has its dangers, but the legislation seemed to minimize many of the most severe. In this case, local committees were given power to summon those who refused to take such oaths, to disarm them (which could be considered a relatively prudent measure under the circumstances), and to limit their movement to within five miles of their residences (*PGM*, I: 248). Their names would to be subject to publication (presumably so neighbors would know to keep an eye on them), and they would be subject to "treble taxes," an illiberal measure that would hardly endear them to the provisional government.

As he had indicated in a letter to Martin Cockburn of August 22, Mason had, in response to a petition from merchants who were British natives and who were clearly caught in a bind, also sought a solution "such as no good Man would object to (*PGM*, I: 251). The Virginia Convention adopted this resolution on August 25, 1775 and ordered that it be published in the two *Virginia Gazettes.* Its sentiments were quite liberal and were arguably calculated with the view of eventual conciliation in mind. It thus recommended that Virginians "treat all natives of *Great Britain,* resident here, as do not show themselves enemies to the common cause of *America,* with lenity and friendship; to protect all persons whatsoever in the just enjoyment of their civil rights and liberty; to discountenance all national reflections; to preserve, to the utmost of their power, internal peace and good order;

and to promote union, harmony, and mutual good-will, among all ranks of people" (*PGM*, I: 253).

ANALYSIS

Loyalty oaths have deservedly gotten a bad name, but the oath that Mason devised is about as liberal as one might have devised in a situation where a governor had dissolved the legislature and was urging slaves to revolt and in which loyalties were divided. Although the threat of treble taxes was hardly mild, the oath did not require incarceration, deportation, or other punishment. By seeking to accommodate both British merchants and Quakers with religious convictions against taking oaths, it pointed in a liberal direction consistent with Mason's later policies with regard to religious liberties.

REFERENCES

Ammerman, David. 1974. *In the Common Cause: American Response to the Coercive Acts of 1775.* Charlottesville: University Press of Virginia.

Aristotle. 1954. *The Politics of Aristotle*, ed. Ernest Barker. New York: Oxford University Press.

Asper, Lewis D. 1969. "The Long and Unhappy History of Loyalty Testing in Maryland." *The American Journal of Legal History* 13 (April): 97-109.

Breen, T.H. 1997. "Ideology and Nationalism on the Eve of the American Revolution: Revisions Once More in Need of Revising." *The Journal of American History* 84 (June): 13-39.

Broadwater, Jeff. 2006. *George Mason: Forgotten Founder.* Chapel Hill: The University of North Carolina Press.

Copeland, Pamela C. and Richard K. Macmaster. 1975. *The Five George Masons: Patriots and Planters of Virginia and Maryland.* Charlottesville: University Press of Virginia.

"Declaration on Taking Arms," July 6, 1775, as found in *The Declaration of Independence in Historical Context: American State Papers, Petitions, Proclamations, & Letters of the Delegates to the first National Congresses,* compiled, edited by Barry Alan Shain. Indianapolis, IN: Liberty Fund, 2014, pp. 277-282.

Farr, James. 2008. "Locke, Natural Law, and New World Slavery." *Political Theory* 36 (August): 495-522.

Ganter, Herbert Lawrence. 1937. "The Machiavellianism of George Mason." *The William and Mary Quarterly* 17 (April): 239-264.

Gould, Philip. 1993. "Virtue, Ideology, and the American Revolution: The Legacy of the Republican Synthesis." *American Literary History* 5 (Autumn): 564-577.

Hamilton, Alexander, James Madison, and James Monroe. 1961 [1787-1788]. *The Federalist Papers.* New York: New American Library.

Hartz, Louis. 1955. *The Liberal Tradition in America: An Interpretation of American Political Thought Since the Revolution.* New York: Harcourt, Brace & World.

Liddle, William D. 1979. "'A Patriot King or None': Lord Bolingbroke and the American Renunciation of George III." *The Journal of American History* 65 (March): 951-970.

[Lind, John]. 1776. *An Answer to the Declaration of the American Congress.* London: J. Walter, Charingcross and T. Sewell.

McDonnell, Michael A. 1998. "Popular Mobilization and Political Culture in Revolutionary Virginia: The Failure of the Minutemen and the Revolution from Below." *The Journal of American History* 85 (December): 946-981.

Maier, Pauline. 1997. *American Scripture: Making the Declaration of Independence.* New York: Alfred A. Knopf.

Mason, George. 1970. *The Papers of George Mason, 1725-1792,* ed. Robert A. Rutland. Chapel Hill: The University of North Carolina Press.

Munves, James. 1978. *Thomas Jefferson and the Declaration of Independence: The writing and editing of the document that marked the birth of the United States of America.* New York: Charles Scribner's Sons.

Parkinson, Robert G. 2016. *The Common Cause: Creating Race and Nation in the American Revolution.* Chapel Hill: University of North Carolina Press.

"Resolve, n." Oxford English Dictionary. http://www.oed.com/view/Entry/163732?rskey=f36sbE&result=1&isAdvanced=false#eis

Rowland, Kate Mason. 1964 [1892] *The Life of George Mason, 1724-1792.* 2 vols. New York: Russell & Russell, Inc.

Sweig, Donald M. 1983. "A New-Found Washington Letter of 1774 and the Fairfax Resolves." *The William and Mary Quarterly* 40 (April): 283-291.

Vile, John R. 2015. *Founding Documents of America: Documents Decoded.* Santa Barbara, CA: ABC-CLIO.

Wills, Garry. 1984. *Cincinnatus: George Washington & the Enlightenment, Images of Power in Early America.* New York: Doubleday.

3

George Mason and the Virginia Declaration of Rights

Of all of George Mason's contributions to political thought, none is better known, or more influential, than the Declaration of Rights, which he and a committee drafted for the Fifth Virginia Convention in 1776. R. Carter Pittman has gone so far as to call the Committee's first official draft, which was printed in Virginia on May 27 of 1776 and widely copied in other newspapers, as "The most influential constitutional document in American history" (1960, 109). Indeed, he classified it with the Magna Carta and the English Bill of Rights as "one of the three most influential constitutional documents in the history of liberty" (1960, 110).

Although scholars thus tend to identify the Virginia Declaration of Rights with contemporary notions of a bill of rights, it is organized differently. Most notably, it was placed at the beginning rather than the end of a constitution, and it began with philosophical assertions about the origin and purposes of government rather than with the list of specific rights like those in the first ten amendments to the U.S.

Constitution.[1] Jeff Broadwater has argued that modern bills of rights are associated with "constitutional status, specificity, and judicial enforceability" (2017, 549). Although the Virginia Declaration was considered to be law, and thus met the first criterion, it listed a fairly limited set of rights and appears to have been regarded largely as a guide for the people to use in assessing whether their leaders were or were not accomplishing the purposes for which they were elected rather than as a set of rights from which individuals might defend themselves from government abuses in court.

In a Ph.D. dissertation, Robert Leroy Hilldrup viewed the Virginia Declaration as "a collection of vague generalities, embodying a political creed for which men would be willing to die, but, like other creeds, capable of sharp restriction when practical problems, such as the framing of a system of government, were encountered" (1935, 187). Writing after World War I, he suggested that it was "easily adaptable to use as war propaganda," and might even be considered as "the Fourteenth Points of the Revolution" (1935, 187). Hilldrup also says, however, that both the Virginia Declaration and its English predecessor, "Were first called 'Declaration of Rights,'

---

[1] When James Madison first introduced his proposals to amend the U.S. Constitution on June 8, 1789, his first two proposals were very close to the philosophical statements within the Virginia Declaration. He thus proposed: "First, That there be prefixed to the Constitution, a declaration, that all power is originally vested in, and consequently derived from, the people. That Government is instituted and ought to be exercised for the benefits of the people; which consists in the enjoyment of life and liberty, with the right of acquiring and using property, and generally of pursuing and obtaining happiness and safety. That the people have an indubitable, unalienable, and indefeasible right to reform or change their Government, whenever it be found adverse or inadequate in the purposes of its institution." (Kurland and Lerner, 1987, V: 25).

and then, after ratification 'Bills of rights.'" He further notes that both "provided new governments," which suggest that they may have had legal force (1935, 210).

CONVENTIONS

Today, political conventions in America typically assemble to nominate candidates for high political office or to revise constitutions, but in early British and early American history, a convention was a collective group of men who met "without warrant from royal authority" (Dunaway 1904, 570). If the king had dismissed or failed to call a parliament, a convention might conduct legislative business or write constitutional documents in his absence. Contemporaries thus designated the English parliament that met in the 1650s under Oliver Cromwell after Charles I had been beheaded, and the parliament that met in 1689 to offer the throne to William and Mary after James II fled England, as "convention" parliaments (Vile 2016, 4). In the most definitive book on the subject in the nineteenth century, Judge John Jameson distinguished four types of conventions, the "spontaneous convention, or public meeting"; "the ordinary legislative convention, or general assembly"; "the revolutionary convention"; and "the constitutional convention" (1887, 3-4). The convention from which the Declaration of Rights emerged shared elements of both a revolutionary law-making convention, which "consists of those bodies of men who, in times of political crisis, assume, or have cast upon them, provisionally, the function of government" (1887, 6) and a constitutional convention, responsible for reframing the fundament law. St. George Tucker, a noted Virginia jurist, thus observed that "It was not the Act of the *ordinary Legislature* that the Bands of Union between us—It was the voice of the people themselves, proclaiming to the world that they were resolved to be free—to be governed only by their own laws;—and to institute such a Government, as in their Opinion was most likely to produce Peace, happiness and safety to the individual as well as to the Community" (Tucker 2013, III:1774).

Virginia conventions began upon Governor Dunmore's dissolution of the House of Burgesses, thus providing that there would be no royal representative in the Virginia legislative body. The first such convention met in Williamsburg from August 1 to August 6, 1774 and was presided over by Peyton Randolph, who had also served as speaker of the House of Burgesses (Dunaway 1904, 570). The convention adopted eleven resolutions limiting trade with Britain, and appointing delegates to the Continental Congress.

A second convention met from March 20-27, 1775, in St. John's Church in Richmond. It approved the actions of the First Continental Congress, proposed the formation of volunteer companies for self defense, and re-elected delegates to Congress, substituting Thomas Jefferson as an alternate for Peyton Randolph (Dunaway 1904, 574-575). This was also the convention where Patrick Henry gave his famous "Liberty or Death" speech.

The third convention, called after fighting had broken out at Lexington and Concord, met in Richmond from July 17, 1775 to August 26, 1775. George Mason was one of its members, albeit a reluctant one. Mason thus wrote a letter to an unknown Englishman on October 2, 1778, in which he indicated that:

> In the Summer 75 I was much against my Inclination Drag'd out of my retirement, by the People of my Country, & sent a Delegate to the General Convention at

> Richmond, where I was appointed a Member of the first Committee of Safety; and have since, at different times, been chosen a Member of the Privy Council, & of the American Congress; but have constantly declined acting in any other public character than that of an independent Representative of the People, in the House of Delegates; where I still remain, from a Consciousness of being able to do my Country more Service there than in any other Department" (*PGM*, I: 434).

Complaining about how his devotion to public business had detracted from his own affairs, he observed that "if I can only live to see the American Union firmly fixed, and free Governments well established in our western world, and can leave to my children a Crust of Bread, & Liberty, I shall die satisfied; and say with the Psalmist 'Lord now lettest thy Servant depart in Peace'": (PJM, I: 434).

The third convention was responsible for appointing Mason, who had replaced George Washington who had left to head the Continental Army, to the colonial Committee of Safety to fill the vacuum left by Governor's Dunmore's flight. The fourth convention, which was moved back to Williamsburg from December 1, 1775 to January 20, 1776, adopted a number of laws.

The fifth convention (Grigsby 1855), at which George Mason was once again a member, and from which the Declaration of Rights and the Virginia Constitution emerged, also met in Williamsburg, this time from May 6, 1776 to July 5, 1776. To utilize Jameson's terminology, it played the role of both a revolutionary and a constitutional body. It was during this time, May 15 to be exact, that the Continental Congress finalized a resolution urging the states to form new governments to replace the colonial governments that were collapsing around them. On that same day, three days before Mason was seated, the Fifth Virginia Convention adopted a resolution, which Richard Henry Lee introduced at the Continental Congress on June 6, 1776, calling for independence from Great Britain and leading to resulting in the writing of the Declaration of Independence.

The Convention also unanimously resolved "that a Committee ought to prepare a Declaration of Rights and such a plan of government as will be most likely to maintain peace and order in this colony and secure substantial and equal liberty to the people" (Revolutionary Virginia, VII, 143). A.E. Dick Howard observed that "Those members of the 1776 convention steeped in Lockean notions of the social contract might well have considered themselves in a 'state of nature' upon the dissolution of the bond with Great Britain. Thus, to declare man's natural rights was a logical step en route to forming a new social compact" (1968, 820).

Perhaps disappointed that he had spent his time in Philadelphia writing the Declaration of Independence while his state was settling on a future government, Jefferson (1964, 188) apparently thought the authority of the convention was limited to drawing up a temporary constitution, one of which he himself proposed, but his view was probably in the minority.[2] This was confirmed by Edmund Randolph, who served in the Fourth and Fifth Virginia Conventions (where he, like Mason, was a member of the Committee to draw up the Declaration of Rights and the state Constitution) as a

---

[2] St. George Tucker thus observed in *Commonwealth v. Rolph Eldridge,* that "a power to demolish the existing fabric of Government, which no one I believe ever denied to that Convention, without Authority to erect a new one could never be presumed" (Tucker 2013, III: 1774).

representative of Williamsburg and later wrote a history of this period. Randolph thus observed that the members of the convention "saw no distinction between the conceded power to declare independence, and its necessary consequence, the fencing of society by the institution of government" (1936, 43).

MASON'S ATTITUDE GOING INTO THE CONVENTION

Mason did not enjoy participating in legislative bodies or conventions. After attending the Third Virginia Convention in Richmond the previous year, Mason had written a letter to George Washington dated October 14, 1775, in which, after referring to "the Partys & Factions which prevail'd at Richmond," he observed that "I never was in so disagreeable a Situation, and almost despaired of a Cause which I saw so ill conducted" (*PGM*, I: 255). Mason was predisposed to fairly regular attacks of gout, and the event had been so distressing that it had physical effects: "Mere Vexation & Disgust threw me into such an ill State of Health that before the Convention rose, I was sometimes near fainting in the House: since my Return Home I have had a severe Fit of Sickness, from which I am now recovering; but am still very weak & low" (*PGM*, I: 255).

As the Fifth Convention approached on May 6, Mason's mood was again disturbed by "a smart fit of the Gout," which, he explained to Richard Henry Lee in a letter from Williamsburg dated May 18, 1776, had "detaine'd me at Home the first of the Session" (*PGM*, I: 271). Sobered by the fact that "We are now going upon the most important of all Subjects—Government" (*PGM*, I: 271), Edmund Pendleton had appointed Mason as part of a committee of 27 or 28 men (Friedman 2002, 935, n. 15), which eventually grew to 36. Archibald Cary, of Chesterfield County, who also headed the

Convention's Committee of the Whole, chaired the committee to draft a Declaration of Rights and a state constitution.

Mason was not particularly sanguine about the process he faced, although he anticipated that he and other Patriots might be able to prevail:

> The Committee appointed to prepare a plan is, according to Custom, overcharged with useless Members. You know our Conventions. I need only say that it is not mended by the late Elections. We shall, in all probability have a thousand ridiculous and impracticable proposals, & of Course, a Plan form'd of hetrogenious, jarring & unintelligible Ingredients; this can be prevented only by a few Men of Integrity & Abilitys, whose Countrys Interest lies next their Hearts, undertaking this Business, and defending it ably thro' every state of opposition. (*PGM*, I: 271)

In a similar, even more pessimistic vein, Patrick Henry wrote a letter to John Adams on May 20, 1776, in which he complained that "Our sessions will be very long, during which I cannot count upon an coadjutor of talents equal to the task" (cited in Oliver 1959, 28).

Mason was added to the Committee when he was seated at the Convention on May 18, 1775. He was also assigned to committees on Proposition and Grievances, Privileges and Elections, a committee tasked to write an ordinance encouraging domestic manufacturing; and another for securing salt, saltpeter, and gunpowder (Rowland 1964, I, 228).

Although he was not the committee chair, Mason took the lead, probably because of his reputation as a draftsman. Edmund Pendleton thus observed in a letter to Thomas Jefferson dated May 24, 1776 that "The Political Cooks are busy in preparing the dish, and as Colonel Mason seems to have the Ascendancy in the great work, I have sanguine hopes it will be framed so as to Answer it's end, Prosperity to the Community and Security to Individuals, but I am yet a stranger to the Plan" (Pendleton, I: 180).

Edmund Randolph recalled that: "A very large committee was nominated to prepare the proper instruments, and many projects of a bill of rights and constitution, discovered the ardor for political notice, rather than a ripeness in political wisdom. That proposed by George Mason swallowed up all the rest, by fixing the grounds and plan, which after great discussion and correction, were finally ratified" (1936, 44).

Randolph went on to identify two broad purposes of what he called "this bill of rights" (1936, 47). The first was "that the legislature should not in their acts violate any of those cannons." The second was "that in all the revolutions of time, of human opinion, and of government, a perpetual standard should be erected, around which the people might rally, and by a notorious record be forever admonished to be watchful, firm and virtuous" (1936, 47). Randolph further identified the document as the "corner stone" of the state constitution that followed (1936, 47).

Mason, who was fearful of judicial activism and therefore generally expected that people would defend their rights through political processes rather than in court (Broadwater 1017, 558), viewed the Declaration of Rights as a way of informing the people of their rights, so they could guard them, but he may have had wider aspirations. Thus, in the previously cited letter to an English friend dated October 2, 1778, Mason employed a Biblical analogy when he observed that "We have laid our new Government upon a broad Foundation, & have endeavoured to provide the most effectual Securities for the essential Rights of human nature, both in Civil and Religious liberty; the People become every Day more & more attach'd to it; and I trust that neither the Power, of Great Britain, nor the Power of Hell will be able to prevail against it" (*PGM*, I: 434-435).

DRAFTING AND PRINTING OF THE DOCUMENT

The Virginia Declaration of Rights had at least three iterations.[3] George Mason drafted the first version of ten propositions sometime during the week of May 20-26, and there is a copy in his handwriting. Thomas Ludwell Lee of Stafford County (elder brother of Richard Henry, Francis Lightfoot, William, and Arthur) made two additions and suggested two others on Mason's copy in Lee's handwriting. Lee further noted that "The above clauses, with some small alterations, & the addition of one, or two more, have already been agreed to in the Committee appointed to prepare a declaration of rights; when this business is finished in the house, the committee will proceed to the ordinance of government" (*PGM*, I: 278).

---

[3] To complicate the situation still further, Mason included a draft of 14 resolutions in a letter to an Englishmen dated October 2, 1778. He described it as "a Copy of the first Draught of the Declaration of Rights, just as it was drawn by me, & presented to the Virginia Convention, where it received few Alterations; some of them I think not for the better; this was the first thing of the kind upon the Continent, and has been closely imitated by all the other States" (*PGM*, I: 434). Displayed in Richmond, Virginia, in the 1840s as the original document, the Document is now known to have been, in the words of Irving Brant, "a composite of the original, the committee draft and the final draft, with one word ["created"] transplanted from the Declaration of Independence." (Brant, I, 236).

On May 27 the Committee reported a total of 18 propositions and ordered them to be printed. After some further emendations, the Convention unanimously adopted 16 Resolutions on June 11, 1776. Ironically, the copy that was most widely printed and circulated within the colonies and available to members of the Second Continental Congress was the second version that the Fifth Virginia Convention ordered printed on May 27 (Billings 1992, 341). Pittmann thus observed that this draft "was published in the Virginia Gazette of June 1, 1777, and therefore republished in newspapers and magazines all over America, in England, and in Europe" (1960, 110). Pittman notes that this was the document that the delegates to the Second Continental Congress would have seen, that Franklin and Adams would have used when respectively constructing the Pennsylvania and Massachusetts declarations of rights, and that other states subsequently imitated (1960, 110). Friedman (2001), has specifically traced its influence on the declarations of rights adopted by Maryland and Delaware. These state declarations further served as one of the inspirations for the Declaration of the Rights of Man and of Citizens in France (Jellinek 1901; Chester 1989, 128-146). Pittman claims that the official Virginia Declaration, the third iteration, was not published in bound volumes with other states declarations until 1811 (1960, 111).

THE SIGNIFICANCE OF A "DECLARATION" OF RIGHTS

This chapter will analyze this document by beginning with the first draft of the Declaration as Mason wrote it, noting its successive changes in the committee draft and in the final document, and suggesting, where possible, some of the subsequent documents that it influenced. I will pay special attention to the Declaration of Independence, the U.S. Constitution, and the first ten amendments to the U.S. Constitution, which have in the 20th Century generally been called the Bill of Rights (Douma 2017; Maier 2017).

Maier (1999, 879) asserts that "the 'ur' document of American liberty," was not the Declaration of Independence but "George Mason's 1776 draft of the Virginia Bill of Rights." Donald S. Lutz has further demonstrated that "The state constitutions and the respective bills of rights, not the amendments proposed by state ratifying conventions, are the immediate source from which the U.S. Bill of Rights was derived" (1992, 67; also see Calabresi, Agudo, and Dore, 2012).

In language that remains virtually unchanged in the succeeding versions, the Virginia Declaration began by identifying itself as a "Declaration of Rights, made by the Representatives of the good People of Virginia, assembled in full Convention; and recommended to Posterity as the Basis and Foundation of Government." Although this appears to be standard boilerplate, it bears some examination. David Armitage observes that a declaration typically referred to "a public document issued by a representative body such as Parliament" (2007, 30), while Pauline Maier described a declaration as "a particularly emphatic pronouncement or proclamation that was often explanatory" (1997, 51). The idea of a Declaration of Rights clearly dates back at least as far of the British Declaration of Rights of 1689, which Parliament issued after the accession of William and Mary. On July 6, 1775, the Continental Congress had adopted a "Declaration on Taking up Arms," and on July 4, 1776, it adopted the Declaration of Independence as an explanation of the action it had taken two days earlier in severing ties with Britain.

Although "conventions" proceeded without the oversight of a king, they could lay claim to being representative bodies if elected by the people, as the Virginia delegates were. The reference to meeting in "full Convention" would further highlight its representative nature.

Of all the Founding Fathers, probably none was more closely associated with the idea that one generation could not bind another than was Thomas Jefferson (Vile 1992, 63-67). He observed in a letter to James Madison dated September 6, 1789 "'that the earth belongs in usufruct to the living'; that the dead have neither powers nor rights over it" (Jefferson 1905, 2: 3-4). In drafting the Bill for Establishing Religious Freedom, which he introduced in the Virginia Assembly in 1778, Jefferson noted that "to declare this act to be irrevocable would be of no effect in law." Still, he declared that "we are free to declare and do declare, that the rights hereby asserted are of the natural rights of mankind, and that if any act shall be hereafter passed to repeal the present or to narrow its operation, such act will be an infringement of natural rights" (Jefferson 1905, II, 48). The introduction to this Declaration probably intended to embody similar sentiments by citing its resolutions as "recommended to Posterity" rather than as legally binding on them.

Whereas the U.S. Constitution preceded the amendments now called the bill of rights (perhaps because its Framers thought that the Declaration of Independence already articulated fundamental principles of the republic), Virginia drafted its Declaration of Rights prior to its Constitution. Moreover, by identifying it as "the Basis and Foundation of Government," Virginia's leaders clearly sought to ground the later document in protection for individual rights.

SOURCES OF THE DECLARATION OF RIGHTS

One analysis of the Declaration asserts that it drew primarily from "Locke's writing, the English bill of rights, and colonial experience and conditions" (Hilldrup 2017, 217). Another believes that Mason may directly, or indirectly, have been influenced by the Jesuit priest Robert Francis Romulus Bellarmine (1542-1621) (Hunt 1917). Although many, if not all, of these sources certainly played a role, they are not exhaustive. Although Mason did not attend college, he was well read, was well acquainted with enlightenment philosophers, and had observed the progress of opinion in the years leading up to independence. Like Jefferson, Mason had the ability to summarize what other patriots, who were also acquainted with contemporary political theory, were thinking and to express this thinking in universal, or near-universal, terms.

PHILOSOPHICAL FOUNDATIONS

Mason's first paragraph related to rights. It proved to be among its most philosophical and controversial. Echoing Remarks on Annual Elections to the Fairfax Independent Company, where he had stated that "All men are by nature born equally free and independent" (Rowland 1964, 430), Mason now proclaimed "That all Men are born equally free and independent,[4] and have certain inherent natural Rights, of which they can not by any Compact, deprive or divest their

---

[4] It may be noteworthy that in introducing Virginia's Resolution for Independence at the Second Continental Congress on June 7, 1776, Richard Henry Lee said that "these states" rather than individual citizens thereof, "are, and of right ought to be, free and independent" (Vile 2015, 95).

Posterity; among which are the Enjoyment of Life and Liberty, with the Means of acquiring and possessing Property, and pursuing and obtaining Happiness and Safety" (*PGM*, I: 277). The Committee accepted the clause but altered it in subsequent convention debate.

The cause of the debate is not difficult to find. Thomas Ludwell Lee thus wrote to his brother Richard Henry Lee in response to reports that the Convention had "been stumbling at the threshold." Somewhat confirming this assessment, he observed that "I will tell you plainly that a certain set of aristocrats—for we have such monsters here—finding that their execrable system cannot be reared on such foundations, have to this time kept us at bay on the first line, which declares all men to be born free and independent." Giving further insight into the drafting process, Lee continued: "A number of absurd or unmeaning alterations have been proposed. The words as they stand are approved by a very great majority, yet by a thousand masterly fetches and stratagems the business has been so delayed that the first clause stands yet unassented to by the Convention" (Quoted in Rowland, 1964, I, 240).

Edmund Randolph further explained that Robert Carter Nicholas of James City County, who was his father-in-law, had opposed Mason's initial clause "as being the forerunner of pretext or civil convulsion" and that "It was answered, perhaps with too great an indifference to futurity, and not without inconsistency, that with arms in our hands, asserting the general rights of man, we ought not to be too nice and too much restricted in the delineation of them; but that slaves not being constituent members of our society could never pretend to any benefit from such a maxim" (1936, 45). Apparently, other slave owners were more concerned about the possibility of slave revolts—and possibly about the hypocrisy of condemning an institution that was a mainstay of their society—than was Mason. The addition of the words "when they enter into a state of society," was clearly designed to exclude such slaves.

The final draft thus declared "That all men are <by nature> equally free and independent, and have certain inherent rights, of which, <when they enter into a state of society,> they cannot, by any compact, deprive or divest their posterity; <namely,> the enjoyment of life and liberty, with the means of acquiring and possessing property, and pursuing and obtaining happiness and safety" (*PGM*, I: 287).

Whereas Mason's previous works had focused on the rights of Englishmen, the Convention had already proposed a resolution for independence, which would preclude further claims based on English citizenship. As Jefferson would soon do in the Declaration of Independence, Mason thus shifted his emphasis from the rights of Englishmen to "inherent natural Rights." Natural rights were, of course, a central topic among English social contract philosophers like Thomas Hobbes and John Locke, but British Whig thinkers, as well as small "r" republicans, would have shared similar sentiments, which were likely grounded in part on Christian conceptions of human brotherhood. Such rights were "inherent" in that they were regarded as being essential to human nature and to human flourishing. Jefferson later chose to use the word "created" rather than "born" and omitted the word "independent,"[5] but

---

[5] In their Essays, No. 45, "On the Equality and Inequality of Men," Trenchard and Gordon had observed that "Men are naturally equal, and none ever rose above the rest but by force or consent: No man was ever born above all the rest, nor below them all: and therefore there never was

none other than John Locke, from whom Mason may have drawn, had asserted that men were "by nature all free, equal and independent" (Locke 1955, par. 95, p. 78).

John Locke regarded the formation of a social contract as a way of escaping an insecure state of nature to protect "life, liberty, and property," the actual words used in the first resolution of the Declaration and Resolves of the First Continental Congress, which it issued on October 14, 1774 (See Vile 2015, 77). Mason's terminology with its reference to "life, liberty, and the pursuit of the Enjoyment of Life and Liberty, with the Means of acquiring and possessing Property, and pursuing and obtaining Happiness and Safety" seemed broader and may have influenced Jefferson's decision to refer in the Declaration of Independence to "life, liberty, and the pursuit of happiness." Jefferson may have been on safer philosophical ground by omitting the word "obtaining" in the elusive pursuit of happiness. Arthur M. Schlesinger believed that Jefferson's decision to cut the words "obtaining happiness and safety" was largely a matter of style (1965, 327).

Mason's next paragraph stated "That Power is, by God and Nature, vested in, and consequently derived from the People; that Magistrates are their Trustees and Servants, and at all times amenable to them" (*PGM*, I: 277). Edmund Randolph chose to summarize this paragraph rather than explaining (if he indeed noticed) why the committee, in both its initial and final drafts, chose to change this to say "That <all> power is vested in, and consequently derived from the people" while dropping Mason's reference "by God and Nature." In the Declaration of Independence, Jefferson would cite both "Nature and Nature's God" in connection with

---

any man in the world so good or so bad, so high or so low, but he had his fellow" (1995, I, 306).

rights, while Congress would add further references to the Deity. Although God and nature might seem to cover all the bases, the Virginia Committee may have omitted references either to derail tensions between the two perspectives or to bypass concerns about church/state separation.

If men were born equally free and independent, then no man, or group of men, would have a divine right, which some English kings had claimed, and which Locke had challenged, to rule over others. The conclusion would logically follow that rulers were "trustees" and "servants" of the people. Any power they exercised was held in trust and could be cabined by those who granted it.

Edmund Randolph summarized the next paragraph by saying that it "affirms the supremacy of a majority in a community" (1936, 46). Mason's original statement, like the Committee restatement and the final draft, was considerably longer and more complex. It stated:

> That government is, or ought to be, instituted for the common benefit and Security of the People, Nation, or Community. Of all the various Modes and Forms of Government, that is best, which is capable of producing the greatest Degree of Happiness and Safety, and is most effectually secured against the Danger of mal-administration. And that whenever any Government shall be found inadequate, or contrary to these Purposes, a Majority of the Community had an indubitable, inalienable and indefeasible Right to reform, alter or abolish it, in such Manner as shall be judge most conducive to the Public Weal" (*PGM*, I: 277).

In addition to changing most of the nouns to lower case, the convention would add the word "protection," after "common benefit," change "had," which was probably a mistaken tense, to "hath," and change the spelling of "public" to "publick" (*PGM*, I: 283, 287).

The first sentence of this paragraph flowed logically from the previous one. If power were vested in, and derived from, the people, then it stands to reason that government should further their "common Benefit and Security." I cannot ascertain with certainty why Mason chose separately to list "the People, Nation, or Community" (the language uncharacteristically reads a bit like a repetitious legal document), although Mason might have intended to progress from larger political units to smaller ones. As one original people previously associated together in an inter-Atlantic empire, Virginians and other Americans were now asserting their current status as a separate people or nation (in the Declaration of Independence, Jefferson would assert that Britons and Americans were now separate peoples), while recognizing that what applied at large also applied within individual states and communities.

Although Mason's next paragraph indicated disdain for governments based on royal birth, at this point, he did not designate the specific form that the new government of Virginia should take. He did say that such "Modes and Forms of Government" are those that best secure "the greatest Degree of Happiness and Safety," and guard against "the Danger of mal-administration" (*PGM*, I: 277). This statement's emphasis on administration is similar to Alexander Pope's widely-known couplet, found in his "Essay on Man" ("Epistle III," lines 303-

304): "For forms of Government let fools contest, whatever is best administered is best."[6]

Whatever form of government was in place, Mason proceeded to recognize the right of "a Majority of the Community" to "reform, alter, or abolish it." At the Constitutional Convention of 1787, Mason would note that "The plan now to be formed will certainly be defective, as the Confederation has been found on trial to be. Amendments therefore will be necessary, and it will be better to provide for them, in an easy, regular and Constitutional way than to trust to chance and violence" (Farrand, I: 203).

Mason's reference to "a Majority" is more specific than the language of "the People," which Jefferson employed in the Declaration of Independence. Just as Mason posed three options, "reform, alter or abolish," Jefferson referred to powers to "alter," "abolish," and "institute new governments" when existing government did not fulfill their purposes.

Mason's successive use of the terms "indubitable, inalienable, and indefeasible" as adjectives to describe the right to reform, alter, or abolish governments provides impressive parallelism (at the cost of some redundancy) and is suggestive of Jefferson's subsequent emphasis on "self-evident" truths. Interestingly, in both cases, printers were apparently responsible for changing the word "inalienable" to

---

[6] At the Constitutional Convention of 1787, records indicate that on September 8, Mason proposed that impeachment should extend to "maladministration" (Farrand, II: 550). After James Madison criticized that term as vague and Gouverneur Morris argued that it was unnecessary, Mason proposed the current language of "other high crimes & misdemeanors" (Farrand, II: 550), a term which, while it had been used by the British Parliament, has presented its own interpretive challenges.

"unalienable." The word indefeasible, meaning unable to be forfeited, seems redundant with the term unalienable, perhaps explaining why Jefferson used only the second of these terms in the Declaration of Independence.

Mason's reference to the "publick weal" is a reminder that, to this day, Virginia and a number of other states, designate themselves as commonwealths. The *Oxford English Dictionary* defines public weal as "the well-being or welfare of a country," or "public good." Virginians would have thought it to be self-evident that elected representatives from their state would better be able to legislate on behalf of such well-being than a distant king or a parliament in England to which they sent no representatives. Gordon Wood has observed that republican thought at the time of the American Revolution focused on the common good and that "No phrase except 'liberty' was invoked more often by the Revolutionaries than 'the public good'" (1969, 55).

Edmund Randolph observed that the fourth numbered resolution "Explodes an inheritance in Office" (1936, 46). This paragraph cautioned that, in choosing governments, the majority should avoid those that confer power based on hereditary privilege. Mason thus wrote: "That no Man, or Set of Men are entitled to exclusive or separate Emoluments or Privileges from the Community, but in Consideration of public Services; which not being descendible, or hereditary, the Idea of a Man born a Magistrate, a Legislator, or a Judge is unnatural and absurd" (*PGM*, I: 277).[7] The final version added

---

[7] In explaining the significance of the Declaration of Independence to Roger C. Weightman, the mayor of Washington, D.C., who had invited him to fiftieth anniversary celebrations of the Declaration of Independence, Thomas Jefferson had observed in a letter of June 24, 1826, that

the words "neither ought the offices" before "of Magistrate" and substituted the phrase "to be hereditary" for "is unnatural and absurd" at the end of the sentence (*PGM*, I: 287).

The idea of hereditary privilege is inconsistent with the idea of human equality. There is general agreement that most Americans accepted the legitimacy of George III and his hereditary kingship prior to Thomas Paine's *Common Sense*. In that book, which he published in January 1776, Paine observed that "Male and female are the distinctions of nature, good and bad are the distinctions of heaven; but how a race of men came into the world so exalted above the rest, and distinguished like some new species, is worth inquiring into" (1776, 270). Like Paine, Mason believed that such distinctions were "absurd."

Mason thus denied that anyone was entitled to special "Emoluments" or "Privileges" as a result of birth. The *Oxford English Dictionary* defines an emolument as "Profit or gain arising from station, office, or employment; dues; reward, remuneration, salary." The term "emoluments" is found in Article I, Section 6, para. 2 of the U.S. Constitution, which prevents members of Congress from being appointed to offices "which shall have been created, or the Emoluments whereof shall have been increased" during their time in

---

is now known to have been borrowed in part from a speech that Colonel Richard Rumbold, a former member of Cromwell's army, had given before his execution (See Adair 1952 and Looney 2004), that "All eyes are opened, or opening, to the rights of man. The general spread of the light of science has already laid open to every view the palpable truth, that the mass of mankind has not been born with saddles on their backs, nor a favored few booted and spurred, ready to ride them legitimately, by the grace of God."

office.[8] It is also found in Article I, Section 9, which prevents persons holding "any Office of Profit or Trust" from receiving "any present, Emolument, Office, or Title, of any kind whatever, from any King, Prince, or foreign State"; and in Article II, Section 1, para. 7, which prohibits the president from receiving any outside "emolument" during the president's term in office, which has been a topic of keen interest and considerable controversy in the Trump Administration.

Mason did not preclude the idea that individuals should be suitably reimbursed for "public Services." He simply indicated that such reimbursement should be for actual services rather than the result of hereditary privilege. Although the term magistrate was sometimes used to refer to both executive and judicial offices, or indeed to all public officials (Friedman 2002, 952), in referring respectively to the offices of "Magistrate," "Legislator," and "Judge," Mason laid the framework for the modern division of government in executive, legislative, and judicial branches, although the U.S. Constitution gives primacy of place (Article I) to the legislative branch, which its Framers, likely including Mason, thought was more representative of the people.

STRUCTURAL GOVERNMENTAL PROTECTIONS

Although both governmental structures and lists of judicially enforceable restraints on governmental powers are

---

[8] A leading article on the subject (O'Connor, 1995) refers to this clause as "an anti-Federalist Intruder in a Federalist Constitution." Mason would, of course, side with the Anti-Federalists with regard to ratification of the U.S. Constitution prior to amendments, including a Declaration of Rights.

designed to secure human rights,[9] modern bills of rights typically focus on the latter rather than the former. By contrast, the Virginia Declaration of Rights mixes both elements. John Locke had proposed dividing governmental powers into legislative, executive, and federative powers, the latter dealing chiefly with matters of war and peace (Locke, 1955, 120-121). Montesquieu's *Spirit of the Laws* was one of the most prominent advocates of dividing governmental powers into multiple branches. In Federalist No. 51, James Madison advocated separation of powers as a way of protecting liberty by pitting ambition against ambition. He viewed such separation as one of the "auxiliary precautions" that was needed to supplement "the primary control on the government," namely, "[a] dependence on the people" (1961, 322).

Mason's next paragraph thus clarified the previous paragraph's link to separation of powers, while somewhat insulating members of the judicial branch, whose members require special expertise and training, from the elections and short terms that applied to the first two. Edmund Randolph observed that this section "separates the legislative, executive and judicial functions, and reduces the members of the two former at fixed periods, to private stations" (1936, 46). Mason's draft thus specified: "That the legislative and executive Powers of the State should be separate and distinct from the judicative; and that the Members of the two first may be restrained from Oppression, by feeling and participating the Burthens they may lay upon the People; they

---

[9] This why Alexander Hamilton was able to assert in Federalist No. 84 that "The truth is, after all the declamations we have heard, that the Constitution is itself, in every rational sense, and to every useful purpose, A BILL OF RIGHTS." (Hamilton, Madison, and Jay, 1961, 515).

should, at fixed Periods be reduced to a private Station, and returned, by frequent, certain and regular Elections, into that Body from which they were taken" (*PGM*, I: 277). The Committee draft made some minor rearrangements and additions (*PGM*, I: 283), while the final draft elaborated the aftermath of elections by adding "in which all, or any part of the former members, to be again eligible, or ineligible, as the law shall direct" (*PGM*, I: 287).

With its emphasis on popular elections, this section is quite reminiscent of Mason's "Remarks on Annual Elections for the Fairfax Independent Company" (*PGM*, I: 229-232). The Declaration of Independence would criticize the King for having "made Judges dependent on his Will alone, for the tenure of their offices, and the amount and payment of their salaries." In stressing the need for judicial independence from both legislative and executive control, Mason presumably agreed.

Having rejected the idea of hereditary appointments, Mason advocated the election of both legislators and executives. Although he did not explicitly support popular instruction of such individuals, he stressed how important it was for them from time to time to resume their role as private citizens who were subject to the laws that they enacted or enforced. Subsequent American constitutionalism has heeded Mason's emphasis on the importance of "frequent, certain and regular Elections." The U.S. Constitution thus provides respectively for 2-year, 4-year, and 6-year terms for members of the U.S. House of Representatives, the U.S. Presidency, and the U.S. Senate. Mason's stance in this paragraph is similar to the provisions in the Fairfax County Resolves, which denied the right of a body to tax individuals who are not represented within it.

The next numbered resolution appears first in the Committee Report rather than in Mason's original draft, but it flows logically from the preceding paragraph and is consistent with Mason's own thoughts. Edmund Randolph observed that one part provided "for the freedom of elections" and another conferred "the right of suffrage on all having sufficient evidence of a permanent common interest with, and of attachment to the community" (1936, 46). Randolph added his own gloss on the provision, however, by observing that "it did not intend to leave this right to the will of the legislature according to capricious views of expediency" (1936, 46).

The resolution provided "That elections of members to serve as representatives of the people, in assembly, ought to be free; and that all men, having sufficient evidence of permanent common interest with, and attachment to, the community, have the right of suffrage" (*PGM*, I: 283). The final draft added "and cannot be taxed or deprived of their property for public uses without their own consent or that of their Representative so elected, nor bound by any law to which they have not, in like manner, assented, for the publick good" (*PGM*, I: 288).

The English Bill of Rights had provided "That the election of members of Parliament ought to be free" (Vile 2015, 48). The principles of representation dated back to the Magna Carta and the creation of Parliament.

Although subsequent constitutional amendments have prohibited discrimination in voting based on race or national origin (Fifteenth Amendment), sex (Nineteenth Amendment), or age above 18 (Twenty-sixth Amendment), the U.S. Bill of Rights does not specifically guarantee a positive right to vote. The provision in the Virginia Declaration came much closer to doing so, although the phrase requiring voters to have "sufficient evidence of permanent common interest with, and attachment to, the community" was almost surely intended to exclude slaves and even poor whites without a freehold—typically 25 or more acres of improved property or 100 acres of total land (Billings 1992, 348)—to say nothing of women. Billings believes that at the time Mason was writing, "perhaps as many as 60 percent of adult white males held the franchise, and about two-thirds of these regularly exercised it" (1992, 348). He notes that Virginians considered freeholders of yeoman farmers to be the guardian against the decline of republican government into tyranny. Billings thus observes that "His cultivation of virtue, his eschewal of licentiousness and luxury, his acceptance of public service as a civic duty rather than a personal reward set this disinterested citizen-patriot apart from the common herd. Ownership of real property was his bulwark against corruptibility" (1992, 345). Jefferson was among those who later identified "Those who labour in the earth" as the "chosen people of God" (Curtis, 2012, 55).

PROPERTY RIGHTS

The next provision in Mason's proposed Declaration provided "That no part of a Man's Property can be taken from him, or applied to public uses, without the Consent of himself, or his legal Representatives; nor are the People bound by any Laws, but such as they have in like Manner assented to for their common good" (*PGM*, I: 277). Although retained as a separate provision in the Committee Draft (*PGM*, I: 283), the final committee draft incorporated this provision into the previous one, adding after the provision for suffrage that individuals "cannot be taxed or deprived of their property for publick uses without their own consent or that of the Representative so elected, nor bound by any law to which they have not, in like manner, assented, for the publick good" (*PGM*, I: 288).

This provision harkened back to provisions of the Fairfax Resolutions and other revolutionary documents that there should be no taxation without representation. It further anticipated the Takings Clause of the Fifth Amendment to the U.S. Constitution, which provides that private property can only be taken for "public use" and which requires compensation for the same. The reference to the "Common Good" was similar to the earlier reference to the "Public Weal."

EXECUTIVE SUSPENSION OF LAWS WITHOUT LEGISLATIVE CONSENT

The next provision of the Virginia Declaration was not in Mason's original draft, but is found in both versions of the Committee's. It provided "That all power of suspending laws, or the execution of laws, by any authority without consent of the representatives of the people, is injurious to their rights, and ought not to be exercised" (*PGM*, I: 283; I: 288). Although this clause is consistent with criticisms of the British king, it is in arguable tension with earlier commendations of separation of powers.

Edmund Randolph linked this clause to English history by observing that it "was suggested by an arbitrary practice of the king of England before the revolution in 1688" (1936, 46). He might further have noted that Governor Dunmore's suspension of the Virginia House of Burgesses had led to the necessity for calling special conventions. The Declaration of Independence would criticize the king for having "forbidden his Governors to pass Laws of immediate and pressing importance, unless suspended in their operation till his Assent should be obtained; and, when so suspended, he has utterly neglected to attend to them." The U.S. Constitution both permits the president to veto laws and permits two-thirds majorities of both Houses of Congress to override them.

DECLARATION'S ADDED AND DELETED PROVISION (EX POST FACTO LAWS)

The original version of Mason's proposals contained two additional provisions that Thomas Ludwell Lee added. The second, which he offered hesitatingly, "Perhaps something like the following," provided "That laws having a retrospect to crimes, & punishing offences committed before the existence of such laws, are generally dangerous, and ought to be avoided" (*PGM,* I: 278). It was incorporated into the Committee's draft (*PGM,* I: 184) but deleted from its final recommendations. Although he used a different term (he referred to bills of attainder, a legislative punishment of a specific individual or individuals without trial, rather than ex post facto laws), Edmund Randolph appeared to refer to this provision when he observed that "An article prohibiting bills of attainder was defeated by [Patrick] Henry, who with a terrifying picture of some towering public offender, against whom ordinary laws would be impotent, saved that dread power from being expressly proscribed" (1936, 47).

Mason was on good terms with Henry and probably was convinced by his rhetoric. In later drafting his comments opposing the U.S. Constitution, Mason thus objected to the prohibitions that the document imposed on ex post facto laws, observing that "there never was nor can be a legislature but must and will make such laws, when necessity and the public safety require them; which will hereafter be a breach of all the constitutions of the Union, and afford precedents for other innovations" (Farrand II: 640). Lee himself had observed that the reservation providing exceptions "in cases of great, & evident necessity, when safety of the state absolutely requires them" was included "to signify to posterity that it is considered not so much as a law of right, as the great law of necessity, which by the well known maxim is—allowed to supersede all human institutions" (*PGM*, I: 278).

THE RIGHTS OF THE ACCUSED

Mason's next paragraph provides a virtual cornucopia of rights that pertain to the rights of criminal defendants. Most of them found their way into subsequent state declarations and into the federal bill of rights. Edmund Randolph observed that the provisions were "similar to those under the English law" (1936, 46). This is the closest the Declaration of Rights comes to resemble the U.S. Bill of Rights and shows, as much as any of the provisions, Mason's own acquaintance with criminal law. The paragraph is as follows:

> That in all capital or criminal Prosecutions, a Man hath a right to demand the Cause and Nature of his Accusation, to be confronted with the Accusers or Witnesses, to call for Evidence in his favour, and to a speedy Tryal by a Jury of his Vicinage; without whose unanimous Consent, he can not be found guilty; nor can he be compelled to give Evidence against himself. And that no Man except in times of actual Invasion or Insurrection, can be imprisoned upon Suspicion of Crimes against the State, unsupported by Legal Evidence. (*PGM*, I: 277-278)

In a move that Mason may well have approved, the Committee omitted the last line and replaced it with a provision, preserved in the final committee report, that "no man be deprived of his liberty except by the law of the land, or the judgment of his peers" (*PGM*, I: 284). The "law of the land provision," which was rooted in the language of the Magna Carta, is often considered to be the origin of modern ideas of "due process of law," which are incorporated in the Fifth and Fourteenth Amendments to the U.S. Constitution (Bodoh 2018).

Although the first clause of this set of rights does not, like provisions of the Fifth Amendment to the U.S. Constitution, specifically call for an "indictment of a Grand Jury," the requirement that individuals be informed of charges against them, would otherwise serve a similar function, especially in conjunction with the provision requiring the support of "Legal Evidence." Both the Virginia Declaration and the U.S. Bill of Rights protect against self-incrimination in criminal cases.

Leonard W. Levy says that Mason was actually the first to constitutionalize this "old English rule of evidence" (1999, 182). Levy believes, however, that by limiting the right to capital and criminal trials, Mason actually offered less protections than existing Virginia practices, which "allowed a right against self-incrimination in all stages of equity and common-law proceedings and also allowed witnesses as well as defendants to invoke the right" (1999, 182). Believing this "was the product of bad drafting, which the Virginia convention failed to remedy" (1999, 182), Levy further finds no evidence "that it was taken literally or regarded as anything but a sonorous declamation of the common-law right of long standing" (1999, 183). He does, however, believe that the provision became the model both for states and for the U.S. Bill of Rights.

The Sixth Amendment, like this provision of the Virginia Declaration, in turn, provided for a speedy trial, for confrontation with witnesses, and for trial by jury, although it does not, like Mason's Declaration, specifically require that such juries be unanimous. Mason's reference to "a Jury of his Vicinage [basically means "neighborhood]," although somewhat antiquated in language, is similar to the Sixth Amendment requirement for a trial "by an impartial jury of the State and district wherein the crime shall have been committed."

For all its breadth, Mason's clause did not include provisions against double jeopardy, which is found in today's Fifth Amendment. Nor did it contain a provision for compulsory processes for obtaining witnesses in favor of the defense or the assistance of counsel, both of which are found in today's Sixth Amendment. Mason's provision for possible imprisonment with legal evidence in cases of "actual invasion or Insurrection" is similar to restrictions on the suspension of the writ of habeas corpus in Article I, Section 9 of the U.S. Constitution.

The provision for a trial in one's vicinage might have been a reaction to British attempts, also critiqued in the Declaration of Independence, to transport individuals out of the colonies for trials relative to customs violations. The provision related to imprisoning individuals on suspicion during "times of actual Invasion or Insurrection" was likely crafted with a view toward protecting the colony against Tories and their supporters during its fight with the British.

Although there is no reason to believe that Mason would have opposed it, the Declaration's ninth numbered set of rights was added by the committee, and originally numbered 11 (*PGM*, I: 284). It provided "That excessive bail ought not to be required, nor excessive fines imposed, nor cruel and unusual punishments inflicted" (*PGM*, I: 288). The first of these provisions continued to emphasize the rights of the accused, whereas the second two dealt with the rights of individuals who were already convicted. Edmund Randolph observed that this section "was also borrowed from England with additional reprobation of cruel and unusual punishments" (1936, 46); in point of fact, all three provisions were found as the tenth of thirteen "ancient rights and liberties" in the British Bill of Rights (Kurland and Lerner 1987, V, 2). Although the Declaration of Rights began with the rights of men, it clearly anticipated continuing rights that the one-time colonists had come to expect under the British common law system with which they were familiar.

Aside from using the word "ought," this provision is strikingly similar to today's Eighth Amendment to the U.S. Constitution. That Amendment provides that "Excessive bail shall not be required, nor excessive fines imposes, nor cruel and unusual punishments inflicted."

On Mason's original copy of the Declaration, Thomas Ludwell Lee noted that the committee had agreed to a provision "condemning the use of general warrants" (*PGM*, I: 278). This provision emerged as proposition 12 in the committee draft and as the tenth numbered paragraph in the final draft. The first such provision provided "That warrants unsupported by evidence, whereby any officer or messenger may be commanded or required to search suspected places, or to seize any person or persons, his or their property, not particularly described, are grievous and oppressive, and ought not to be granted" (*PGM*, I: 284). The final version inserted the word "general" before warrants, and added "without evidence of a fact committed" after the phrase "suspected places," "not named, or whose offence is" before "not particularly described," "and supported by evidence" after "described" (*PGM*, I: 288).

In a letter that he sent to an unidentified British correspondent, which was dated October 2, 1778, Mason added a marginal note to the accompanying manuscript mistakenly purporting to be his original draft of the Declaration. In this letter he indicated that although the Convention had added two more provisions, he did not think this provision of the final document, or the 14th detailing the right to "uniform government," was "of fundamental nature" (*PGM*, I: 438).

Others not only in Virginia, but elsewhere, evidently disagreed. In explaining the provision against general warrants, Edmund Randolph wrote that it "was dictated by the remembrance of the seizure of Wilkes's paper under a warrant from a Secretary of State" (1936, 46). Wilkes was, of course, the British parliamentarian, who had expressed support for the colonists who had, in turn, protested the search and seizure of his papers and his exclusion from Parliament (Cash 2006). John Adams said that "the child of Independence was born" when James Otis argued in 1761 against writs of assistance and general warrants, which were especially hated by merchants in New England where the British had used them to target smuggling (Adams 1969, 2:124). Robert Hilldrup further noted that Virginia colonial courts had denied writs of assistance to British officials, suggesting that committee members may have thought they were asserting a long-standing right (Hilldrup 1935, 198).

Unlike the warrants described in today's Fourth Amendment, general warrants provide broad authority to conduct searches, usually during the entire life of the monarch under whose authority such warrants were issued, without particularly specifying the person or place to be seized. Although, like the original committee draft of the Virginia Declaration, today's Fourth Amendment omits the term "general," it was designed to stop this practice. It also contained requirements that warrants shall not issue "but upon probable cause, supported by Oath or affirmation." These requirements, like the introductory phrase "The right of the people to be secure in their persons, houses, papers, and effects against unreasonable searches and seizures," are missing from the Virginia Declaration.

Notably, like other provisions within the Virginia Declaration, this provision was listed as an action that "ought" not to be practiced rather than something which it specifically prohibited. I am thus uncertain whether Laura K. Donohue (2016, 1267) is correct is saying that "Mason's decision to include a prohibition on promiscuous search and seizure took an aspect of the common law and turned it into a written, guaranteed right, as held against the government. It could not be abridged by mere statute."

JURY TRIALS IN CIVIL CASES

The next right that that the Virginia Declaration listed switched positions (it was originally the last of Mason's ten proposals), but otherwise remained unchanged, except for altering the spelling from Mason's "Tryal" to "trial," in the drafting process. Mason's proposal stated "That in all controversies respecting Property, and in Suits between Man and Man, the Ancient Tryal by Jury is preferable to any other, and ought to be held sacred" (*PGM*, I: 278). Like other provisions within the Declaration, it employed the hortatory "ought" instead of the mandatory "shall" or "must." Whereas the previous provision had dealt with trial by jury in capital criminal cases, this extended the right to civil cases, or disputes between private citizens.

Mason's reference to the "ancient Tryal by Jury," accentuated by Mason's original antiquated spelling, indicated that, even while recognizing that the colony was declaring independence, Mason was once again thinking of English common law rights that the colonists would have brought with them from the mother country. Mason may have drafted this language intentionally to allow for some leeway. Edmund Randolph thus observed that "the trial by jury was not considered as a mandate to legislatures without the possibility of exception" (1936, 46). Moreover, Billings believes that few Virginians chose jury trials over summary trials and that "the ringing endorsement of civil juries perhaps spoke more to hope than to reality" (1992, 350).

This link to English law is even more explicit in the Seventh Amendment to the U.S. Constitution. It provides that "In Suits at common law, where the value in controversy shall exceed twenty dollars, the right of trial by jury shall be preserved, and no fact tried by a jury shall be otherwise reexamined in any Court of the United States, than according to the rules of common law."

FREEDOM OF THE PRESS

Although there is no reason to believe that Mason opposed it, the twelfth provision of the Virginia Declaration of Rights was not in Mason's original draft. It was listed as the fourteenth paragraph in the Committee draft and remained unchanged in the final draft. It provided "That the freedom of the Press is one of the greatest bulwarks of liberty, and can never be restrained but by despotick Governments" (*PGM* I: 278). This has been described as "the first constitutional guarantee of freedom of the press" (Bogen 1983, 429). Edmund Randolph observed that this provision and the one that followed "were the fruits of genuine democracy and historical experience" (1936, 46).

The reference to a bulwark of liberty in this resolution was apparently taken from the fifteenth essay by John Trenchard and Thomas Gordon (1995, I, 110-117) of *Cato's Letters,* which were originally published from 1720 to 1723. That essay was entitled "Of Freedom of Speech: That the Same is Inseparable from Publick Liberty." The document left no obvious clues as to why the Virginia Convention chose to apply this analogy to freedom of the press rather than freedom of speech (although the two are obviously quite closely related) or why the Virginia Declaration did not include related First Amendment rights of assembly and petition. Robert Hilldrup observed that in addition to the Zenger case in New York, Virginians had their own experience with prior restraint, as when Governor Dunmore had seized a press belonging to James Holt and used it to publish his own paper (1935, 197).

In seeking to account for omitted rights, it is important to realize that no list of rights is likely to include them all and that subsequent writers often add rights to earlier lists. Warren Billings has observed that as "A well-schooled politician, Mason obviously understood the practical purpose for which his draft was intended; it was a debating paper, no more, no less. As such, it need only delineate major structural components as the basis for the finished version" (1992, 341).

WELL-REGULATED MILITIA VERSUS STANDING ARMIES

Although the next right that the Virginia Declaration of Rights listed was not included in Mason's original, it is so consistent with his other writings that it seems quite likely not only that it had his full approval but that he also wrote it. The provision in the final document, which varies from the committee draft only in capitalization and number (it is number 15 in the original draft), was as follows: "That a well-regulated Militia, composed of the body of the people, trained to arms, is the proper, natural, and safe defence of a free State; that Standing Armies, in time of peace, should be avoided as dangerous to liberty; and that, in all cases, the military should be under strict subordination to, and governed by, the civil power" (*PGM*, I: 288). Edmund Randolph observed that this provision was known for "preferring militia to standing armies" and was, like the previous right, one of the "fruits of genuine democracy and historical experience" (1936, 46). Billings provides further context by observing that "Virginians had endured a period of garrison government when the Crown dispatched over a thousand Redcoats to crush Bacon and his rebels [Bacon's Rebellion had occurred in 1676]," and that they had remained "into the next decade at colonial expense" (Billings 1992, 352).

Of all the principles that small "r" republicans espoused, few were as sacred as the emphasis on the need for citizen "virtue," which included a willingness to defend their homes and families. Ironically, one of the factors that compelled George III to rely upon German and other mercenaries in carrying out war in America was that British republicans had opposed standing armies for fear that they would have separate interests from the people they were designed to protect. As demonstrated in his Remarks on Annual Elections for the Fairfax Independent Company the previous year, Mason's conception of a citizen army was more egalitarian than that of many of his contemporaries, as he believed that such an army should have the power to choose their own officials, who should be rotated on a yearly basis.

The provision made some concession to necessity in indicating that standing armies might sometimes be needed during times of war. The clause is a reminder that security was not the only reason for civil society, and that liberty was also quite important.

Although this provision is not found either in the U.S. Constitution or the first ten amendments to that Document, the provision that "in all cases, the military should be under strict subordination to, and governed by, the civil power" is arguably reflected in the provision within Article II, Section 1 of the U.S. Constitution, which makes the President, who is an elected official, the Commander-in-Chief of the armed forces. Moreover, the Second Amendment provides that "A well regulated Militia, being necessary to the security of a free State, the right of the people to keep and bear Arms, shall not be infringed." Mason was among those who had expressed fears that without such an amendment, the government might disarm the citizens (Cornell 2004, 257-258).

UNIFORM GOVERNMENT

The next provision in the Virginia Declaration was not found in Mason's original draft, and it is one of two such provisions that he later said were "not of fundamental nature" (*PGM*, I: 438). The final draft, which differed very little from that of the committee, provided "That the people have a right to uniform Government; and, therefore, that no Government separate from, or independent of, the Government of *Virginia*, ought to be erected or established within the limits thereof" (*PGM*, I: 288). Edmund Randolph's explanation of this provision is quite helpful: "The fourteenth prohibiting the erection of a government within the limits of Virginia proceeded partly from local circumstances; when the charter boundaries of Virginia, were abridged by royal fiats in favor of Lord Baltimore and Lord Fairfax, much to the discontent of the people: and partly from recent commotions in the west" (1936, 46-47). As Chapter 1 of this book reveals, partly as a result of his role as long-time treasurer of the Ohio Company, Mason had engaged in extensive analyses of Virginia's charters (*PGM*, I: 163-179).

Hilldrup believes that this provision emerged from the "real danger of anarchy on the border between Virginia and Pennsylvania" where, "as a result of rival land claims," Virginians were concerned that companies might attempt to create a new state (1935, 199). Hilldrup also noted that attempts had already begun to organize an independent government in today's Kentucky (1935, 199).

Although Virginia eventually gave up most of its claims in the West (smaller states demanded this before they agreed to sign the Articles of Confederation), Article IV, Section 3 of the U.S. Constitution provided that while new states could be admitted to the Union, "no new States shall be formed or erected within the Jurisdiction of any other State; nor any State be formed by the Junction of two or more States, or Parts of States, without the Consent of the Legislatures of the States concerned as well as of the Congress." Ironically, the only state ever so formed was West Virginia, which broke from Virginia during the Civil War over the issue of slavery.

Residents of western parts of Virginia did not believe they were adequately represented in state councils, and Kentucky eventually became a separate state just as Tennessee parted from North Carolina. At the Constitutional Convention of 1787, Mason consistently sided with those who favored treating new states equally to the original thirteen. He thus observed in debates on July 11, 1787 that: "If the Western States are to be admitted into the Union as they arise, they must, he wd. Repeat, be treated as equals, and subjected to no degrading discriminations. They will have the same pride & other passions which we have, and will either not unite with or will speedily revolt from the Union, if they are not in all respects placed on an equal footing with their brethren" (Farrand, I: 579).

JUSTICE AND FUNDAMENTAL PRINCIPLES

One of the most strikingly republican sentiments within the Virginia Declaration of Rights was found in the penultimate paragraph, which was originally the eighth of Mason's original proposals (*PGM*, I: 278) and the seventeenth in the Committee's Draft Proposals (*PGM*, I: 284). The final draft differed from the previous two only in matters of capitalization. It provided "that no free Government, or the blessing of liberty, can be preserved to any people but by a firm adherence to justice, moderation, temperance, frugality, and virtue, and by frequent recurrence to fundamental principles" (*PGM*, I: 289). It thus put greater emphasis on responsibilities than on rights.

Edmund Randolph attributed the provision "recommending an adherence and frequent recurrence to fundamental principles" to Patrick Henry (1936, 47). Both Henry and Mason were dedicated to republican principles, but, as indicated in Chapter 2 of this book, Mason had used an almost identical phrase in his "Remarks on Annual Elections for the Fairfax Independent Company" in April of 1775. There he had observed "that no institution can be long preserved, but by frequent recurrence to those maxims on which it was formed" (*PGM*, I: 229). Julian Boyd succinctly summarized the phrase "frequent recurrence to fundamental principles" when he observed that "The implication is clear—rights so hardly won impose the responsibility to defend them" (1976, 871). Consistent with this provision's emphasis on "moderation and temperance," in crafting nonimportation agreements, Mason had targeted luxury, and at the Constitutional Convention of 1787, he called for a power to make sumptuary laws (Farrand, II: 606).

This provision's emphasis on the necessity for moral virtues is reminiscent of both classical political thought and of earlier colonial compacts, especially from New England. The Preamble to the U.S. Constitution later mentioned both the "blessings of liberty" and the need "to secure Justice." Republicans like Mason were concerned that "corruption" would lead to the downfall of governments, hence their need to recur to "fundamental principles." Whereas contemporary Americans chiefly view bills of rights as a set of prescriptions and prohibitions through which individuals can secure their rights in courts of law, many of the Founders saw them more as standards or principles around which people could rally when they perceived governmental abuses.

DECLARATION'S SIXTEENTH NUMBERED RIGHTS (FREE EXERCISE OF RELIGION)

The final right that the Virginia Declaration articulated began as the ninth in Mason's original draft. That draft was among the longest that Mason proposed. His original draft was as follows:

> That as Religion, or the Duty which we owe to our divine and omnipotent Creator, and the Manner of discharging

> it, can be governed only by Reason and Conviction, not by Force or Violence; and therefore that all Men shou'd enjoy the fullest Toleration in the Exercise of Religion, according to the Dictates of Conscience, unpunished and unrestrained by the Magistrate, unless under Colour of Religion, any Man disturb the Peace, the Happiness, or Safety of Society, or of Individuals. And that it is the mutual Duty of all, to practice Christian Forbearance, Love and Charity towards Each other. (*PGM*, I: 278)

Despite its presence in Mason's original draft, Edmund Randolph traced this provision, which he summarized as "unfettering the exercise of religion," to Patrick Henry (1936, 47). He further observed that the provision relative to religion, "coming from a gentleman, who was supposed to be a dissenter, caused an appeal to him, whether it was designed as a prelude to an attack on the established church, and he disclaimed such an object" (1936, 47). It seems likely that Randolph incorrectly assumed that because Henry had introduced the provision that he must also have originated it.[10] James Madison provided evidence for Mason's original authorship in his short Autobiography, where he observed, specifically with reference to the provision dealing with freedom of religion that, "This important and meritorious instrument was drawn by Geo. Mason, who had inadvertently adopted the word *toleration* in the article on that subject" (Adair 1945, 199). Madison went on to observe that "The change suggested and accepted, substituted a

---

[10] It is possible that Randolph also remembered Henry's later defense of the Virginia law, which Madison and Jefferson so adamantly opposed, to provide state financial support for sectarian teachers.

phraseology which declared the freedom of conscience to be a natural and absolute right" (Adair 1945, 199).

The Committee made some minor changes in Mason's original resolution (*PGM*, I: 284), but the most important development occurred sometime between the Committee's first printing and the final draft. In the first occasion where James Madison is known to have influenced such a constitutional document, he proposed redrafting the first part of the resolution as follows:

> That Religion or the duty we owe to our Creator, and the manner of discharging it, being under the direction of reason and conviction only, not of violence or compulsion, all men are equally entitled to the full and free exercise of it accord[in]g to the dictates of Conscience; and therefore that no man or class of men ought, on account of religion to be invested with peculiar emoluments or privileges; nor subjected to any penalties or disabilities under &c. (Madison's Papers, I: 174).

In addition to elevating the discussion from mere "toleration" of religion to its "full and free exercise," according to their consciences" and in downplaying Mason's references to disturbing the peace, which might be used as a pretext to squelch religious dissent, this provision envisioned that one religion had no more right to special privileges than did hereditary monarchs.

If Henry, who probably introduced this resolution on behalf of the neophyte Madison, participated in the debates, it was likely at this point because Madison's proposal quite clearly threatened the established church. Showing that Madison was already learning how to concede a point that could be argued on another day to attain an immediate goal, Madison drafted a subsequent modification that avoided disestablishing the Anglican Church (Dreisbach 2000, 15). It provided:

> That religion, or the duty which we owe to our CREATOR, and the manner of discharging it, can be directed only by reason and conviction, not by force or violence; and therefore, that all men are equally entitled to enjoy the free exercise of religion, according to the dictates of conscience, unpunished and unrestrained by the magistrate. Unless the preservation of equal liberty and the existence of the State are manifestly endangered; And that it is the mutual duty of all to practice Christian forbearance, love, and charity towards each other. (Madison, I: 171).

The final version became more succinct and much closer to the language of the opening words of the First Amendment to the U.S. Constitution. Its language was as follows:

> That Religion, or the duty which we owe to or Creator, and the manner of discharging it, can be directed only by reason and conviction, not by force or violence; and, therefore, all men are equally entitled to the free exercise of religion, according to the dictates of conscience; and that it is the mutual duty of all to practice Christian forbearance, love, and charity, towards each other. (*PGM*, I: 289).

Although this history might suggest that Mason and Madison were at loggerheads, Daniel Dreisbach has observed that "Madison apparently offered his amendments without sharp objection from Mason" (2000, 16). Dreisbach thus notes that in a letter that Madison wrote to Mason's grandson on December 27, 1827, he observed that his suggestion for a substitute to the word toleration "was readily exchanged for the phraseology excluding it" (Quoted in Dreisbach 2000, 16). Moreover, as Dreisbach documents, Mason clearly allied himself with Madison and Jefferson in later efforts to disestablish the Anglican Church in Virginia. This work included an amendment introduced on December 5, 1776 exempting dissenters holding differing opinions from, or requiring them to attend the established church (*PGM*, I: 318) and another law, introduced on November 18, 1779, repealing parish taxes used to provide their salaries (*PGM*, II: 553-554).

Whereas the Declaration of Independence introduced the Creator relatively early in the text ("all men are created equal"), the Virginia Declaration of Rights waited until the last paragraph. Despite the revised clause's liberal sentiments, its definition of religion as "the duty which we owe to our *Creator*," is distinctively monotheistic. The juxtaposition of "reason and conviction" against "force and violence" is a reminder of the kinds of religious persecution that led to the eventual disestablishment of religion, which both Mason and Madison supported.

The last phrase of the Declaration with its reference "the mutual duty of all to practice Christian forbearance, love, and charity, towards each other," while distinctly Christian, embodies virtues that non-Christians might also support. This phrase seems to echo John Winthrop's sermon from 1630 entitled "A Model of Christian Charity" in which he advised "[T]hat every man might have need of other, and from hence they might all be knit more nearly together in the bond of brotherly affection" (Vile 2015, 20). This clause set up the possibility of what Kendall and Carey described as "a Christian *society* with a secular, that is precisely *not* religious, form of government" (1970, 70).

Of all the provisions in the Virginia Declaration, the last may have been the most consequential. Michael Meyerson observed that it "fundamentally altered the treatment of minority religions in Virginia," and quotes a much earlier historian (Hamilton James Eckenrode) as observing that "Prosecution for religious causes cease. Disabilities on account of religion were removed. . . . Anglicans, Roman Catholics, Evangelicals, Jews, and unbelievers were placed on the same civil footing" (2012, 70). In time, of course, Jefferson, Madison, and Mason all played a role in disestablishing the Anglican Church in the state.

SUMMARY AND ANALYSIS

Although it is possible to trace many of the provisions of the Virginia Declaration of Rights to earlier English documents and colonial practices, the Declaration remains an eloquent statement of revolutionary principles that provided sources for the Declaration of Independence, other state Declarations of Rights, the U.S. Bill of Rights, and even international documents. As the term "Declaration" suggests, the document retains some elements, particularly its philosophical preface and its reference to separation of powers, that do as much to hearken back to past history as to point forward to modern conceptions of rights. The fact that the Virginia Convention found it necessary to modify the opening references to equal birth and independence shows that Mason's sentiments, while arguably hypocritical (he was, after all, a slave owner) were recognized as challenging the status quo, not only within the British Empire but within Virginia itself. Much as Thomas Paine had done in *Common Sense,* Mason used the Declaration to strike a particularly powerful blow against hereditary public offices.

The Declaration does not contain as many rights as the first ten amendments to the U.S. Constitution, but most of the rights mentioned in the former are contained within the latter. In time the hortatory use of the word "ought" that is characteristic of similar declarations was replaced by the more easily enforced "shalls." Perhaps the most remarkable aspect of the Virginia Declaration is that it was largely drafted by a man who lacked a college education and was not trained as a lawyer but who could hold his ground with contemporaries with such backgrounds. Hugh Grigsby observed that Mason's Declaration "is the philosophical embodiment of the elemental principles which lie at the foundation of society, and which, gathered from the universal experience of man, and refined in the alembic of a mighty mind, are digested and expressed with a distinctness and with a severe simplicity intelligible alike by the young and the old, by the unlettered and the wise" (1855, 164).

REFERENCES

Adair, Douglass. 1945. "James Madison's Autobiography." *The William and Mary Quarterly* 2 (April): 191-209.

Adair, Douglass. 1952. "Rumbold's Dying Speech, 1685, and Jefferson's Last Words on Democracy, 1826," *The William and Mary Quarterly* 9 (October): 521-531.

Adams, John. 1969. *The Works of John Adams, Second President of the United States,* ed. by Charles Francis Adams. Freeport, NY: Books for Libraries Press.

Armitage, David. 2007. *The Declaration of Independence: A Global History.* Cambridge, MA: Harvard University Press.

Billings, Warren M. 1992. "'That all Men Are Born Equally Free and Independent' Virginians and the Origins of the Bill of Rights." *The Bill of Rights and the States: the Colonial and*

Revolutionary Origins of American Liberties, ed. Patrick T. Conley and John P. Kaminski. Madison, WI: Madison House, 335-369.

Bodah, Andrew T. 2018. "The Road to 'Due Process': Evolving Constitutional Language from 1776 to 1789." *Thomas Jefferson Law Review* 40 (Spring): 102-169.

Bogen, David S. 1983. "The Origins of Freedom of Speech and Press." *Maryland Law Review* 42 (Spring): 429-465.

Boyd, Julian P. 1976. "On the Need for 'Frequent Recurrence to Fundamental Principles.'" *Virginia Law Review* 62 (June): 859-871.

Brant, Irving. 1941. *James Madison: The Virginia Revolutionist, 1751-1780.* New York: Bobbs-Merrill.

Broadwater, Jeff. 2017. "George Mason, James Madison, and the Evolution of the Bill of Rights," *Georgetown Journal of Law & Public Policy.*" 15 (Summer): 547-568.

Calabresi, Steven G. Sarah E. Agudo, and Kathryn L. Dore. 2012. "State Bills of Rights in 1787 and 1791: What Individual Rights Are Really Deeply Rooted in American History and Tradition?" *Southern California Law Review* 85 (September): 1451-1550.

Cash, Arthur H. 2006. *John Wilkes: The Scandalous Father of Civil Liberty.* New Haven: Yale University Press.

Chester, Edward W. 1989. "George Mason— Influence Beyond the United States." *George Mason and the Legacy of Constitutional Liberty*, ed. Donald J. Senese. Fairfax County History Commission, 128-146.

Cornell, Saul. 2004. "Beyond the Myth of Consensus: The Struggle to Define the Right to Bear Arms in the Early Republic," *Beyond the Frontiers: New Approaches to the Political History of the Early American Republic*, ed. Jeffrey L. Pasley, Andrew W. Robertson, and David Waldstreicher," Chapel Hill: University of North Carolina Press.

Curtis, Christopher Michael. 2012. *Jefferson's Freeholders and the Politics of Ownership in the Old Dominion.* New York: Cambridge University Press.

Donohue, Laura K. 2016. "The Original Fourth Amendment." *The University of Chicago Law Review* 83 (Summer): 1181-1328.

Douma, Michael J. 2017. "How the First Ten Amendments Became the Bill of Rights." *Georgetown Journal of Law & Public Policy* 15 (Summer): 593-614.

Dreisbach, Daniel L. 2000. "George Mason's Pursuit of Religious Liberty in Revolutionary Virginia." *The Virginia Magazine of History and Biography* 108: 2+5-44.

Dunaway, W.F., Jr. 1904. "The Virginia Conventions of the Revolution." *The Virginia Law Register* 10 (November): 567-586.

Farrand, Max, ed. 1966. *The Records of the Federal Convention of 1787.* 4 vols. New Haven, CT: Yale University Press.

Friedman, Dan. 2002. "Tracing the Lineage: Textual and Conceptual Similarities in the Revolutionary-Era State Declarations of Rights of Virginia, Maryland, and Delaware." *Rutgers Law Journal* 33 (Summer): 929-1028.

Grigsby, Hugh Blair. 1855. *The Virginia Convention of 1855.* Richmond, VA: J.W. Randolph.

Hamilton, Alexander, James Madison, and John Jay. 1961. *The Federalist Papers.* New York: New American Library.

Heymsfeld, Carla R. and Joan W. Lewis. 1991. *George Mason, Father of the Bill of Rights.* Alexandria, VA: Patriotic Education Incorporated.

Hilldrup, Robert Leroy. 1935. *The Virginia Convention of 1776: A Study in Revolutionary Politics.* Dissertation for Ph.D., University of Virginia.

Howard, A.E. 1968. "'For the Common Benefit': Constitutional History in Virginia as a Casebook for the Modern Constitution-Maker." *Virginia Law Review* 54 (June): 816-902.

Hunt, Gaillard. 1917. "The Virginia Declaration of Rights and Cardinal Bellarmine." *The Catholic Historical Review* 3 (October): 276-289.

Jameson, John Alexander. 1887. *A Treatise on Constitutional Conventions; Their History, Powers, and Modes of Proceeding.* 4th ed., Intro by John R. Vile. Clark, NJ: The Lawbook Exchange, 2014.

Jefferson, Thomas. [1781] 1964. *Notes on the State of Virginia.* New York: Harper & Row.

Jefferson, Thomas. June 24, 1826. "Letter to Roger C. Weightman." Teaching American History.org. http://teachingamericanhistory.org/library/document/letter-to-roger-c-weightman/

_____. 1905. *The Works of Thomas Jefferson,* ed. Paul Leicester Ford. New York: G.P. Putnam's Sons, Knickerbocker Press.

Jellinke, Georg. 1902. *The Declaration of the Rights of Man and of Citizens: A Contribution to Modern Constitutional History,* trans. By Max Farrand. New York: Henry Holt and Company.

Kendall, Willmoore, and George W. Carey. 1970. *The Basic Symbols of the American Political Tradition.* Baton Rouge: Louisiana State University Press.

Kurland, Philip B. and Ralph Lerner, eds. *The Founders' Constitution.* 5 vols. Chicago: The University of Chicago Press.

Levy, Leonard W. 1999. *Origins of the Bill of Rights.* New Haven, CT: Yale University Press.

Locke, John. 1955. *Of Civil Government: Second Treatise.* Chicago: Henry Regnery Company.

Looney, J. Jefferson. 2004. "Thomas Jefferson's Last Letter." *The Virginia Magazine of History and Biography* 112:178-184.

Lutz, Donald S. 1992. *A Preface to American Political Theory.* Lawrence: University Press of Kansas.

Madison, James. 1962. *The Papers of James Madison,* ed. by William T. Hutchinson, et al. 17 vols. Chicago: University of Chicago Press; Charlottesville: University Press of Virginia.

Maier, Pauline. 1997. *American Scripture: Making the Declaration of Independence.* New York: Alfred A. Knopf.

_____. 1999. "John Randolph Tucker Lecture: The Strange History of 'All Men Are Created Equal,'" *Washington & Lee Law Review* 56 (Summer): 873-888.

Mason, George. 1970. *The Papers of George Mason, 1725-1792.* Robert A. Rutland, ed. Chapel Hill: University of North Carolina Press.

Meyerson, Michael I. 2012. *Endowed by Our Creator: The Birth of Religious Freedom in America.* New Haven: Yale University Press.

O'Connor, John F. 1995. "The Emoluments Clause: An Anti-Federalist Intruder in a Federalist Constitution." *Hofstra Law Review* 24 (Fall): 89-178.

Oliver, George Brown. 1959. *A Constitutional History of Virginia 1776-1860.* Diss. For Doctorate of Philosophy in Department of History in the Graduate School of Arts and Sciences at Duke University.

Paine, Thomas. *Common Sense* [1776]. *Classics of American Political & Constitutional Thought,* vol. 1, *Origins through the Civil War,* ed. By Scott J. Hammond, Kevin R. Hardwick and Howard L. Lubert. Indianapolis, IN: Hackett Publishing Company, Inc., 2007), pp. 267-280.

Pendleton, Edmund. 1967. *The Letters and Papers of Edmund Pendleton 1734-1803,* ed. by David John Mays. Charlottesville: The University Press of Virginia.

Pittman, R. Carter. 1960. "Review of Sources of Our Liberties by Richard L. Perry." *The Virginia Magazine of History and Biography* 68 (January): 109-112.

Randolph, Edmund. 1936. "Edmund Randolph's Essay on the Revolutionary History of Virginia 1774-1781 (Continued)." *The Virginia Magazine of History and Biography* 44 (January): 35-50.

Revolutionary Virginia, The Road to Independence. 1983. Vol VII, Part One *Independence and the Fifth Convention, 1776,* ed. Brent Tarter. Charlottesville: University Press of Virginia.

Rowland, Kate Mason. 1964 [1892]. *The Life of George Mason, 1724-1792.* 2 vols. New York: Russell & Russell, Inc.

Schlesinger, Arthur M. 1964. "The Lost Meaning of 'The Pursuit of Happiness,'" *The William and Mary Quarterly* 21 (July): 325-327.

Trenchard, John and Thomas Gordon. 1995. *Cato's Letters or Essays on Liberty, Civil and Religious, and Other Important Subjects.* Ed. Ronald Hamowy. 2 vols. Indianapolis: Liberty Fund.

Tucker, St. George. 2013. *St. George Tucker's Law Reports and Selected Papers 1782-1825,* 3 vols. Ed. Charles F. Hobson. Chapel Hill: University of North Carolina Press.

Vile, John R. 2016. *Conventional Wisdom: The Alternate Article V Mechanism for Proposing Amendments to the U.S. Constitution.* Athens: The University of Georgia Press.

_____. 2015. *Founding Document of America: Documents Decoded.* 2015. Santa Barbara, CA: ABC-CLIO.

_____. 1992. *The Constitutional Amending Process in American Political Thought.* New York: Praeger.

Wood, Gordon S. 1969. *The Creation of the American Republic 1776-1787.* Chapel Hill: The University of North Carolina Press.

4

George Mason and the Virginia Constitution of 1776

On May 15, 1776, the Continental Congress adopted a resolution encouraging states to create new governments to replace royal authority. Even before this resolution, New Hampshire had adopted a constitution on January 5, 1776, and South Carolina had adopted one on March 26, 1776, but both were provisional documents designed only for the duration of the Revolutionary War (Adams 2001, 66-70). The Fifth Virginia State Convention, which had, also on May 15, 1776, sent a request from Williamsburg to Congress asking that it declare the colonies to be independent, began by drafting a Declaration of Rights. George Mason, who took the lead in that project, is also believed to have been the chief drafter of the Constitution that followed. Unfortunately, the paper trail for this document does not begin, as with the Virginia Declaration of Rights, with a hand-written draft from Mason but with a printed draft of "A Plan of Government" reported by the committee on which he served sometime between June 8 and June 10, 1776.

The Convention subsequently prefaced the Constitution with a list of grievances against the king, which Thomas Jefferson supplied, and issued a final draft on June 29, 1776.

Again, there is no way to ascertain which of these changes Mason proposed and which he did not. Mason was not as careful as other Founders in keeping his correspondence and other papers, but given Mason's later criticism of the U.S. Constitution, it is not unreasonable to expect that had he had serious reservations, he might have voiced them. Moreover, it would be logical for the convention to entrust primary responsibility for drafting the Constitution to the individual who had drafted the prefatory Declaration of Rights.

MODELS

Although former colonists undoubtedly drew inspiration from their ancient charters (and few of his contemporaries knew them better than Mason), it is important to realize that Britain had operated under a largely unwritten constitution that recognized parliamentary sovereignty. Mason and his compatriots were therefore treading on relatively virgin territory when it came to drafting new constitutions, and they did not undertake the task lightly.

Mason had a number of models from which he may have drawn. First, there was a handbill that Richard Henry Lee had published in the *Virginia Gazette* (Alexander Purdie) on May 10, 1776 under the title of "Government Scheme" (Selby 1976). Lee appears to have drawn considerably from the thinking of John Adams, with whom he had conversed on the subject and whose pamphlet, *Thoughts on Government,* was published in April of 1776. Carter Braxton likewise published an Address about the time that the Virginia Constitution was being drafted urging the colonies to emulate the British system. Thomas Jefferson, who seemed to spend much of his time at the Second Continental Congress in Philadelphia wishing he were back in Virginia drafting its fundamental law, sent a number of proposals, most of which appeared to have arrived too late to affect the final outcome.

It is important to remember that while it had no prior written constitution, Virginia did have a long history of representative government. Fashioning a system that did not depart radically from past practice would have helped reassure those, especially among the elites, who might otherwise be wary about declaring independence and waging war against Great Britain.

LEE'S HANDBILL

The proposal that Richard Henry Lee published as a handbill was divided into seven sections. The first provided that the people would "as usual" choose a "Representative body" and that it would, in turn choose 24 men to serve 7-year terms in an upper house. The houses would jointly choose a governor, although he might have been closer to a prime minister since Lee said that the two houses and governor would collectively constitute "the legislative power." There would also be a 12-member Governor's Council, or Council of State, chosen annually from both houses by a joint ballot. Both Houses would also choose judges who would serve "during good behavior, with fixed, adequate, but not splendid salaries." If charged with "misbehavior" they could defend themselves before the legislature. If convicted, they would be dismissed and subject to "other pains, penalties, and disabilities." Both houses would chose the Lieutenant-Governor, Secretary, Commissary, Attorney and Solicitor-General by joint ballot every seven years and the Treasurer each year. The Governor would appoint Justices of the Peace and Sheriffs, with the consent of the Council of State. The

Governor and this Council would also appoint militia officers and provide for its government (Selby 1976, 390).

ADAMS'S THOUGHTS ON GOVERNMENT

As indicated above, Lee had conversed with John Adams, whose *Thoughts on Government,* which did not initially identify him as the author, were published in April 1776 (Adams 1776). Adams provided greater details about possible state governments, which he prefaced with considerably more philosophical justification. Connecting "the divine science of politicks" to "the science of human happiness," Adams had argued that "the happiness of society is the end of government," and that "the happiness of man, as well as his dignity consists in virtue." Noting that some forms of government were based on fear, and some on honor, Adams said that Republican government, which he defined as "an Empire of Laws, and not of men," was "the best form of government." Such government rested chiefly on a representative assembly, which "should be in miniature, an exact portrait of the people at large," and which should represent people equally.

Adams, who was anxious to refute Thomas Paine's calls for simple government, offered six reasons why he favored a bicameral legislature. He thought that unicameral legislatures were "[s]ubject "to all the vices, follies and frailties of an individual"; were "avaricious"; were "ambitious" and sought to perpetuate themselves; lacked "secrecy and dispatch"; were "too numerous, too slow, and too little skilled in the laws"; and would act arbitrarily. Adams also feared that a unicameral legislature would be in constant conflict with a single executive.

Adams thus favored a bicameral legislature with a Representative Assembly, which would choose a Council of from 20 to 30 men "from among themselves or their constituents," both of which would be required to adopt legislation. The two houses would choose a governor and other state officials through a joint ballot. The governor would have a "negative upon the legislative." One-year terms would make it unlikely that he would abuse this veto power.

Adams had no objection to rotating offices, and he thought that seven members of the Council could serve as a Privy Council to advise the governor. The governor would command the militia, and, with the Council, have the power to issue pardons. The governor would nominate members of the judiciary with the advice and consent of the Council.

The judicial power should be distinct from and independent of both the legislative and executive authorities. Judges would serve "during good behavior" but be subject to impeachment before the Governor and council. Adams further favored a militia law to provide for self-defense, "[l]aws for the liberal education of youth," and "sumptuary laws" to promote frugality.

One of the most quoted lines in Adams' work was found in his last full paragraph in which he had opined that he and fellow Americans "have been sent into life, at a time when the greatest law-givers of antiquity would have wished to have lived. How few of the human race have ever enjoyed an opportunity of making an election of government more than of air, soil, or climate, for themselves or their children. When! Before the present epoch, had three millions of people full power and a fair opportunity to form and establish the wisest and happiest government that human wisdom can contrive?"

In several letters in which he had summarized his sentiments, including one that he had sent to Lee, Adams had stressed that his plan could "be varied in any one particular an infinite number of ways, so as to accommodate it to the different genius, temper, principles and even prejudices of different people" (Selby 1976, 391). This council would have gone over very well in Virginia, which, by 1776, already had a long history of legislative experience. One way of assuring that the population continued to support revolution was to keep the essence of the old forms, without their monarchical aspects.

BRAXTON ADDRESS TO THE CONVENTION

Carter Braxton, who was a long-time member of the House of Burgesses from Tidewater, Virginia, and who may therefore have previously shared his sentiments with individual members of the Convention (see Dill 1983), published essays in the June 8 and June 15 editions of the *Virginia Gazette.* The first of these essays, which stressed his overall approach, might have been available to members of the Convention, but the second would not have been available until after the printing of the first committee draft, and might even have reflected some of its provisions.

Braxton's first essay appears to have been designed to respond to Adams' since it referred to an author who "blended *private* with *public* virtue, as if for the purpose of confounding the two." Braxton denied that public virtue had ever "characterized the mass of the people in any state." Rather than favoring democratic-republican government, Braxton favored emulating as closely as possible the system of mixed government that he thought had brought such prosperity to Britain.

The plan of government that he outlined in the second essay proposed continuing allowing the people to "choose their usual number of Representatives" for three-year terms.

They would, in turn, elect a governor who would serve "during his good behavior" as judged by the Representative and the Council of State.

This Council would consist of 24 men. They would be chosen by the representatives who, like members of the British House of Lords, would also "hold their places for life, in order that they might possess all the weight, stability and dignity due to the importance of their office."

Braxton would prohibit members of either house, other than the Treasurer, from holding "a post of profit in the government." Braxton further recommended "a Privy Council of seven" advisors to the Governor who would not be drawn from either house. The Governor would appoint judges with the Council's advice; the lower house would choose the Treasurer and other officers of state; the Governor would appoint military officers; and courts would appoint their own clerks. Braxton signed his essays "A Native." It was so aristocratic that Patrick Henry called it "a silly thing . . . an affront and disgrace to this country" (Quoted in Jefferson 1950, I, 335).

JEFFERSON'S PROPOSALS

Whereas Braxton's proposals were quite conservative, Thomas Jefferson's were more liberal. He sent three drafts of a constitution to the convention through his mentor, George Wythe, that were far more detailed than those that the Committee proposed or that the Convention adopted (Jefferson 1950, I: 329-369), but by the time Wythe arrived, the new constitution was nearly complete (Cogliano 2013, 37). Jefferson favored a bicameral legislature and three branches of government that included a relatively weak executive who would serve a one-year term. He also favored land reform, the elimination of capital punishment, barring slavery from lands west of the Alleghenies, and religious disestablishment. He devoted an entire section of his final draft devoted to "Rights Private and Public."

COMMITTEE'S INITIAL DRAFT

Mason's Plan consisted of 15 sections, all but the last of which began with the word "Let." This was the same construction that Lee's handbill had used. Consciously or otherwise, this word hearkened back to the original act of creation of the Universe. Genesis 1:3 thus notes that God said "Let there be light, and there was light" (KJV). The final version of the document omitted this construction and replaced it with a simpler declarative construction, as in Section 1, no longer numbered, which simply began with "The legislative, executive and judicial Departments, shall be separate and distinct" (*PGM*, I: 304).

In addition to prefacing the new constitution with Jefferson's list of grievances against the British crown, the final constitution of 1776 added a paragraph. It specified that, in light of these grievances and the dangers that the state would face "unless some regular adequate mode of civil polity is speedily adopted . . . the delegates and representatives of the good people of VIRGINIA . . . do ordain and declare the future form of Government of *Virginia* to be as followeth" (*PGM*, I: 304). Although speaking on behalf of the people, the Convention thus chose, perhaps because of the perceived exigencies of the situation, not to require a direct referendum by the people, or the selection of a separate ratifying convention, both of which would later become fairly standard practice.

SEPARATION OF POWERS

The initial committee draft was divided into 16 numbered sections. The first, anticipated by the Declaration of Rights, provided for the division of power among "the legislative, executive, and judicative departments" "so that neither exercise the powers properly belong to the other" (*PGM*, I: 299). In fleshing this out further, the final draft of the Constitution provided for an exception, thus allowing "The Justices of the county courts" to be eligible to either house (*PGM*, I: 304).

THE LEGISLATIVE BRANCH

The second section, which remained virtually unchanged in the final iteration, provided for a bicameral legislature. Designated as the General Assembly, this body was to meet "once, or oftener" every year (*PGM*, I: 299). In creating a bicameral legislature, Mason would have been following both the suggestions of Richard Henry Lee and John Adams. Those who had read Adams' document would know some of the reasons for it.

In Parliament, the House of Commons held (and now holds even greater) power than the upper-house of Lords. The Virginia House of Burgesses traced its history back to 1619. As under that system, Section 3 provided that the Lower House of Assembly, would have two delegates from each county. From the standpoint of equal representation, one flaw in this plan was that it did not vary representation according to population. Nor would it provide representation for western areas of the state that were not yet organized into counties. The final version attempted to remedy these defects by providing for representation for West Augusta, for

Williamsburg, and for Norfolk and for other cities that the legislature might designate. It further provided that such representation would cease for cities that for seven consecutive years had half the voters of comparable counties (*PGM*, I: 305).

Consistent with Mason's earlier stance on the heads of militia companies, elections would take place annually. Despite the liberal aspirations for voters in Section 6 of the Virginia Declaration of Rights (*PGM*, I: 283), this section limited actual office-holding to men of rank. The one-year residence requirement was not particularly unusual, but members of the lower house were also required to "possess an estate of inheritance of land, in Virginia, of at least one thousand pounds value" (*PGM*, I: 299). In a close approximation of the age later required for members of the U.S. House of Representatives (25 years), they were also required to be 24 years of age or older. Although the final draft kept the committee recommendations for annual elections, it chose to allow voting to resident freeholders who were "duly qualified according to law" thus either leaving existing provisions, or future legislation, to govern this issue (*PGM*, I: 305). It also designated this house as the House of Delegates.

Section 4 specified that the Upper House of Assembly was to be a smaller body of 24 men selected for terms of four years. To this end, the Constitution proposed dividing counties into 24 districts, with each county choosing 12 electors, each of whom were freeholders holding lands valued at 500 pounds or more. These deputies would, in turn, select one member of the Upper House, who would be a freeholder for at least a year, with property valued at 2000 pounds or more and 28 years of age. Much as the U.S. Senate now provides that one-third of its members be elected every two years, Section 4 provided that six members of the Upper House would be selected every four years, after which they would be ineligible for the next term. The latter provision was consistent with Mason's known predilection for rotation in office.

The final document changed a few details. It specified, for example, that senators would have to be at least 25 years of age but kept the system for rotation.

In attending to legislative housekeeping matters, Section 5 allowed each House to issue writs of election for vacancies. Consistent with the emphasis on broad suffrage in Article 6 of the Virginia Declaration, this section provided for voting rights to those "having leases for land, in which there is an unexpired term of seven years" (*PGM,* I: 300). It also extended such rights to householders with one year of residence and three children, presumably because both groups would have a strong stake in society. By contrast, the final version specified that suffrage "shall remain as exercised as present" (*PGM,* I: 305), thus presumably no longer guaranteeing the right to men with three or more children.

Section 2 had provided that the two branches of the government should together "be a complete legislature" (*PGM,* I: 299). Section 6 indicated that the lower houses, whose members were elected directly by the people for shorter terms, would have special control over the purse strings. It provided that all legislation would require the consent of both houses, but that money bills, would not only originate in the lower house but could not be altered by the upper one. This provision was retained in the final document and was less subject to evasion that the one that was incorporated into the U.S. Constitution.

GOVERNOR AND PRIVY COUNCIL

Although early U.S. state constitutions provided for separation of powers, many, probably reacting to what they considered to be arbitrary behavior by King George III, provided for relatively weak executive authority (Wood 1969, 148-150). Moreover, shorn of the monarchy, the British model suggested that the executive authority should be vested in a prime minister, who was head of the majority party or coalition.

The Virginia Constitution, as Mason proposed it, was similar. It provided for annual elections of governors by a "joint ballot of both Houses" (*PGM* I: 300). The Constitution limited the governor to three successive terms, and made him ineligible to reelection for three more. Wisely leaving specific details to legislation, this provision also provided for "an adequate, but moderate salary . . . during his continuance in office" (*PGM,* I: 300). In a mechanism that Mason later advocated at the U.S. Constitutional Convention, and which it seems likely that he originated, this Section also provided that he would exercise his powers "with the advice of a Council of State" (*PGM,* I: 300). In addition to the general "executive powers of government," the governor and council would have "the power of proroguing or adjourning the General Assembly, or of calling it upon emergencies, and of granting reprieves or pardons" (*PGM,* I: 300). The latter power was to be limited in cases "where the prosecution shall have been carried on by the Lower House of Assembly" (*PGM,* I: 300). Consistent with actions taken with respect to the Declaration of Rights, this would presumably allow for so-called bills of attainders in emergency situations.

The convention made relatively few changes to this provision. It did add a provision, which Mason may very well have approved, specifying that the governor "shall not, under any pretence, exercise any power or prerogative by virtue of any law, statue, or custom of *England*" (*PGM*, I: 306). It also added a subsequent paragraph allowing houses to adjourn, and prohibiting the governor from proroguing, adjourning, or dissolving them. It did allow the governor, with the advice of the Council of State or petition by a majority of the House of Delegates, to call them back into session earlier than planned.

The discussion of the Privy Council or Council of State (the constitution used both terms) was the most detailed in the committee draft. It was to consist of eight members chosen by joint ballot of the General Assembly either from among their members (which might be more consistent with a parliamentary system than with separation of powers) or from "the people at large" (*PGM*, I: 300). The Governor would serve as President of the council, but each year, the Council would choose a member as Vice-President, to act as lieutenant-Governor in the death or absence of the Governor.

This section further specified that three members would be sufficient to act as a quorum, that they would select a salaried clerk, that they would take an "oath of secrecy" unless "called upon by the Lower House of Assembly for information" (*PGM*, I: 300). They would receive pay, "divided annually among the members, in proportion to their attendance" (*PGM*, I, 300), and were barred from sitting in either house during their service on the Council, thus seemingly remedying separation of powers concerns. Like members of the Assembly, members would be rotated out every three years and be eligible for reelection for a similar period.

The final document was quite similar. However, with a view to the other colonies, it added a paragraph specifying that a joint ballot of both houses would annually select delegates to the Continental Congress.

APPOINTMENTS

Just as the U.S. President currently appoints most federal officers with the advice and consent of the Senate, so too, the Governor would, "with the advice" of the Council appoint militia officers "under the laws of the country" (*PGM*, I: 301). This would complement the provision within the Virginia Declaration of Rights that called for civilian control of the military.

The final draft of the 1776 constitution began by continuing existing militia officers. It further provided for suspending officers and ordering court martials "on complaint of misbehavior" (*PGM*, I: 307).

Whereas the Governor would appoint militia officers with the "consent" of the General Assembly, Section 10 provided that the Assembly itself, would by joint ballot, appoint members of "judges in chancery, judges of admiralty, and the attorney general, to be commissioned by the Governour, and continue in office during good behavior" (*PGM*, I, 30). The latter provision showed concern for the principle of judicial independence. In cases of "death or incapacity, the Governor with "the advice of the Privy Council, would appoint successors "to succeed in office pro tempore" and "to be approved or displaced by both Houses" (*PGM*, I: 301). Again leaving details to legislation, legislative salaries should be "fixed and adequate" (*PGM*, I: 301), which was consistent with Lee's suggestion that the salaries should not be "splendid." Judicial officers would be barred from the General Assembly or Privy Council, "except the attorney-general and the treasurer," who, much as in a parliamentary system, "may be permitted to a seat in the Lower House of Assembly" (*PGM*, I: 301). The final document retained the proposed method of choosing judges but gave more formal names to Virginia courts.

To this point, the Constitution had provided for the direct election of members of the lower, house, for an indirect election of members of the upper house and the privy council, and for selection of the governor by a joint ballot of both houses of the assembly. It had also provided that the governor, with the advice of the privy council, would appoint militia officers and that both houses of the legislature would appoint judges. Section 11 further provided that the Governor and members of the Privy Council would appoint county justices of the peace and that the courts would, in turn, appoint clerks, sheriffs, and coroners, with justices specifically designated to appoint constables.

The final version of the Constitution added a provision. It specified that "all fees of the aforesaid Officers [would] be regulated by law" (*PGM*, I: 308).

SECTION 12 (IMPEACHMENT)

Even though most officials other than judges and their clerks would serve relatively short terms, Mason provided in Section 12 that the governor, members of the privy council, judges, and other administrative officials would be subject to impeachment by the Attorney General in the Lower House "for mal-administration, or corruption" (*PGM*, I: 301), the former term being one that Mason later proposed at the U.S. Constitutional Convention of 1787 before he substituted the language of "high crimes and misdemeanors" (Farrand II, 550). The final version of the Virginia Constitution limited the impeachment of governors to those who were no longer in office and added, as impeachable offenses, actions "by which the safety of the state may be endangered" (*PGM*, I: 308). Both drafts differed from the U.S. Constitution which later provided for impeachment in one house and trial in the second. In a provision that is similar to current national rules, however, Section 12 provided that guilt would result in removal from office and possible exclusion to future offices as well as to "such pains or penalties as the laws shall direct" (*PGM*, I: 301).

The final version of the Virginia Constitution further distinguished impeachment of the governor and other officials from judicial officers. Unlike the governor and other officials, judges would be "prosecuted in the Court of Appeals" rather than in the body that had accused them (*PGM*, I: 308). This was likely intended to protect them against politically-motivated accusations.

OTHER MATTERS

The remaining sections again dealt chiefly with housekeeping and implementation rules. Section 13 thus provided that commissions would be awarded "in the name" and "with the seal of the commonwealth annexed" (*PGM*, I: 301). Indictments were to be worded, "Against the peace and dignity of the Commonwealth" (*PGM*, I: 301).

Section 14 followed the advice of Lee's broadside in providing that both houses would annually appoint a treasurer (considered to be a legislative rather than an executive official) by a joint ballot. The fifteenth, and final, provision proposed initiating the new government through elections for the Lower Assembly, to set in motion the rest of the Constitution, which would replace existing offices.

The final draft of the Virginia Constitution further provided that all penalties that previously went to the king should now go to the commonwealth. It ceded Virginia's claims to lands within Maryland, Pennsylvania, and North and South Carolina, retaining other lands guaranteed by Virginia charters "unless by act of <this> legislature, one or more territories shall hereafter be laid off, and governments established westward of the *Allegheny* mountains." It also prohibited purchases from Native-Americans that were not approved by the General Assembly (*PGM*, I: 309).

ANALYSIS

The Virginia Constitution essentially continued the kind of representative government that was already familiar to its citizens. Although it arguably did not vest adequate powers (such as a veto) in the governor or give him a term of sufficient length, it did incorporate checks and balances through the establishment of a bicameral legislature and through separating the legislative, executive, and judicial powers. It was also prefaced by a Declaration of Rights, which sought to protect individual liberties. Perhaps because it was written at such an early stage of constitution making, it did not provide a formal constitutional amending process, although the Declaration of Rights had asserted a general right to "reform, alter, or abolish" governments. As noted above, the Virginia Convention further failed to secure more popular grounding for the state constitution either by requiring a popular referendum or by vesting subsequent ratification in another convention called specifically for this purpose. It did not, as Adams had proposed, specifically provide for governmental support of education or endorse sumptuary laws.

Although it is impossible to discern the precise contributions that George Mason made to this Document, he appears to have played a major role in its drafting, likely aided by proposals that Richard Henry Lee and John Adams had circulated. It seems likely that Virginia later chose Mason to attend the Constitutional Convention of 1787 in part because of his experience in fashioning the Virginia document.

It is important to recognize that the creation of republican government put in motion a process through which further reforms—like Jefferson's desire to abolish primogeniture and entail and to disestablish the church—could later be effected. Although Mason was later appointed to the committee to revise state laws, he soon resigned, deferring to lawyers on the committee, including Jefferson, who largely led the way to enacting through legislation portions of this reform program that were not effected through the constitution.

REFERENCES

Adams, John. April 1776. *Thoughts on Government.* From *The Papers of John Adams,* Vol. IV. Posted at https://www.masshist.org/publications/apde2/view?&id=PJA04dg2.

Adams, Willi Paul. 2001. *The First American Constitutions: Republican Ideology and the Making of the State Constitutions in the Revolutionary Era,* trans. By Rita and Robert Kimber. Lanham: Rowman & Littlefield.

Braxton, Carter. 1983 [1776]. "An Address to the Convention of the Colony and Ancient Dominion of Virginia on the Subject of Government in General, and Recommending a Particular Form to Their Attention." *American Political Writing During the Founding Era, 1760–1805,* vol. I of 2, ed. by Donald S. Lutz and Charles S. Hyneman. Indianapolis: Liberty Fund.

Dill, Alonzo. 1983. *Carter Braxton, Virginia Signer: A Conservative in Revolt.* Lanham, MD. University Press of America.

Cogliano, Francis D. 2013. "'The Whole Object of the Present Controversy': The Early Constitutionalism of Paine and Jefferson." *Paine and Jefferson in the Age of Revolutions*, ed. Simon P. Newman and Peter S. Onuf. Charlottesville, VA: University of Virginia Press, 26-48.

Dinan, John J. 2006. *The American State Constitutional Tradition.* Lawrence: University Press of Kansas.

Farrand, Max, ed. 1966. *The Records of the Federal Convention of 1787.* 4 vols. New Haven, CT: Yale University Press.

Howard, A.E. Dick. 1968. "'For the Common Benefit': Constitutional History in Virginia as a Casebook for the Modern Constitution-Maker." *Virginia Law Review* 54 (June): 816-902.

Jefferson, Thomas. 1950. *The Papers of Thomas Jefferson.* Volume 1 *1760-1776*, ed. Julian Boyd. Princeton NJ: Princeton University Press.

Mason, George. 1970. *The Papers of George Mason, 1725*-1792, Vol. I. ed. Robert A. Rutland. Chapel Hill: The University of North Carolina Press.

Selby, John E. 1976. "Richard Henry Lee, John Adams, and the Virginia Constitution of 1776." *The Virginia Magazine of History and Biography* 84 (October): 387-400.

Washington, Henry Augustine. 1852. *The Virginia Constitution of 17776: A Discourse Delivered Before the Virginia Historical Society at their Annual Meeting.* Richmond: MacFarlane & Fergusson.

Wood, Gordon S. 1969. *The Creation of the American Republic, 1776-1787.* Chapel Hill: The University of North Carolina Press.

5

George Mason and the Articles of Confederation

The Articles of Confederation, which Congress had proposed in 1777, were ratified on March 1, 1781. These Articles continued with a unicameral Congress in which states were equally represented by delegates who served one-year terms that could be renewed for up to three consecutive years. Congress exercised a limited number of powers (often requiring the consent of nine or more states), which, significantly, did not extend to the control of interstate commerce. All unspecified powers, and the exercise of most aspects of domestic sovereignty, remained with the states. After being proposed by Congress, constitutional amendments, none of which were ever adopted, required the unanimous consent of the states. The Articles lacked an independent executive or an independent judicial system, although it had provided a procedure to settle disputes over state boundaries.

Because the government under the Articles was confederal, Congress had no means to operate directly upon individuals and had to requisition states for troops and taxes, which they were often unable or unwilling to provide. In time, leading statesmen came to see the Articles as an inadequate mechanism for preserving America's place in the world, for preserving order, or for protecting civil rights and liberties, over which state legislatures sometimes rode roughshod (Dougherty 2001; Hoffert, 1992; Jensen 1966; McLaughlin 1962).

The battle of Yorktown, the last such engagement of the Revolutionary War, ended on October 19, 1781. In time, Mason was among those who concluded that the Articles needed to be amended, and yet many of his concerns during the Articles would point to future reservations that he would have with the Constitution that replaced it. Mason, who would later object to the necessary and proper clause on similar grounds, was particularly concerned about interpretations of either state or national documents that went beyond the text. This concern is reflected in a number of letters and documents that he wrote during the Confederation period. Although they are not as extensive as his writings for some other periods of his life, they are arguably fundamental for understanding why Mason ultimately refused to sign the U.S. Constitution

PRIVATE LETTERS

Mason expressed his concerns soon after the Articles were ratified. Thus writing to Thomas Jefferson on September 17, 1781, Mason informed him of what he considered to be "the factious, illegal, & dangerous Schemes now in Contemplation in Congress, for dismembering the Commonwealth of Virginia, & erecting a new State or States to the Westward to the Alleghany Mountains" (*PGM*, II: 697). He further cited arguments that Thomas Paine had advanced in his *Public Good, Being an Examination into the Claims of Virginia to the Vacant Western Territory* (1780), in which Paine had argued that the Revolution had transferred the sovereignty previously exercised by Great Britain to Congress. Mason feared that, were this the case, "the Revolution, instead of securing, as was intended, our Rights & libertys, will only change the Name & place of Residence of our Tyrants" (*PGM,* II: 697). Mason proceeded to cite several provisions in the Articles of Confederation questioning the power of Congress to create new states, at least without the consent of at least nine of them.

In a subsequent letter to Samuel Purviance dated July 17, 1782, Mason repeated and elaborated on many of these themes. As he would do in his later criticisms of the U.S. Constitution, Mason feared that congressional actions were either tyrannical or aristocratic in nature, and he was often inclined to believe the worse. Observing that "Some of the late proceedings of Congress must give thinking men great Uneasiness, and convince them that our foederal Union can not be lasting, or that we are in Danger of establishing as tyrannical a Power in America, as that against which we have drawn the Sword," he observed that congress cannot exceed its powers "without establishing an arbitrary & tyrannical Aristocracy; for if, under pretense of public Utility, Necessity, or under any Pretence whatsoever, they can, in one Instance, exceed the Powers delegated to them, they may in another, or in a hundred; every repetition of Wrong will be considered, & urged as a precedent for others" (*PGM,* II: 739).

Acknowledging that experience might show that the "present Powers" of Congress, are, "in some Instances, insufficient," Mason argued that they be increased "by additional Articles to the Confederation, acceded to (after due Deliberation) by all the States; but upon no Pretence, however plausible, without" (*PGM,* II: 740). Mason's eyes were watchful, believing that "the Few have always encroached upon the Rights of the Many" (*PGM*, II: 741). If Congress were to be vested with new powers, it should be so empowered by constitutional amendments rather than by liberal constitutional construction.

As he revealed in another letter to William Cabell dated May 6, 1783, Mason thought that it was important to give "strict adherence to the Distinctions between Right & Wrong for the future" (*PGM*, II: 768). He feared that "Frequent Interferance with private Property & Contracts, retrospective Laws destructive of all public Faith, as well as Confidence between Man & Man, and flagrant Violations of the Constitution must disgust the best & wisest Part of the Community, occasion a general Depravity of Manners, bring the Legislature into Contempt, and finally produce Anarchy & public Convulsion" (*PGM*, II: 768).

PETITION OF FREEHOLDERS OF PRINCE WILLIAM

If Mason feared the newly authorized congress, he had similar qualms about his own state legislature. He was accordingly largely responsible for drafting "A Petition and Remonstrance from the Freeholders of Prince William County" to the General Assembly, which was dated December 10, 1781. At a time when others might well have been commending the forceful executive actions that had arguably contributed to the victory at Yorktown, Mason remained focused on their implications for the rights and liberties of the people and not a little concerned that his own state might be getting the short end of the stick.

Mason, who had a major hand in the design of the Virginia Constitution and who would consider the lack of a council of state as a major defect of the U.S. Constitution, was especially concerned that in the events leading up to

Yorktown, Governor Thomas Nelson had violated the state constitution by acting with respect to a number of matters without the consent of the Council. Although Mason thought that such lawless actions were, in and of themselves, undesirable, he was even more concerned about what they might portend. As he explained, "such Precedents are of the most dangerous & fatal Tendency; sapping the Foundations of the Commonwealth, and the Rights & Libertys of the People" (*PGM*, II: 704).

Mason directed particular ire at the governor's authorization, sometimes directly to military officials, to seize property, mostly horses and cattle. He argued that in many cases the French soldiers could have paid to purchase such livestock for themselves and that, in some cases, the livestock that was so confiscated had gone not to Virginians but to troops from other states. He further believed that such seizures had violated the principle of civilian control of the military and that they had fallen particularly heavily on poor families.

Pointing out that many of the commissioners had not taken required oaths of offices, Mason portrayed a scene not far different from that which had led to the American Revolution: "the Enormity & Tyranny of these Proceedings can hardly be paralleled in the most despotic Governments; and that, without exemplary Punishment upon the Guilty, a Man can have no Security in his Property; or must be reduced to the fatal Necessity of punishing the Aggressor with his own Hand; as in a State without Laws, every Man has a Right to do" (*PGM*, II: 707). Mason further likened the seizures to "public-Robbery" (*PGM*, II: 707).

Mason also objected to the embargo on exports which the state had adopted (presumably to insure supplies for troops) but which other states had dropped, and which had apparently been ended by the time that the General Assembly received his petition. Mason observed that "without speedy and proper Alterations, and due Encouragements to Industry, Tillage is in great Danger of being totally neglected; and real Scarcity introduced to prevent an imaginary one; as it is not to be expected that Men will labour to have the Produce perish upon their Hands, or seized from them by Violence" (*PGM*, II: 708).

Mason further objected to Virginia shouldering the main burden for providing for British prisoners (he also later charged that uniforms that Virginians had made for their soldiers had been given to those of other states), and to the issuance of paper currency, which had led to rapid depreciation. In a connection that does not appear altogether clear, Mason further believed that the depreciation of currency had "enfeebled or frustrated our whole System of Penal-Laws, prevented the Performance of many necessary public Dutys, and the Punishment of public Delinquents & Offenders: that they have stained the national character, destroyed all Confidence between Man & Man; and by encouraging Knavery, & legalizing Fraud, have corrupted & depraved the Morals of the People" (*PGM*, II: 709).

Mason tied depreciation of currency at the state level to a similar depreciation by Congress and suggested that Virginia having somewhat profited by this situation should refuse to send more of its quota to Congress. He also thought that current tax burdens could be distributed more equally "If the Taxes were imposed in Specie, with the Power of discharging a certain proportion (sufficient to sink the Paper-Money in a limited time) in the said Paper Currency at its present value" (*PGM*, II: 710).

The petition ended with a set of specific recommendations. They included:

- establishing mechanisms for detecting and punishing fraud;
- eliminating seizures and reining in military authority;
- ending the embargo;
- repealing currency laws;
- adhering to "Economy and Frugality . . . in all public measures";
- informing Congress that the state would no longer "submit to any Encroachment upon it's just right" or assuming unequal burdens; and
- adopting electoral regulations so as "to procure a proper Representation, by the general Suffrage of the Freeholders, who should receive "moderate Penalties" should they fail to vote (*PGM*, II: 711)

In his preview to these resolutions, Robert Rutland says that the General Assembly took most of Mason's concerns seriously and adopted several pieces of legislation as a result. Although Governor Thomas Nelson resigned, the Assembly did not find that he had been a fault. Still, Rutland believes that "the remedial legislation passed in answer to Mason's petition helped Virginia return to more stability in its fiscal affairs and to more equanimity in the transition period between 1782 and 1789" (*PGM*, II: 703)

FAIRFAX COUNTY FREEHOLDER'S ADDRESS AND INSTRUCTIONS

Early Americans, who often thought that representative bodies should be direct reflections of the people who elected them, exercised the right both to instruct and to recall representatives that did not heed such instructions (Bresler 1991). In a document dated May 30, 1783, George Mason compiled a list of 13 instructions that he and other Fairfax County Freeholders sent to their delegates to the Virginia General Assembly. The Document presents a window into Mason's thinking just two years after ratification of the Articles of Confederation, under which states retained those aspects of sovereignty not specifically delegated to Congress. Given that some of the concerns expressed in the document relate directly to acts of Congress, it is significant that Mason addressed his concerns directly to members of the Virginia General Assembly.

Addressing state legislators as "Gentlemen," the first paragraph noted that the freeholders "have committed to you the greatest and most sacred trust, which a free people can repose in any of their fellow-citizens," namely "the care of our dearest and most important interests, the protections of our rights and liberty, and the power of making, on our behalf, those laws by which we are to be governed, and this commonwealth preserved in safety and prosperity" (*PGM,* II: 779). Affirming confidence in the representatives' "integrity and attachment to the public good," Mason nonetheless affirmed "our undoubted right of instructing you, as our immediate Representatives in the Legislature" (*PGM,* II: 779).

Altogether, Mason and his fellow freemen addressed 13 unnumbered concerns. The first instructed their representatives to oppose "the smallest infraction of the late Treaty of Peace, either with respect to the payment of debts, or in any other matter whatsoever, whereby the public faith. . . . may be violated" (*PGM,* II: 779). Quite practically, Mason indicated that such violations could lead either to renewed "calamities of war, or the danger or reprisals" (*PGM,* II: 779).

The second instruction called for the representatives "to enact a law for repayment of the principal and interest to each and every individual, who hath paid paper money into the public treasury, in discharge of the debts due to British creditors, according to its real value in specie, to be adjusted by the legal scale of depreciation, at the time each sum was respectively placed in the Treasury; and that such debts, as well as all other private debts and contracts, be thereafter left to the common course of the laws of the land" (*PGM*, II: 779). This instruction further called upon delegates to make sure that a roll-call vote was taken on any such measures so that, using a Biblical analogy, the voters would be able "to separate the *tares* from the *corn*" (*PGM*, II: 780).

The third instruction called upon delegates to oppose granting any special trade privileges "other than what may be stipulated in the Commercial Treaties concluded by the authority of Congress" (*PGM*, II, 780). Mason and his compatriots clearly stood on the side of free trade, wanting prices to be determined by "the goodness and cheapness of" individual commodities rather than by the dispensing of special favors (*PGM*, II: 780).

Although Mason remained constantly vigilant against judicial overreach, instruction four was directed to opposing "any further occlusion," or closure, of courts. With concern for "the due and regular administration of justice," Mason feared that such closures "must loosen the bonds of society, corrupt the morals of the people, and tend to produce anarchy and public confusion" (*PGM*, II: 780).

Instruction five through seven dealt with monetary and fiscal issues. At a time when such matters largely lay with the states, the fifth asked delegates to oppose "emissions," or printings, of paper money, interferences with private contracts, or the adoption of an ex post facto laws, "except such only as are warranted by the greatest emergencies, and the plain principles of justice," (*PGM*, II: 780) and to repeal existing laws that provided for any of these. Instruction six opposed any further delays in tax collections other than those that might give the people "the benefit of this summer's market, for their commodities now on hand" (*PGM*, II: 780). Mason feared that such delays were "highly injurious to public credit" (*PGM*, II: 780). Instruction seven further directed delegates to investigate public expenditures and to bring to account "all public delinquents and defaulters" (*PGM*, II: 780).

On a related matter, the eighth instruction called for procuring "ample justice to the officers and soldiers of the American army" who "have so bravely defended the rights and liberties of their country" (*PGM*, II: 780). Similarly instruction 9 called for opposition to laws "preventing extensive credits upon open accounts" or for higher duties on "imported iron or cordage [ropes]" than upon other goods (*PGM*, II: 780-81).

The final instructions are especially important because they all related to actions of Congress. Instruction 10 shows that Mason and his fellow citizens remained vigilant with respect to states' rights and that they favored strict construction of a document, which had provided that "Each state retains its sovereignty, freedom, and independence, and every power, jurisdiction, and right, which is not by this Confederation expressly delegated to the United States, in Congress assembled." Mason thus called for opposition to "all encroachments of the American Congress upon the sovereignty and jurisdiction of the separate States; and every assumption of power, not expressly vested in them, by the Articles of Confederation" (*PGM*, II: 781). Mason further argued that if additional powers were necessary, they should "be granted only by additional articles to the Confederation, duly acceded to by all the States" (*PGM,* II: 781). As justification for such a strict interpretation of constitutional provisions, Mason observed that if Congress could claim such powers in one instance, "They may in another, or in an hundred; every repetition will be strengthened and confirmed by precedents" (*PGM,* II: 781).

Becoming somewhat more specific, Mason mandated opposition to "any attempts which may be made by Congress to obtain a perpetual revenue, or the appointment or revenue officers" (*PGM,* II: 781). Were Congress to enact such measures, it would show both the Articles and state constitutions to be "mere parchment bulwarks to American liberty" (*PGM,* I: 781),

In an obvious reference to the *Address and Recommendations to the United States in Congress Assembled,* which had proposed a 25-year tariff for making care of the nation's debts ("Report"), Mason said that they exhibited "strong proofs of lust of power" (*PGM,* II: 781). Mason likened them to the requests of British kings for ship money, and found the "very style" of the congressional report to be alarming. Mason believed that "The proposed duties may be proper, but the separate States only can safely have *the power of levying taxes.* Congress should not have even the appearance of such a power" (*PGM,* II: 781). Noting that "forms generally imply substance," Mason further observed that "when the same man, or set of men, holds both the sword and the purse, there is an end of liberty" (*PGM,* II: 781). As in his letters, Mason expressed further opposition to the congressional resolution allowing it to dispose of unappropriated lands or to create new states.

The final instruction, which demonstrated continuing concern over congressional expenditures, urged members of the General Assembly to instruct members of Congress against sending ambassadors to Europe. Although the central concern appears to have been expense, this concern was tied to larger issues, dear to the heart of republicans: "Such appointments can hardly fail of producing dangerous combinations, factions, and cabals, in the great council of America. And from the great distance and the difficulty of knowing and examining their conduct, there is danger, too, that courts some of the persons so sent, may be corrupted and pensioned by the courts where they reside" (*PGM*, II: 782). Mason argued that "consuls to superintend our trade (at less than a tenth part of the charge of ambassadors) will be sufficient to answer every good purpose" (*PGM*, II: 272). Advocating a form of early American isolationism, he further thought that "nature having separated us, by an immense ocean, from the European nations, the less we have to do with their quarrels or politics, the better" (*PGM*, II: 782). Mason ended by affirming "sentiments of great respect and esteem" from "your friends and fellow-citizens" (*PGM*, II: 782).

ANALYSIS

By the time the Constitutional Convention met in 1787, general sentiment, especially among elites, had come to accept that both state and national governments were seriously flawed. James Madison delineated many of these flaws in an essay that he drafted in April of 1787 entitled "Vices of the Political System of the United States" that influenced his extensive contributions to the Virginia Plan (Meyers 1972, 82-93). From the letters that he wrote and the resolutions that he helped draft during the Confederation period, it seems clear that Mason shared many of these concerns and that he was willing to accede to an increase in congressional powers.

Whereas Madison and other Federalists at least initially thought that he had constructed a government that might largely transcend the problems of the Articles of Confederation, Mason remained more cautious. Indeed, he continued to project his fears that the general government was headed either in a monarchical or aristocratic direction onto the new government and remained extremely suspicious of any openings for implied powers or any exercises of power by a president without the guide of an executive council like the one Mason had helped to create in Virginia.

At the state level, even when there might be general agreement that a particular exercise of executive power might have been for the public good, Mason remained concerned that such precedents might have long-term negative consequences. He did not believe that the election of delegates from larger districts, or many of the other mechanisms that the Constitutional Convention of 1787 proposed would be adequate to quench the lust for power that he believed he had witnessed at both state and local levels.

As the next chapter shows, although Mason played an important role at the Constitutional Convention of 1787, he thus stumbled at the threshold of ratifying a new constitution without either a declaration of rights or additional structural changes including the addition of a council to rein in executive powers and check its possible collusion with the U.S. Senate.

REFERENCES

Bresler, Kenneth. 1991. "Rediscovering the Right to Instruct Legislators." *New England Law Review* 26 (Winger): 335-394.

Dougherty, Keith L. 2001. *Collective Action under the Articles of Confederation*. Cambridge: Cambridge University Press.

Hoffert, Robert W. 1992. *A Politics of Tensions: The Articles of Confederation and American Political Ideals*. Niwot, CO: University Press of Colorado.

Jensen, Merrill. 1966. *The Articles of Confederation*. Madison: University of Wisconsin Press.

McLaughlin, Andrew C. 1962 [1905]. *The Confederation and the Constitution, 1783-1789*. New York: Collier Books.

Mason, George. 1970. *The Papers of George Mason, 1725*-1792. 3 vols. ed. Robert A. Rutland. Chapel Hill: The University of North Carolina Press.

Meyers, Marvin, ed. 1973. *The Mind of the Founder: Sources of the Political Thought of James Madison*. Indianapolis: The Bobbs-Merrill Company, Inc.

"Report on Address to the States by Congress." April 25, 1983. Founders Online. https://founders.archives.gov/documents/Madison/01-06-02-0180.

6

George Mason and the U.S. Constitutional Convention of 1787

The longest distance that George Mason ever traveled was the trip that took him from Virginia to Philadelphia to attend the Constitutional Convention of 1787. After having long resisted calls for him to represent Virginia in the Continental Congresses, this would indicate that Mason was among those who were concerned about the weaknesses of the government under the Articles of Confederation and believed that changes were needed to correct them. In contrast with his general dislike of being away from home and his sporadic attendance to his duties at the Fairfax Court (Horrell 1983), Mason attended the Convention from beginning to end. After all this effort, he ultimately refused to sign the Constitution that it produced.

Mt. Vernon Conference

There were two primary meetings that led to the Constitutional Convention, and Mason was a key figure in the first, albeit almost inadvertently. A key problem under the Articles of Confederation was that it did not vest Congress with power over interstate commerce so states with conflicts with one another had to fend for themselves. To this end, the Virginia General Assembly adopted a resolution in June of 1784 appointing four commissioners (Mason, Edmund Randolph, Alexander Henderson, and James Madison) to meet with a Maryland commission to deal with "jurisdiction and navigation of the river Potomac" (*PGM*, II: 813).

Neither the Governor nor the Assembly had supplied the commissioners with copies of the resolution or with notice of their appointments. Mason thus reported in a letter to James Madison dated December 7, 1785, that he found out about his commission "by mere Accident," when two of three Maryland Commissioners headed to Alexandria, Virginia wrote to him just before the meeting was about to begin (*PGM*, II: 836). George Washington furnished Mason and Henderson with a similar resolution respecting Pennsylvania, and he invited the three Maryland commissioners (Daniel of St. Thomas Jenifer, Thomas Stone, and Samuel Chase) to meet at his home at Mt. Vernon On March 25, 1785.

Fortuitously, but mistakenly, believing that they had authority to act (the resolution had required a quorum of three commissioners) and that this authority included power to discuss navigation of the Chesapeake Bay and Pocomoke River as well as the Potomac River (*PGM*, II: 836), the commissioners successfully arrived at a compact between the two states. They prepared this for the Virginia House of Delegates on March 28, and the House accepted it. James Madison used the success of this compact to call for a meeting in Annapolis Maryland the following September to discuss issues of navigation throughout America. Although Mason was appointed, he did not attend because of illness, and only five state delegations arrived in Annapolis. Madison, Alexander Hamilton, John Dickinson and others, however, used this meeting to call for a wider convention, which, aided by fears generated by Shay's Rebellion in Massachusetts, resulted in the Constitutional Convention of 1787 (Morris 1985).

MASON'S ATTITUDE AS THE CONVENTION BEGAN

Those who knew Mason's sentiments going into the Convention may have found his ultimate decision not to sign to be puzzling. Writing to his son, George Mason, Jr., on May 20, 1787, six days after the Convention had been scheduled to convene, Mason observed that he was meeting regularly with fellow members of the Virginia delegation and that "The Expectations & Hopes of all the Union center in this Convention. God grant that we may be able to concert effectual Means of preserving our Country from the Evils which threaten us" (*PGM*, III: 880).[1] Moreover, in another letter to the same son dated June 1, Mason expressed far greater optimism than he had expressed at the start of the Fifth Virginia Convention. Observing his fear "that soured & disgusted with the unexpected Evils we had experienced from

---

[1] One of the most fascinating aspects of this letter is that, writing before the Convention had adopted its rules of secrecy, Mason gave a remarkable preview of the central elements of what would become the Virginia Plan: "The most prevalent Idea, in the principal States seems to be a total Alteration of the present federal System and substituting a great National Council, or Parliament, consisting of two Branches of the Legislature, founded upon the Principles of equal proportionate Representation, with full legislative Powers upon all the Objects of the Union; and an Executive: and to make the several State Legislatures subordinate to the National, by giving the latter the Power of a Negative upon all such Laws, as they shall judge contrary to the Interest of the federal Union" (*PGM*, III: 880). Mason wrote a similar description in a letter to Arthur Lee dated May 21, 1787 (*PGM*, III: 882).

the democratic Principles of our Governments, we shou'd be apt to run into the opposite Extreme, and in endeavouring to steer too far from Scilla, we might be drawn into the Vortex of Charybdis" (*PGM,* III: 892), Mason was quite complimentary of his fellow delegates. He thus observed that: "I have the Pleasure to find, in the Convention, many Men of firm Republican Principles. America has certainly, upon this Occasion, drawn forth her first Characters; there are upon this Convention many Gentlemen of the most respectable Abilities, and, so far as I can yet discover, of the purest Intentions" (*PGM,* III: 892). Perhaps reflecting his typical distaste for public gatherings, Mason affirmed that he would not "upon pecuniary Motives, serve in this Convention for a thousand pounds per Day" (*PGM,* III: 892). However, he observed that the work of the Revolution and the formation of the Articles of Confederation "were nothing compared with the great Business now before us," which involved nothing less than "the Happiness or Misery of Millions yet unborn" (*PGM,* III: 893).

Early during its deliberations, Mason seconded a motion opposing the recording of delegate votes under individual names, lest, in cases where delegates changed their minds, this "furnish handles to the adversaries of the Result of the Meeting" (Farrand, I: 10). This rather clearly suggested that he did not anticipate being among such opponents. Although he may not have had the same enthusiasm for the Convention as did Madison and Washington, Mason observed on May 30th that the Articles of Confederation had been unable to deal with "delinquent States" and "that such a Govt. was necessary as could directly operate on individuals" (Farrand, I: 34). On June 20th, Mason supported the dominant Virginia Plan over the rival New Jersey Plan.

In his famed character sketches of delegates to the Constitutional Convention, Georgia's William Pierce described him as follows: "Mr. Mason is a Gentleman of remarkable strong powers, and possesses a clear and copious understanding. He is able and convincing in debate, steady and firm in his principles, and undoubtedly one of the best politicians in America. Mr. Mason is about 60 years old, with a fine strong constitution" (Vile, 2015d, 159).

On July 5, James Madison summarized a speech that Mason had given indicating that although "It could not be more inconvenient to any gentleman to remain absent from his private affairs, than it was for him . . . he would bury his bones in this city rather than expose his County to the consequences of a dissolution of the Convention without any thing being done" (Farrand, I: 533). Similarly, more than a month later, on August 10, Madison recorded that although Mason "wished to guard agst abuses as much as possible," "He thought the Constitution as now moulded was founded on sound principles, and was disposed to put into it extensive powers" (Farrand, II: 252).

MASON'S ATTITUDE CHANGES

By August 31, however, Mason favored a motion by Elbridge Gerry of Massachusetts to postpone consideration of the provision sending the Constitution to state conventions for ratification. According to Madison's notes, Mason said that "he would sooner chop off his right hand than put it to the Constitution as it now stands" (Farrand, II: 479). Moreover, should certain points "be improperly settled, his wish would then be to bring the whole subject before another general Convention" (Farrand, II: 479).

In a letter to Thomas Jefferson dated October 24, 1787, James Madison, who would later take a somewhat kinder view,[2] observed that "Col. Mason left Philadea. In an exceeding ill humour indeed. A number of little circumstances arising in part from the impatience which prevailed towards the close of the business, conspired to whet his acrimony. He returned to Virginia with a fixed disposition to prevent the adoption of the plan if possible" (*PGM*, III: 1007).

After the Convention ended and Mason opposed ratification of the Constitution without prior amendments even more wholeheartedly, there is hearsay evidence that Mason's attitude further hardened and began to take a more negative personal tone. Despite his early praise for the devotion of delegates to "fine republican principles, and their "most respectable abilities" and "purest intentions," a letter that Tobias Lear wrote to John Langdon on April 3, 1788, and affirmed by others, indicated that he was now taking the low road. Mason had "declared that the Convention, generally speaking, was made up of block-heads from the northern, coxcombs from the southern, & office-seekers from the middle states" (Quoted in Henriques 1989, 200).

---

[2] In answering a letter by George Mason of Green Springs about the role of his ancestor in the Founding, Madison responded, perhaps with some consideration to the lineage of the inquirer: "The public situation in which I had the best opportunity of being acquainted with the genius, the opinions, and the public labours of Col. Mason, was that of our co-service in the Convention of 1787, which formed the Constitution of the United States. The objections which led him to withhold his name from it have been explained by himself. But none who differed from him on some points will deny that he sustained throughout the proceedings of the body the high character of a powerful reasoned, a profound statesmen, and a devoted Republican" (Farrand, III: 476).

On September 30, 1782, just a week before Mason's death, Thomas Jefferson, who had been in France during the Constitutional Convention of 1787, visited Mason at Gunston Hall and took notes summarizing what Mason told him about the proceedings. He observed that Mason said that he could "have set his hand & heart to" the Constitution, had it provided that "The presidt was to be elected for 7. Years, then ineligible for 7. more. 2. Rotation in the senate. 3. A vote of 2/3 in the legislature on particular subjects, & expressly on that of navign." (*PGM*, III: 1275). Mason had proceeded to explain how toward the end of the convention, the southernmost states had combined with three New England states to delete the two-thirds vote required on commercial regulations in exchange for the right to import slaves for 20 additional years. Mason had observed that "Under this coalition the great principles of the Constn were changed in the last days of the Convention" (*PGM*, III: 1276).

THE CONSTITUTION AS A BUNDLE OF COMPROMISES

The Constitutional Convention achieved a quorum on May 25, and delegates signed the resulting Document on September 17. Rather than simply revising the Articles of Confederation, as many arriving delegates probably anticipated, the Virginia Plan, which had dominated initial discussion, proposed an entirely new federal government. It was to consist of three branches of government that, in contrast to the Articles, could act directly on individual citizens. These were to be composed of a bicameral Congress with extensive new powers apportioned according to population, a president or presidents to serve as chief executive, and an independent judiciary.

Although it is common to call James Madison the "father" of the Constitution, no delegate to the Constitution Convention got everything he wanted. The Great Compromise thus provided for equal state representation in the U.S. Senate, compromising between large and small states. Compromises between northern and southern states permitted states that wished to do so to continue importing slaves for another 20 years. A variety of compromises led to the Electoral College mechanism for choosing presidents, determined qualification for federal officers, and settled on lengths of terms of office.

Any delegate who came with a set of ideas as to what the Constitution should be likely found himself disagreeing with at least some elements of the plan. In a justifiably famous speech that fellow Pennsylvanian James Wilson presented on his behalf on the day the delegates signed the Document, Benjamin Franklin began by observing that "there are several parts of this constitution which I do not at present approve" (Farrand, II: 641). He went on to argue, however that he could not be sure that his own initial opinions had been correct because he valued collective wisdom and because "I think a general government necessary for us" (Farrand, II: 642). Noting that in addition to their "joint wisdom," the assembly has also brought "their prejudices, their passions, their errors of opinion, their local interests, and their shellfish views," he professed that he was astounded "to find this system approaching so near to perfection as it does" (Farrand, II: 642), and argued for unanimity. In contrast to Edmund Randolph (who would later support the Document at the Virginia ratifying convention), who arose to express his apologies for not signing, and to Elbridge Gerry, who rose to express "the painful feelings of his situation, and the embarrassment" he felt in following suit (Farrand, II, 646), Mason did not deliver any speeches on that final day. At that time, however, his reservations about the Document remained stronger than the reasons he had come to the Convention.

MASON'S WORK AT THE CONVENTION

Anti-Federalists John Lansing and Robert Yates of New York, like Luther Martin of Maryland, were among those who left the Convention early rather than continuing to participate in debates that they thought were leading to an overly consolidated national government that they could not approve. By contrast, Mason not only attended the Convention from beginning to end, but was one of six delegates who spoke more than 100 times—with 136 speeches, he was fifth among delegates in this regard ("Constitutional Convention," 1861, 18). Mason served on three committees at the Convention, although the last (on Sumptuary Legislation) never issued a report. He was a member of one of the most illustrious and influential state delegations, had initially supported the Virginia Plan, and arguably won more battles at the Convention than he lost.[3]

On August 31, Mason circulated a document to some members of the Committee on Postponed Parts with a dozen proposed changes, which, if they could be obtained, would make the document "unexceptional" (this term is Madison's, Hudson, 1987, 251). These proposed the following: that the Council of State of from five to seven members would be appointed by two-thirds majorities in the Senate and rotate in

---

[3] Note, the analysis that follows draws heavily from my essay on George Mason, in *The Constitutional Convention of 1787*, 2016a, I: 502-514.

office; that the "Objects of the National Government" be "expressly defined"; that two-thirds, rather than three-fourths majorities of Congress should be able to override presidential vetoes; that navigation laws require a two-thirds vote of Congress; that duties on imports be uniform throughout the United States; that Congress should "be restrained from establishing perpetual Revenue"; that laws for raising revenue or fixing salaries should originate in the House of Representatives; that members of congress be ineligible to any offices under the national government other than military posts; that the president be limited to a single term; that treaty-making and the appointment of ambassadors require the mutual concurrence of the Senate and the Council of State; that the president appoint all offices created by Congress with Senate concurrence; that the president's power to grant pardons not extend to impeachment or treason; and that the Senate be prohibited from altering money bills (Hutson 1987, 251-252). Notably, between the writing of Mason's proposals and the end of the Convention, the delegates adopted a number of these proposals including the two-thirds requirement for overturning presidential vetoes, uniform tariffs, presidential appointment and senatorial confirmation of most appointments, and limiting the president's power to pardon impeachments.

Just two days before delegates signed the Constitution, Mason successfully supported a motion by Connecticut's Roger Sherman providing that states could petition for a convention to propose constitutional amendments in the event that Congress proved unresponsive in proposing amendments that the people desired (Farrand, II: 629). Earlier in the Convention, Mason, who may have learned from the omission of a similar provision in the Virginia Constitution, had stressed that:

> The plan now to be formed will certainly be defective, as the Confederation has been found on trial to be. Amendments therefore will be necessary, and it will be better to provide for them in an easy, regular and Constitutional way than to trust to chance and violence. It would be improper to require the consent of the Natl. Legislature, because they may abuse their power, and refused their consent on that very account. (Farrand, I: 203).

Nonetheless, at the end of the Convention, Mason listed a set of his "Objections to this Constitution of Government," which he initially printed on his copy of a draft of the Document that was published for the Convention on September 12th after the Committee of Style had made its report. It is possible that Mason had originally intended to introduce his objections, which he later printed with minor emendations for the public, at the Convention. He thus noted, in a letter to Thomas Jefferson dated May 26, 1788, that he had drawn up "some general Objections; which I intended to offer, by way of Protest; but was discouraged from doing so, by the precipitate, & intemperate, not to say indecent Manner, in which the Business was conducted, during the last week of the Convention, after the Patrons of this new Plan found they had a decided Majority in their Favour; which was obtained by a Compromise between the Eastern & the two Southern States, to permit the latter to continue the Importation of Slaves for twenty odd Years; a more favourite Object with them, than the Liberty and Happiness of the People" (Farrand, III: 305).

Mason's document, in conjunction with arguments that Mason made during the course of the Convention, will serve as the guide to understanding why Mason ultimately opposed adoption of an unamended Constitution.[4] Essay No 6 published by Oliver Ellsworth, under the title of "The Landholder" on December 10, 1787 (Ford 1892, 161-166), an unattributed essay published in the *Virginia Independent Chronicle* on January 30, 1788 under the pseudonym "Civis Rusticus," meaning "Country Citizen" (Bailyn 1993, 353-362),[5] and essays by James Iredell, a future U.S. Supreme

---

[4] Edmund Randolph offered a similar laundry lists in debates on September 10. As summarized by Madison, "They turned on the Senate's being made the Court of Impeachment for trying the Executive—on the necessity of ¾ instead of 2/3 of each house to overrule the negative of the President—on the smallness of the number of the Representative branch,—on the want of limitation to a standing army—on the general clause concerning necessary and proper laws—on the want of some particular restraint on Navigation acts—on the power to lay duties on exports—on the Authority of the general Legislature to interpose on the application of the *Executives* of the states—on the want of a more definite boundary between the General & State Legislatures—and between the General and State Judiciaries—on the unqualified power of the President to pardon treasons—on the want of some limit of the President to pardon treasons—on the want of some limit to the power of the Legislature in regulating their own compensations" (Farrand, II: 563-564).

[5] The author of this essay remained highly complimentary to Mason. He observed at the outset that he considered Mason to be a "respectable and worthy gentleman; to whose great and eminent talents, profound judgment, and strength of mind, no man gives a larger credit" (Bailyn 1993, I: 353). At the conclusion of his essay, he added that, as a "man of abilities, firmness, and integrity," Mason had the courage "to judge, and act for himself" and that "his principles have not the pliancy of his gloves, neither has he his mind to make up at every revolution of the hour: authority with him is not the guide to truth, nor does infallibility rest in numbers" (Bailyn 1992, I: 362).

Court justice, published in the *Norfolk and Portsmouth Journal* from February 20 to March 19, 1788, under the name of "Marcus" (Bailyn, 1993), provide some public comment on Mason's thoughts.

CRITICISM OF THE OMISSION OF A DECLARATION OF RIGHTS

The first objection that Mason listed, and the one that has done the most to boost his reputation among modern civil libertarians, was the one that Mason apparently raised on the very day that delegates received the proposed wording of the Constitution from the Committee of Detail. At that time, Mason thus observed that "There is no Declaration of Rights, and the laws of the general government being paramount to the laws and constitution of the several States, the Declaration of Rights in the separate States are no security" (Farrand, II: 637). As I have elaborated elsewhere, however, Mason appeared to be looking back to the kind of "oughts" that he had articulated in the Virginia Declaration of Rights rather than forward to the more judicially enforceable "shalls" articulated in the Bill of Rights that Madison would later advance in Congress (Vile, 2016a, I: 511; Also see Broadwater 2017).

In thus responding on September 12 to observations that the Convention had yet to provide for juries in civil cases, Nathanial Gorham of Massachusetts had argued that "It is not possible to discriminate equity cases from those in which juries are proper" (Farrand, II: 587). Agreeing that this presented a problem, Mason observed, in comments that further illuminated the nature of the kind of bill of rights that he favored, that "A general principle laid down on this and some other points would be sufficient. He wished the plan had been prefaced with a Bill of Rights, & would second a

Motion if made for the purpose—It would give great quiet to the people: and with the aid of the State declarations, a bill might be prepared in a few hours" (Farrand, II: 587-588).

Mason's comments were notable for four reasons. First, he seemed more interested in articulating general principles than he did in establishing specific rights, like those we now depend upon courts to enforce. Second, he envisioned a bill that would "preface" the Constitution rather than being integrated into the text, as Madison would later advocate, or appended to it, as Congress would eventually decide, at Roger Sherman's urging, to do. Third, Mason appeared as motivated by the desire to placate public opinion as by concerns that such a bill of rights was actually necessary. Fourth, Mason was confident that the task could be achieved fairly quickly by working from existing state examples, undoubtedly including his own.

Elbridge Gerry then proposed, and Mason seconded, a motion creating a committee to prepare a bill of rights. After Connecticut's Roger Sherman suggested that state declarations of rights would be sufficient, Mason sagely observed that "The Laws of the U.S. are to be paramount to State Bills of Rights" (Farrand, II: 588). Nonetheless, delegates from the states that were present rejected the resolution by a vote of 10 to 0, indicating that Mason did not even carry a majority of his home state.

Debates on September 14 reveal that Mason continued to favor adding provisions articulating general aims and principles rather than categorical prohibitions such as those in contemporary bills of rights. Mason thus indicated that he favored adding a preface to the clause vesting Congress with the power to organize, arm, and discipline the militia with the statement "And that the liberties of the people may be better secured against the danger of standing armies in time of peace" (Farrand, II: 617).[6] Moreover, Mason moved to strike the provision in Article I, Section 9 outlawing ex post facto laws because he did not think the wording made it clear that the prohibition was limited only to criminal cases since "no Legislature ever did or can altogether avoid them in Civil cases" (Farrand, II: 617).

The plea for a declaration, or bill, of rights turned out to be the most potent Anti-federalist argument against adoption of an un-amended constitution, but many Federalists continued to argue against such an addition fairly late in the game. Oliver Ellsworth of Connecticut was among those who thought that such bills of rights were more necessary in a kingdom like England, where the king claimed all power, than in a government where the people would rule (Ford, 1892, 163). The author of Civis Rusticus observed that if Mason were correct in thinking that the state bills of rights would be no security against the national government, then "neither would a general declaration of rights be any security, for the sovereign who made it could repeal it" (Bailyn 1993, I: 356). "Marcus," largely following the approach that Publius would take, observed that "the future government which may be formed under that authority [the new Constitution] certainly cannot act beyond the warrant of that authority." (Bailyn 1993, I: 364).

---

[6] Although this amendment failed by a vote of 2 to 9, the Second Amendment, proposed by the first session of the new Congress, adopted a similar construction when it provided that "A well regulated Militia, being necessary to the security of a free State, the right of the people to keep and bear Arms, shall not be infringed."

CRITICISMS OF THE CONSTITUTION AND COMMON LAW

It is difficult to know whether Mason listed his objection to the omission of a bill of rights first because he thought it was most important (what rhetoricians call primacy), or because it was the argument that he had made closest to the time that he wrote (recency). It is even more difficult to ascertain why Mason added to this criticism "Nor are the people secured even in the enjoyment of the benefit of the common law" to which, in the print edition, he added, "which stands here upon no other foundation than its having been adopted by the respective acts forming the constitution of the several States" (Farrand, II: 637).

This topic was not a major issue at the Convention, which might have found it somewhat indelicate to underline the manner in which many state court decisions relied on English precedents. The first apparent mention of the common law, which took place on August 17, had to do with the congressional power to punish piracies and felonies on the high seas. Although Mason had registered some concern over "taking the power in all these cases wholly from the States" (Farrand, II: 315), he does not appear to have participated in discussion precipitated by Madison's motion to insert the word "define &" before punish. Nor had Mason, who was not trained as a lawyer, taken part in a second discussion on August 27, which involved giving courts jurisdiction over matters of both law and facts during which Pennsylvania's James Wilson had said that the believed the Committee that had proposed this had "meant facts as well as law & Common as well as Civil law" (Farrand, I: 431).

In a letter that he wrote to George Washington on October 18, 1787, James Madison expressed perplexity regarding Mason's criticism. He thus asked: "What can he mean by saying that the Common law is not secured by the new Constitution, though it has been adopted by the State Constitutions" (Farrand, III: 130). He continued: "The Common law is nothing more than the unwritten law, and is left by all the Constitutions equally liable to legislative alterations. I am not sure that any notice is particularly taken of it in the Constitutions of the States. If there is, nothing more is provided than a general declaration that it shall continue along with other branches of law to be in force till legally changed" (Farrand, III: 130). As if to clinch the argument, Madison further observed that "The Constitution of Virga. Drawn up by Col Mason himself, is absolutely silent on the subject" (Farrand, III: 130).

As Madison further warmed to the subject, he observed that, if common law remained in place, it would continue the law of primogeniture giving first-borns the lion's share of an inheritance and thus widening economic inequality. Moreover, if the delegates "had in general terms declared the Common law to be in force, they would have broken in upon the legal Code of every State in the most material points: they wd. Have done more, they would have brought over from G.B. a thousand heterogeneous & antirepublican doctrines, and even the *ecclesiastical Hierarchy itself*, for that is a part of the Common law. This objection surely was not brought forward in the Convention or it wd. Have been placed in such a light that a repetition of it out of doors would scarcely have been hazarded" (Farrand, III: 130).

Writing as "Marcus," James Iredell had professed, like Madison, that "It is difficult to know what is meant by that part of the objection" (Bailyn, 1993,I: 364). Iredell saw no reason to believe that the new Constitution would mandate any deviations from the common law other than which it already specified.

CRITICISMS OF REPRESENTATION IN THE U.S. HOUSE OF REPRESENTATIVES

Mason's next objection focused on representation in the U.S. House of Representatives. He complained that "In the House of Representatives there is not the substance but the shadow only of representation; which can never produce proper information in the legislature, or inspire confidence in the people; the laws will therefore be generally made by men little concerned in, and unacquainted with their effects and consequences." In his printed objections, Mason observed that this objection had been somewhat corrected by a last-minute change, supported by George Washington on September 17, to provide that there could be one representative for every 30,000 rather than for every 40,000 people (Farrand, II: 638). This strongly suggests that Mason penned his objections sometime between September 12 and September 17, thus casting light on the specific reasons that he refused to sign in Philadelphia rather than possible subsequent rationalizations.

Throughout the Convention, Mason had been proponent of popular election to the House of Representatives. On May 31 he referred to the House as "the grand depository of the democratic principles of the Govt." and likened it to the British House of Commons, in which every class would be represented (Farrand, I: 48-49). Largely for reasons of regional equity and the difficulty of sending representatives from distant states, he favored biennial, rather than annual, elections (Farrand, I: 363), a minimum age of 25 for its members (Farrand, I: 375), and origination of money bills in that body, all of which the Constitution included. Mason had supported the Connecticut Compromise, giving states equal representation in the Senate (indeed, he had served on the Committee, chiefly staffed with moderates, that proposed this compromise), and he had been one of the strongest proponents of periodic reapportionment of the House of Representatives, which made the new Congress far more democratic than the one that it was replacing. Indeed, on July 11, arguing that those with power would never give it up unless forced to do so, Mason said that he could not support the Constitution unless it was periodically apportioned (Farrand, I: 578). On the same day, he made a powerful argument for admitting new western states "as equals, and subjected to no degrading discriminations" (Farrand, I: 579). He had taken the same stance on July 5 (Farrand, I: 534).

As he would make clearer in his debates at the Virginia Ratifying Convention, it appears that Mason's primary objection to the House centered on the size of its membership. Although this body now consists of 435 voting members, its initial allocation was 65 members, which Mason wanted to double. Mason who probably knew that attendance had been a major issue under the Articles of Confederation, had explained his reasoning on July 10, when he observed that "A *majority* of a *Quorum* of 65 members, was too small a number to represent the whole inhabitants of the U. States; They will not possess enough of the confidence of the people, and wd. be too sparsely taken from the people, to bring with them all the local information which would be frequently wanted" (Farrand I: 568). In an argument in apparent tension with his later stance that it would be too expensive to raise the number of senators from two to three per state (Farrand, II: 94), Mason had argued that "the additional expense" of doubling the size of the House "was too inconsiderable to be regarded in so important a case" (Farrand, I: 569). He thought that such an objection "was over-balanced by its effect on the hopes of a greater number of the popular Candidates" (Farrand, I: 569). Mason was not the only one with this objection. In addition to those who focused on the specific size of their own state representation in that body, on September 10, Edmund Randolph also commented "on the smallness of the number of the Representative branch" (Farrand, II: 573).

In answering Mason's objection, the author of the "Civis Rusticus" essay observed that the size of the new House was larger than that of the Congress under the Articles of Confederation. The author further suggested that the delegates to the Constitutional Convention may have kept the number low in order to minimize expenses (Bailyn, 1993, I: 357), which is a concern that would likely have appealed to Mason.

CRITICISMS OF THE SENATE

In considering Mason's critique of the U.S. Senate, it is important to remember that under the original Constitution (later amended by the Seventeenth Amendment), state legislatures were to choose its members, who would serve for six-year terms, thus giving it a somewhat elite cast. Moreover, after the adoption of the Connecticut Compromise in which Mason had concurred, states would be represented equally in the Senate, thus magnifying sectional imbalances (Banning, 1989, 272). Given his republicanism, Mason's objections to the U.S. Senate, which he delineated in two paragraphs, are thus somewhat easier to understand. Mason complained that

> The Senate have the power of altering all money bills, and of originating appropriations of money, and the salaries of the officers of their own appointment, in conjunction with the president of the United States, although they are not the representatives of the people or amenable to them.
>
> These with their other great powers, viz.: their power in the appointment of ambassadors and all public officers, in making treaties, and in trying all impeachments, their influence upon and connection with the supreme Executive from these causes, their duration of office and their being a constantly existing body, almost continually sitting, joined with their being one complete branch of the legislature, will destroy any balance in the government, and enable them to accomplish what usurpations they please upon the rights and liberties of the people. (Farrand, II: 638).

Mason consistently advocated limiting the origination of money bills to the House of Representatives, which he expected to be closer to the people than the Senate, and he apparently believed that the provision in Article I, Section 7 allowing the Senate to amend such bills made the restriction largely nugatory. Noting in debates on August 13 that "the Senate did not represent the *people*, but the *States* in their political character," he had contended that "the purse strings should be in the hand of the Representatives of the People" (Farrand, II: 273, 274).

Whereas his objections indicated that he thought membership in the House of Representatives might be too small, Mason had, for reason of expense, opposed raising the number of Senators from two to three for each state (Farrand, II: 94), and the Convention had agreed. Apparently, Mason thought that the House of Representatives, and it alone, should determine the salaries of appointed officials, although I can find no evidence that he had raised this point in earlier debates. He had, during the discussion of money bills on July 6th, indicated that if the Senate "have the power of giving away the people's money, they might soon forget the Source from whence they received it. We might soon have an aristocracy" (Farrand, I: 544). Similarly, on August 15 in discussions on the same subject, Mason had observed that "He was extremely earnest to take this power from the Senate," which, he feared, "could already sell the whole Country by means of Treaties" (Farrand, II: 297).

Mason's complaints about the Senate thus appear to be more of crystallization of his general concern over a more aristocratic body that might encroach on "the rights and liberties of the people" than a repetition of specific objections that he had made, or defeats that he had sustained, during the Convention. Mason's criticisms might also relate to concerns, detailed below, that the President had no constitutional council.

The author of the Civis Rusticus essay responded to Mason's criticisms of senatorial power to alter money bills by distinguishing that body, whose members rotated in office, from the hereditary English House of Lords, and by observing that both the U.S. House and Senate would still have to agree before such measures could be adopted (Bailyn 1993, I, 357). Similarly, Iredell considered Mason's objections to be a type of "visionary skepticism" consisting of "a great deal of gloomy prediction, without any solid foundation" (Bailyn 1993, I: 366). Iredell argued that both the House of Representatives and the electoral system would result in adequate constraints on the Senate.

CRITICISMS OF THE JUDICIARY

As a body appointed by the President with the advice and consent of the Senate and serving "during good behavior," judges and justices were even farther removed from the people than were Senators, and, as a republican, Mason remained concerned about its powers. In outlining his objections to the new government, Mason therefore noted that: "The Judiciary of the United States is so constructed and extended, as to absorb and destroy the judiciaries of the several States; thereby rendering law as tedious, intricate and expensive, and justice as unattainable, by a great part of the community, as in England, and enabling the rich to oppress and ruin the poor" (Farrand, II: 638).

In debates on July 18 over whether Congress should be able to appoint inferior judicial tribunals, Mason had thought that cases might arise that would make such power "absolutely necessary" (Farrand, II: 46) so his criticism, now largely based on states' rights concerns, is difficult to interpret. It is possible that he had initially anticipated that the appointment would be made by the House of Representatives, or by the Congress collectively, rather than by the president with the advice and consent of the Senate. His charge that the federal judiciary would displace that of the states has proven inaccurate, although the number of issues brought under the authority of the U.S. Constitution has certainly increased, especially since the adoption of the Fourteenth Amendment in 1868. His concern that the judicial system might oppress the poor likely stemmed from the belief that federal courts, being farther away, would be more difficult for them to access.

In his letter to George Washington dated October 18, 1787, Madison again expressed some perplexity over Mason's criticisms: "What he means by the dangerous tendency of the Judiciary I am at some loss to comprehend. It never was intended, nor can it be supposed that in ordinary cases the inferior tribunals will not have final jurisdiction in order to prevent the evils of which he complains. The great mass of suits in every State lie between Citizens & Citizens, and related to matters not of federal cognizance" (Farrand, III: 130). Similarly, the author of the Civis Rusticus essay observed that Mason had exaggerated the degree to which laws would be "tedious and expensive" (Bailyn 1993, I: 358). Iredell further argued that the Constitution left state courts free with respect to purely internal matters (Bailyn 1993, I: 371).

CRITICISMS OF THE PRESIDENCY AND THE OMISSION OF A CONSTITUTIONAL COUNCIL

The Virginia Constitution had not provided for a strong executive, and it had included a Council for him to consult, and Mason expressed concern early at the Constitutional Convention that a single executive might corrupt the legislature through use of the veto power. On June 4, he thus opined that: "The Executive may refuse its assent to necessary measures till new appointments shall be referred to him; and having by degrees engrossed all these into his own hands, the American Executive, like the British, will by bribery & influence, save himself the trouble & odium of exerting his negative afterwards" (Farrand I: 101). In notes that he apparently made for his speech of that day, Mason observed that: "If strong and extensive powers are vested in the Executive, and that executive consists only of one person, the government will of course degenerate (for I will call it degeneracy) into a monarchy—a government so contrary to the genius of the people that they will reject even the appearance of it" (Farrand, I: 113).

Mason's critique of the presidency was his longest, and it chiefly centered on the failure of the Convention to provide the president with a "Constitutional Council" (Farrand, II: 638). As one who had played a major role in the drafting of the Virginia Constitution, Mason observed that such an omission was "a thing unknown in any safe and regular government" (Farrand, II: 638). He thus feared that the president "will therefore be unsupported by proper information and advice, and will generally be directed by minions and favorites; or he will become a tool to the Senate —or a Council of State will grow out of the principal officers of the great departments; the worst and most dangerous of all ingredients for such a Council in a free country" (Farrand, II:628). As he further explained in his published version, "They may be induced to join in any dangerous or oppressive measures, to shelter themselves, and prevent an inquiry into their own misconduct in office" (Farrand, II: 638-639). Had a Council of six members been formed (two from each of three major sections of the country), it could have provided the advice, the Council president could have served as the vice-president, and the U.S. Senate would not have had to remain in session. Notably, Mason referred to this as a "fatal defect." Perhaps fearing the kinds of corruption many republicans had attributed to the British Parliament, he explained that allowing the Senate to concur in appointments could lead to "the alarming dependence and connection between that branch of the legislature and the supreme Executive" (Farrand, II: 639).

In critiquing Mason's argument, Oliver Ellsworth argued that such a council would be expensive and unwise. He further argued that such a council would be likely to detract from the "secrecy, vigor, dispatch and responsibility" of the executive branch (Ford, 1892, 163). Civis Rusticus appeared to agree that it might have been better to leave executive power unrestrained either by a Council of Revision or by the Senate but thought that this action had proceeded from "A jealousy of executive government; and a jealousy in the minor states, which made them anxious to add every weight to the scale of the senate, considering it as the inexpugnable barrier of their privileges, and the soul of their existence" (Bailyn 1993, I: 359). Iredell observed that the English Privy Council had been "a mere creature of the Crown," and said that there was no more reason to believe that the president would be "a tool to the Senate" than there was to believe that he might be one for such a Council (Bailyn 1993, I:374-375). He further lauded the provision in the Constitution allowing the President to demand the opinions of his cabinet officers in writing, thus making it more likely that he would get their considered judgments rather than eliciting political posturing.

In addition to providing for such a Council, the Virginia Constitution had created a much weaker executive who served for one-year terms and did not have a veto over state legislation. Moreover, Mason had expressed concerns over a strong executive throughout his time at the Convention. On June 4, Mason had combined concerns over a unitary executive with reservations over its power of appointment. Mason feared that "The Executive may refuse its assent to necessary measures till new appointments shall be referred to him; and having by degrees engrossed all these into his own hands, the American Executive, like the British, will by bribery & influence, save himself the trouble & odium of exerting his negative afterwards" (Farrand, I: 101). Mason further pointed to the dangers of an "elective monarchy," argued that the American people would never approve of an hereditary king, and suggested that the president should only have the power "to suspend offensive laws, till they shall be coolly revised, and the objections to them overruled by a greater majority than was required in the first instance" (Farrand, I: 101) which, as it turns out, is essentially what the delegates decided to do!

Mason apparently missed the vote in which the Convention decided on a unitary executive (Farrand, I: 101), but, in addition to favoring the creation of an executive council, Mason appears to have favored a plural executive consisting of three men (Farrand, I: 111). Mason had commended the Electoral College for removing "some capital objections, particularly the danger of cabal and corruption" (Farrand, II: 500). He had also been influential in seeing that the more democratic House of Representatives, rather than the more aristocratic Senate, would choose among presidential candidates in cases where none received a majority.

In his Objections to the Constitution, Mason had further criticized the creation of the vice-presidency, which he thought was both "unnecessary" and "dangerous." He believed that making the Vice-President the president of the Senate violated separation of powers by blending executive and legislative powers, and gave the state from which the vice-president hailed a special advantage (Farrand II: 639). He had made a similar objection on September 7, where had also reiterated the need for what he then called "a privy Council of six members" (Farrand, II: 537).

The author of the Civis Rusticus essay thought Mason's criticism of the vice-presidency was overwrought. Apparently he believed, like Mason, that the vice-president would serve only as an interim until a new election could be held; he pointed out that the vice-president would only exercise powers upon "the death, resignation, or inability of the president; and, if he should, he will exercise it for a short time (Bailyn 1993, I: 359). He further assessed Mason's concerns over the pardon power as having less "validity and force" than as being built upon "chimera and imagination" (Bailyn 1993, I: 359). Focusing on Mason's fear that a state might gain an extra vote through vice-presidential election, Iredell observed that the vice-president would only cast votes in cases of ties and that "Such a reason is utterly unworthy [of] that spirit of amity, and rejection of local views, which can alone save us from destruction" (Bailyn 1993, I: 378). Iredell further thought it highly unlikely that the president would engage in treason and posed cases where a broad pardoning power might be necessary.

Mason's final objection to the presidency was that "the unrestrained power of granting pardons for treason. . . may be sometimes exercised to screen from punishment those whom he had secretly instigated to commit the crime, and thereby prevent a discovery of his own guilt" (Farrand, II: 639). On September 15, Mason had unsuccessfully supported a motion by fellow Virginian Edmund Randolph who had used almost identical reasoning to support exempting treason from the offenses that a president could pardon (Farrand, II: 626).

In answering this objection, Iredell had observed that: "The probability of the President of the United States committing an act of treason against his country is very slight; he is so well guarded by the other powers of government, and the natural strength of the people at large must be so weighty, that in my opinion it is the most chimerical apprehension that can be entertained" (Bailyn 1993, I: 380).

CRITICISMS OF TREATY MAKING

Mason moved from his discussion of the Senate and the President to a critique of the treaty power, which involved both—the president negotiates treaties, and the Senate ratifies or disapproves them. He thus observed that "By declaring all treaties supreme laws of the land, the Executive and the Senate have, in many cases, an exclusive power of legislation; which might have been avoided by proper distinctions with respect to treaties, and requiring the assent of the House of Representatives, where it could be done with safety" (Farrand, II: 639). In critiquing Mason, Ellsworth doubted that the president and the senate would be any less threatening than the president and a council and further observed that the Senate was both "elective and rotative," and, more broadly, that "The danger of the constitution is not aristocracy or monarchy, but anarchy" (Ford 1892, 165).

Although Mason did not specifically tie this fear of treaty-making power to concern over civil rights and liberties, concerns that the former might undermine the latter have persisted into modern times (See entry on "Bricker Amendment" In Vile, 2015b, I: 53-55). Moreover, On August 15, Mason had feared that "the Senate by means of treaty might alienate territory &c. without legislative sanction" (Farrand, II, 297). He observed that the British had ceded the West Indies by treaty and feared, somewhat improbably, that if Spain conquered Georgia, "the Senate might by treaty dismember the Union" (Farrand, II: 298).

The author of Civis Rusticus argued that it was essential that treaties have the force of law, and he believed that popular opinion would provide adequate protections against those that might be ill advised (Bailyn, 1993, I: 359). Iredell observed that "The power of making treaties is so important, that it would have been highly dangerous to vest it in the Executive alone, and would have been the subject of much greater clamour" (Bailyn 1993, I, 370). He also challenged Mason to specify a more proper place for trying impeachments than in the Senate. For his part, Iredell added that the Articles of Confederation also considered treaties to be law of the land and that the new Constitution was closer to the people than it was.

CRITICISM OF THE MAJORITY REQUIRED FOR COMMERCIAL AND NAVIGATION LAWS

Although it seems logical that Mason might have preferred participation by the more popular House of Congress in treaty making, if he expressed his concern previously in the Convention, I have been unable to find evidence of it. By contrast, Mason's next critique allowing majorities of Congress to enact commercial and navigation laws was not a new-found cause but a deep-seated concern. It stemmed from fears generated by the Jay-Gardoqui Negotiations of 1785 in which John Jay, the U.S. Secretary of Foreign Affairs, had, in negotiations with Don Diego de Gardoqui of Spain, considered bargaining away for 25 to 30 years the right to navigate the Mississippi River, which was particularly important to the South and West, for other commercial advantages for the North. This measure, which had done much to heighten sectional fears, had only been blocked by a coalition of five southern states—the Articles of Confederation required the concurrence of nine or more states on such matters (Vile 2015a, I: 416-417).

At the Convention, the Committee of Detail had attempted to placate southern demands by requiring a two-thirds vote in Congress on commercial regulations, prohibiting a tax on exports, and banning federal interference with the slave trade. The first of these provisions had been subsequently bargained away for the latter two and for assuring that money bills could only originate in the House (Banning 1989, 270), but Mason remained concerned. On August 29, he thus observed that:

> If the Govt. is to be lasting, it must be founded in the confidence & affections of the people, and must be so constructed as to obtain these. The *Majority* will be governed by their interests. The Southern States are the *minority* in both Houses. Is it to be expected that they will deliver themselves bound hand & foot to the Eastern States, and enable them to exclaim, in the words of Cromwell on a certain occasion— 'the lord hath delivered them into our hands'" (Farrand, II: 451).

Just two days before the delegates signed the Constitution, Mason had repeated this concern "at the power given to Congress by a bare majority to pass navigation acts" (Farrand, II: 631). Again, he expressed clear distrust of other regions, which "would not only enhance the freight, a consequence he did not so much regard—but would enable a few rich merchants in Philada N. York & Boston, to monopolize the Staples of the Southern States & reduce their value perhaps 50 Per ct." (Farrand, II: 631). Only Maryland, Virginia, and Georgia supported his motion on that day to require a two-thirds vote on such matters until 1808, the same date during which Congress would have power to restrict the slave trade.

Making much the same argument in his final objections to the Constitution, Mason added language suggesting that he viewed this issue as a zero-sum game in which regulations favoring northern and eastern states would harm the five southern states. By contrast, he believed that "requiring two-thirds of the members present in both Houses would have produced mutual moderation, promoted the general interest, and removed an insuperable objection to the adoption of this government" (Farrand, II: 640). The term "insuperable" sounds as strong as his further reference to the "fatal defect" stemming from the role of the President and the Senate in making appointments.

Mason's argument could be regarded as a prescient anticipation of later controversies over tariffs and other matters that caused such division between North and South prior to the Civil War or as an excessive regard for purely regional interests. In critiquing Mason, Oliver Ellsworth, who had represented Connecticut at the Constitutional Convention, argued that that navigation "ought to be left on the same footing with other national concerns" and sought to contrast what Ellsworth believed to be Mason's parochialism against such "liberal, just and federal men in Virginia" as such Virginia delegates as Washington, Blair, and Madison (Ford 1892, 162). As he interpreted Mason's objections, they amounted to "Make a federal government that will secure Virginia all her natural advantages, promote all her interests regardless of every disadvantage to the other states, and I will subscribe to it" (Ford 1892, 166). Although not quite so harsh, the author of Civis Rusticus thought it was more important to accept this provision as an "American" than to oppose it as a "Virginian" (Bailyn 1993, I: 359).

Criticism of Implied Powers

The final power that Article I, Section 8 of the Constitution vests in Congress is "To make all Laws which shall be necessary and proper for carrying into execution the foregoing Powers, and all other Powers vested by this Constitution in the Government of the United States, or in any Department or Officer thereof." This clause differs significantly from Article II of the Articles of Confederation, which had provided, much more restrictively, that "Each state retains its sovereignty, freedom, and independence, and every Power, Jurisdiction and right, which is not by this confederation expressly delegated to the United States in Congress assembled" (Vile, 2015c, 113).

In examining the necessary and proper clause, Mason complained that "the Congress may grant monopolies in trade and commerce, constitute new crimes, inflict unusual and severe punishments, and extend their powers as far as they think proper; so that the State legislatures have no security for the powers now presumed to remain to them, or the people for their rights" (Farrand, II: 640). Edmund Randolph had made a similar, albeit far less specific, criticism on September 10 when he cited "the general clause concerning necessary and proper laws" as one of his concerns (Farrand, II: 573).

Mason proved fairly prescient in identifying the clause that Alexander Hamilton and other leading Federalists would use to expand congressional powers under the new government, although it is not altogether clear whether the same might have happened even without the clause. Hamilton would thus argue in Federalist No. 33 that "it may be affirmed with perfect confidence that the constitutional operation of the intended government would be precisely the same if these clause were entirely obliterated as if they were repeated in every article" (Hamilton, Madison, and Jay, 1961, 202). Similarly, the essayist writing as Civis Rusticus responded with "Valeat quantum valere potest" (Bailyn 1993,

I: 360), meaning that constitutional provisions would have effect as far as they could have effect. For his part, Iredell observed that "If Congress, under pretence of exercising the power delegated to them, should, in fact, by the exercise of any other power, usurp upon the rights of the different Legislatures, or any private citizens, the people will be exactly in the same situation as if there had been an express provision against such power in particular, and yet they had presumed to exercise it" (Bailyn 1993, I, 385). He further pointed to existing constitutional restrictions. In time, the Eighth Amendment to the Constitution specifically addressed Mason's concern about the infliction of cruel punishments.

ADDITIONAL CRITICISMS RELATED TO CIVIL LIBERTIES

As Mason continued, he circled back to concerns over the lack of a bill of rights. Grouping three omissions together, he thus observed that "There is no declaration of any kind, for preserving the liberty of the press, or the trial by jury in civil cases, nor against the danger of standing armies in time of peace" (Farrand, II: 640). Mason had, of course, listed liberty of the press in the Virginia Declaration of Rights. On August 20, Charles Pinckney of South Carolina introduced a number of proposals including a provision specifying that "The liberty of the Press shall be inviolably preserved," and another providing that "No troops shall be kept up in times of peace, but by consent of the Legislature" (Farrand, II: 341), which were sent to the Committee of Detail for consideration, but neither was included in the final un-amended document.

In answering Mason's objections, Ellsworth observed that it was no more necessary to preserve such freedoms that to single out "liberty of conscience, or of matrimony, or of burial of the dead." He believed that "it is enough that congress have no power to prohibit either, and can have no temptation.... the states have all the power originally, and congress have only what the states grant them" (Ford, 1892, 164). Similarly, the author of the Civis Rusticus essay observed that any attempts to suppress the press would be unlikely to stem from republican government but be "the last efforts of a despotic government" (Bailyn, 1993, I: 360). Iredell observed that the new constitution did not vest Congress with any power over the press and that while there was high regard for jury trials, state practices varied with respect to such trials in civil cases (Bailyn, 1993, I:389).

Mason's fear over standing armies in times of peace was a quintessential republican concern. On June 29, in expressing fears over executive power, James Madison had observed that "A standing military force, with an overgrown Executive will not long be safe companions to liberty. The means of defence agast. Foreign danger, have been always the instruments of tyranny at home." He further noted that "Throughout all Europe, the armies kept up under the pretext of defending, have enslaved the people," and that Britain had escaped such a fate because it was largely able to defend itself through the use of sea power, "wch. Cd. Not be used for the purpose of oppression" (Farrand, I: 465).

The main problem that the Convention faced with respect to military forces had been practical. When Elbridge Gerry had suggested a specific limit of 2000 to 3000 regular troops during peace time, Washington was said to have remarked that such a provision would only work if the U.S. could guarantee that a foreign power did not send a larger number of invading troops (Fleming 1997, 365)! Ultimately, the Convention had responded to concerns over standing armies by limiting military appropriations to two years and by making a civilian president commander-in-chief.

On September 14, Mason, having recognized "that an absolute prohibition of standing armies in time of peace might be unsafe," nonetheless proposed prefacing the clause granting congress power to organize the militia with the statement "And that the liberties of the people may be better secured against the danger of standing armies in times of peace" (Farrand, II: 617). Although Randolph had seconded, and Madison had supported, the resolution, it failed by a 9 to 1 vote after New York's Gouverneur Morris expressed reasonable fears that such a clause might set "a dishonorable mark of distinction on the military class of Citizens" (Farrand, II: 617). Iredell contended that Mason's arguments against standing armies were overblown and "that those who can seriously suggest the danger of a premeditated attack on the liberties of the people from such a government as this, could with ease assign reasons equally plausible for distrusting the integrity of any government formed in any manner whatever" (Bailyn 1993, I: 392).

As to jury trials, Article III, Section 3 of the Constitution had provided that "The Trial of all Crimes, except in Cases of Impeachment, shall be by Jury; and such Trial shall be held in the State where the said Crimes shall have been committed," but it had not included a similar provision for civil cases. When he had introduced his motion to add a Bill of Rights on September 12, Mason had agreed with Nathanial Gorham's view that "It is not possible to discriminate equity cases from those in which juries are proper," but, as indicated above, had suggested that "A general principle laid down on this and some other points would be sufficient" (Farrand, II: 587).

Criticism of Prohibition of State Export Duties

Mason's next objection to the Constitution was the shortest. He thus observed that "The State legislatures are restrained from laying duties on their own produce" (Farrand, II: 640). This restriction is found in Article I, Section 10, and qualified by the phrase "without the Consent of Congress" and excluding "what may be absolutely necessary for executing it's inspection Laws." This had followed a similar provision in article I, Section 9 limiting the power of Congress to impose such taxes.

Mason had arguably gotten much of what he wanted with respect to this provision. On August 16, he had thus argued that the congressional power to tax should be limited by the restriction on taxing exports. He thought that this guarantee would be especially important to the southern states, which he identified with the "staple states" (Farrand, II: 305-306). Gouverneur Morris had argued that "it would not in some cases be equitable to tax imports without taxing exports" (Farrand, II: 306). Madison had argued that it was appropriate for the national government, but not the states to do so. He observed that "it would be unjust to the States, whose produce was exported by their neighbours, to leave it subject to be taxed by the latter" (Farrand, II: 306).

Mason weighed in again on August 21 in arguments that revealed that he was willing to raise regional considerations that other delegates might have preferred to ignore. Arguing from the principle that "a majority when interested will oppress the minority," he found that the eight northern states had different interests than the five southern states, giving the latter "good ground for their suspicions." (Farrand, II: 362-363). Whereas imports were "the same throughout the

United States," exports were not (Farrand, II: 363). He did not, however, specifically argue for a state right to tax its own exports noting, in fact that the "impolicy" of taxing tobacco exports "has been demonstrated by the experiment of Virginia" (Farrand, II: 363).

CRITIQUE OF EX POST FACTO PROVISIONS

Mason's next objection is reminiscent of debates that accompanied the Virginia Declaration of Rights, where Mason had joined in opposition with Patrick Henry to kill a provision prohibiting ex post facto laws. In what is generally considered to be a protection for individual rights, the proposed U.S. Constitution prohibited both Congress (Article I, Section 9) and the states (Article I, Section 10) from adopting such laws. Mason observed in response that "though there never was nor can be a legislature but must and will make such laws, when necessity and the public safety require them; which will hereafter be a breach of all the constitutions in the Union, and afford precedents for other innovations" (Farrand, II: 640).

Mason's critique was almost identical to one that he made on September 14. On that date he observed that the Document did not make it clear that the ex post facto law provision was meant to apply only to criminal laws since "no Legislature ever did or can altogether avoid them in Civil cases" (Farrand, II: 616).

The author of the Civis Rusticus responded that "Ex post facto laws have ever been considered as abhorrent from liberty: necessity and public safety can never require them" (Bailyn, 1993, I: 361). Similarly, Iredell lauded the prohibition against ex post facto laws, believing that although they sometimes proved to be "convenient," they were never "absolutely necessary" (Bailyn, 1993, I: 396).

CRITIQUE OF ARISTOCRACY AND TYRANNY

Mason's penultimate criticism of the new Constitution again said more about his general fears than his specific objections. His fear, previously reflected in both his criticisms of the presidency and the judiciary, was that the government would commence as an "aristocracy" but might degenerate either into a "monarchy," or a corrupt, tyrannical aristocracy" (Farrand, II: 640).

From time to time, delegates had raised such concerns at the Convention. On June 1, not long after the introduction of the Virginia Plan, South Carolina's Charles Pinckney had feared the possibility of an "elective" Monarchy (Farrand, I: 65). On June 4, Mason had expressed the hope "that nothing like a monarchy would ever be attempted in this Country" (Farrand, I: 102). On June 26, Elbridge Gerry had said that he thought that fewer than one in 1000 Americans supported monarchy. When discussing the origination of money bills on August 8, Mason had noted the encroaching power of an aristocratic body, which "like the screw in mechanics, working its way by slow degrees, and holding fast whatever it gains, should ever be suspected of an encroaching tendency" (Farrand, II: 224).

Mason strongly favored making legislators ineligible for other offices during their service and for some time thereafter. On August 14, Madison thus noted that Mason "ironically" proposed to strike such a proposal from the version then being considered "as a more effectual expedient for encouraging that exotic corruption which might not otherwise thrive so well in the American Soil—for compleating that Aristocracy—which was probably in the contemplation of some among us, and for inviting into the Legislative service, those generous & benevolent characters who will do justice to each other's merit, by carving out offices & rewards for it" (Farrand, II: 284). On September 3, Mason further observed that such provision would not exclude merit but "will keep out corruption, by excluding office-hunters" (Farrand, II: 491).

One reason that Mason was so concerned about both aristocracy and tyranny was that he had a clear sense that families, including his own, who were privileged in one generation could easily lose their class status. During the opening days of the Convention (May 31), in lauding the House of Representatives and his hope that it would be "the grand depository of the democratic principle of the Govt" (Farrand, I 48), Mason had thus observed that "We ought to attend to the rights of every class of the people." He further noted that:

> He had often wondered at the indifference of the superior classes of society to this dictate of humanity & policy, considering that however affluent their circumstances, or elevated their situations, might be, the course of a few years, not only might but certainly would, distribute their posterity throughout the lowest classes of Society. Every selfish motive therefore, every family attachment, ought to recommend such a system of policy as would provide no less carefully for the rights— and happiness of the lowest than of the highest orders of citizens. (Farrand, I: 49).

In supporting another convention that would consider amendments proposed by the states, Mason repeated his fears on September 15. On that day, he animadverted "on the dangerous power and structure of the Government, concluding that it would end either in monarchy, or a tyrannical aristocracy; which, he was in doubt. But one of other, he was sure" (Farrand, II: 632). Although Mason was unsure which direction would prevail, he did not anticipate that either would be good.

Iredell noted the ambiguity of Mason's predictions about the future direction of the new government. Iredell suggested that Mason's criticisms were not infallible, and that its prospects were quite different. Viewing the time at hand as one of those "critical periods in the fate of nations," he suggested that the new constitution can stand the nicest examination, if reason and not prejudice is employed in viewing it," and that any errors that were discovered in practice could be corrected "at leisure" once the Constitution was adopted (Bailyn, 1993, I: 397).

CRITIQUE OF THE SLAVERY IMPORTATION COMPROMISE

Mason's last critique, which he would later highlight in his letter to Thomas Jefferson (Farrand III: 304-305), complained that "The general legislature is restrained from prohibiting the further importation of slaves for twenty odd years; though such importations render the United States weaker, more vulnerable, and less capable of defence" (Farrand, II: 640). Perhaps because he anticipated that his objections would be circulated, Mason did not emphasize the fact that the Constitution continued to allow slavery but highlighted its permission of such importation for the next 20 years. A Committee of Eleven had reported a plan on August 24 that would have permitted slave importation until the year 1800, but after complaints from delegates from the Carolinas and Georgia, on August 25, the delegates had extended this date to 1808 (Farrand, II: 416).

Two notable speeches at the Constitutional Convention condemned slavery. On August 8, Gouverneur Morris of New York had called it "a nefarious institution," which "was the curse of heaven on the States where it had prevailed" (Farrand, II: 221). Mason had delivered the second on August 22, largely in an attempt to prevent further slave importation. Claiming that the slave trade had "originated in the avarice of British Merchants," and repeating the claim that Jefferson had included in his original draft of the Declaration of Independence blaming the King for failing to allow the colonists to stop it, Mason pointed to the dangers of slave insurrections and to the possibility that it might expand into the West (Farrand, II: 370). Using arguments similar to those that Morris had advanced, Mason sometimes depended on racial stereotypes in opposing the further growth of the institution:

> Slavery discourages arts and manufacturers. The poor despise labor when performed by slaves. They prevent the immigration of Whites, who really enrich & strengthen a Country. They produce the most pernicious effect on manners. Every master of slaves is born a petty tyrant.
>
> They bring the judgment of heaven on a Country. As nations can not be rewarded or punished in the next world they must be in this. By an inevitable chain of causes & effects providence punishes national sins, by national calamities. (Farrand, II, 370).

Oliver Ellsworth of Connecticut responded with apparent scorn for Mason's moralism. Observing that "As he had never owned a slave [he] could not judge of the effect of slavery on character," he suggested that "if it was to be considered in a moral light we ought to go farther and free those already in the Country" (Farrand, II: 370-371). In a Landholder essay, Ellsworth skeptically observed that Mason owned about 300 slaves and that he apparently thought that it was "more humane to breed than import slaves—those imported having been bred and born free, may not so tamely bear slavery as those born slaves, and from their infancy inured to it" (Ford 1892, 164). This comment reflected the widespread belief that Mason and other upper-South delegates did not so much oppose slave importation because it was immoral but because they feared that such importation would lower the value of their slave property by increasing its supply.

Civis Rusticus responded by observing that while South Carolina and Georgia might choose to import slaves for an additional 20 years, the provision would not effect Virginia and thus represented "the excess of criticism" (Bailyn, 1993, I: 361). Similarly, "Marcus" (Iredell) thought that "Our situation makes it necessary to bear the evil as it is," leaving slave importation as "a matter between God and their own consciences" (Bailyn, 1993, I: 395). Mason undoubtedly knew that were he to make such an argument, he would be far more likely to alienate supporters than to gain them. Ellsworth captured the difficulty that Mason and other slave owners faced when trying to argue for restraints on the institution that provided their livelihood.

THE THREAT OF ANOTHER CONVENTION

As indicated above, Benjamin Franklin articulated the view of many supporters of the Constitution that it was not perfect but was the best that could be expected. Mason came from another camp, initially led by Edmund Randolph, which would grant power to states to offer amendments to the plan, which would then go before another general convention (Farrand, II: 631). Supporting this view on September 15, Mason pointed out that "This Constitution had been formed without the knowledge or idea of the people" (Farrand, II: 632), by which he most certainly meant not that they were unaware that it was meeting but of the drastic changes it was proposing to the present form of government. He further argued that "A second Convention will know more of the sense of the people, and be able to provide a system more consonant to it." This would be better than telling the people "take this or nothing" (Farrand, II: 632).

South Carolina's Charles Pinckney had countered that "Conventions are serious things, and ought not to be repeated" (Farrand, II: 632). He favored adopting an imperfect plan, rather than "the danger of a general confusion, and an ultimate decision by the Sword" (Farrand, II: 632). After Gerry offered a laundry list of concerns about the document,[7] the convention voted unanimously against calling yet another.

---

[7] Most of the fascinating aspects of this list, which pointed to a potential problem with calling another convention, was that it overlapped very little with that of Mason. Gerry has thus objected to: "1. The duration and re-eligibility of the Senate. 2. The power of the House of Representatives to conceal their journals. 3—the power of Congress over the places of election. 4 the unlimited power of Congress over their own compensations. 5. Massachusetts has not a due share of Representatives allotted to her. 6. 3/5 of the Blacks are to be represented as if they were freemen 7. *Under* the power over commerce, monopolies may be established. 8. The vice president being made head of the Senate" (Farrand II, 633). Saying that he could accept each of these "If the rights of the citizens were not rendered insecure" he elaborated with "1. By the general power of the Legislature to make what laws they may please to call necessary and proper. 2. Raise armies and money without limit. 3. To

Much of Madison's strategy in latter shepherding a bill of rights through the first Congress was his fear that a second convention might undue the work of the first (Goldwin 1997; Labunski 2006). In his previously mentioned letter of October 18, 1787 to George Washington, after complaining that Mason had never raised his objection relative to the common law, Madison observed that "This objection surely was not brought forward in the convention, or it wd. have been placed in such a light that a repetition of it out of doors would scarcely have been hazarded. Were it allowed the weight which Col. M. may suppose it deserves, it would remain to be decided whether it be candid to arraign the Convention for omissions which were never suggested to them—or prudent to vindicate the dissent by reasons which either were not previously thought of, or must have been willfully concealed" (Farrand, III: 130-131).

Madison and other supporters of the Constitution hoped to avert a second convention. Although they succeeded in offering the Constitution for ratification on an all-or-nothing basis (permitting states to propose amendments as long as their ratifications were not dependent on their acceptance), they would have many questions to answer at the state ratifying conventions. This would constitute the next stage of Mason's opposition.

For his part, Mason continued to adhere to his criticisms, which he enclosed in a letter to George Washington dated October 7, 1787. Mason believed that "a little Moderation & Temper in the latter End of the Convention, might have removed" his objections (Farrand, III: 102). Mason further observed that "You will readily observe, that my Objections

---

establish a tribunal without juries, which would be a Star-chamber as to Civil cases" (Farrand, II: 633).

are not numerous (the greater Part of the inclosed paper containing Reasonings upon the probable Effects of the exceptionable Parts) tho' in my mind, some of them are capital ones" (Farrand, III: 102).

Mason's objections were undoubtedly a factor, arguably an important one, in the eventual adoption of the bill of rights that included liberty of the press and trial by jury in civil cases, which he had proposed, and many additional provisions that he had not. A proposed amendment that might have been designed to address Mason's concern over representation in Congress remains the only one of the original twelve that failed (Vile, 2015b, I: 105-106), although the size of the house jumped from 65 to 106 members after the first census. Although most of Mason's objections centered on structural changes that he thought needed to be enacted, most of the provisions of the first ten amendments (and especially the first eight) instead delineated protections for individual rights and liberties, while the Tenth Amendment, which was designed to protect states' rights, did so only in very general language that differed from that in the Articles of Confederation.

REFERENCES

Bailyn, Bernard, ed. 1993. *The Debate on the Constitution: Federalist and Antifederalist Speeches, Articles, and Letters During the Struggle Over Ratification.* N.p.; The Library of America. 2 vols.

Banning, Lance. 1989. "Sectionalism and the General Good," *Ratifying the Constitution,* ed. Michael Allen Gillespie and Michael Lienesch. Lawrence: University Press of Kansas, 261-299.

Broadwater, Jeff. 2017. "George Mason, James Madison, and the Evolution of the Bill of Rights." *Georgetown Journal of Law and Public Policy* 15 (Spring): 547-568.

"Constitutional Convention, 1787." 1861. *The Historical Magazine* 2st ser. V (January): 18.

Farrand, Max, ed. 1966. *The Records of the Federal Convention of 1787.* 4 vols. New Haven, CT: Yale University Press.

Fleming, Thomas. 1997. *Liberty! The American Revolution.* Viking: New York.

Ford, Paul Leicester, ed. 1892. *Essays on the Constitution of the United States Published During its Discussion by the People, 1787-1788.* Brooklyn, NY: Historical Printing Company.

Gates, George Marion. 1930. *The Influence of George Mason on the Framing and Adoption of the Constitution.* A thesis presented to the Department of History University of Southern California for Master of Arts degree.

Goldwin, Robert A. 1997. *From Parchment to Power: How James Madison Used the Bill of Rights to Save the Constitution.* Washington, DC: AEI Press.

Hamilton, Alexander, James Madison, and John Jay. 1961. *The Federalist Papers.* New York: New American Library.

Henriques, Peter R. 1989. "An Uneven Friendship: The Relationship between George Washington and George Mason." *The Virginia Magazine of History and Biography.* 97. (April): 185-204.

Horrell, Joseph. 1983. "George Mason and the Fairfax Court." *The Virginia Magazine of History and Biography.* 92 (October): 418-439.

Hudson, James H. ed. 1987. *Supplement to Max Farrand's The Records of the Federal Convention of 1787.* New Haven, CT: Yale University Press.

Labunski, Richard. 2006. *James Madison and the Struggle for the Bill of Rights.* New York: Oxford University Press.

Mason, George. 1970. *The Papers of George Mason, 1725-1792.* 3 vols. Ed. Robert A. Rutland. Chapel Hill, NC: The University of North Carolina Press.

Morris, Richard B. 1985. "The Mount Vernon Conference: First Step Toward Philadelphia." *this Constitution*, no. 6 (Spring): 38-49.

Vile, John R. 2016a. *The Constitutional Convention of 1787: A Comprehensive Encyclopedia of America's Founding*. Rev. 2nd edition. 2 vols. Clark, NJ: Talbot Publishing.

_____. 2015b. *Encyclopedia of Constitutional Amendments, Proposed Amendments, and Amending Issues, 1789-2015*. 4th ed. 2 vols. Santa Barbara, CA: ABC-CLIO.

_____. 2015c. *Founding Documents of America: Documents Decoded*. Santa Barbara, CA: ABC-CLIO.

_____. 2015d. *The Wisest Council in the World: Restoring the Character Sketches by William Pierce of Georgia of the Delegates to the Constitutional Convention of 1787*. Athens: The University of Georgia Press.

7

George Mason and the Virginia Ratifying Convention of 1788

Whereas Section XIII of the Articles of Confederation had specified that constitutional amendments required proposal by congress and the consent of all the state legislatures, Article VII of the Constitution, which was proposed to replace it, provided that it would go into effect among ratifying states when nine or more approved in special conventions. This not only bypassed the state legislatures whose members would be losing power under the new plan, but it was also designed to heighten the legitimacy of the Constitution by grounding it on a more popular base.

By the time the Virginia Ratifying Convention began, eight states had ratified (New Hampshire would ratify during the Virginia Convention), giving Virginia a particularly critical role. Even if other states had ratified the U.S. Constitution, it is unlikely that the new government could have gotten off to a credible start without this most populous state. Its absence would also have divided Northern and Southern states and deprived the nation of the services of George Washington, Thomas Jefferson, James Madison, and other notable statesmen. The role of Virginia's Ratifying

Convention, over which Edmund Pendleton presided, thus assumed special importance.

Although the final vote, 89 votes for ratification and 79 against it, came down to a choice between Federalists who wanted to ratify the Constitution and Anti-Federalists who did not, Jon Kukla has argued that it is more accurate to think of delegates in terms of Federalists, Anti-Federalists, and Federalists who favored amendments prior to ratification (1988). Delegates like James Madison and John Marshall were in the first group, delegates like Patrick Henry in the second, and delegates like James Monroe, and George Mason, were somewhere in the third. Still others like Edmund Randolph had initially opposed adoption but now thought that it was essential to continuing union among the states.

Although George Washington let it be known that he firmly supported the new Document, he stayed at Mount Vernon during the proceedings, relying on his own reputation with apparent confidence that Madison and others had the situation in hand. By contrast, his neighbor George Mason was in the middle of the fray. Scholars still argue over whether the proceedings actually changed many minds. Despite days of debate, most delegates ultimately lined up on the same side that they had been expected to support at the beginning of the Convention (Johnston, 1988). Nonetheless, reports of the debates could affect public attitudes about the new constitution for years to come and would be particularly important for those who continued to seek out flaws once it was ratified.

On October 20, 1787, Mason wrote a letter to Elbridge Gerry of Massachusetts, who, like Mason, had refused to sign the Constitution. In this letter, Mason hoped that yet another convention would propose some amendments. He thus observed:

> I have no Doubt of our Legislatures referring it to a Convention of the People; where it will probably undergo some Alterations. It wou'd be fortunate for America, if the Conventions in the different States cou'd meet upon this important Business about the same time: by a regular & cordial Communication of Sentiments, confining themselves to a few necessary amendments, & determining to join heartily in the System so *amended,* they might, without Danger of public convulsion or Confusion, procure a general Adoption of the new Government (*PGM,* III: 1006)

As revealed in the previous chapter, the objections to the Constitution that Mason raised in Philadelphia centered on a number of fairly specific complaints, many of which sought to reverse decisions made during the convention's last two weeks. These included the following: the omission of a bill of rights; the failure to secure common law; representation within the House of Representatives; the aristocratic nature of the Senate; fear that the federal judiciary would swallow state courts; the omission of a constitutional council; concerns over treaty making; the lack of a supermajority requirement for laws regulating commerce and navigation; fear of implied powers; the omission of protections for specific civil liberties; the prohibition of state export duties; the ex post facto prohibition; fear of aristocracy and tyranny; and the restraint on taxing slave importation for 20 years.

By contrast, Mason's criticisms of the Constitution at the Virginia Ratifying Convention dealt with the entire Document. Mason's critiques are thus far more diffuse. This makes them somewhat more difficult to assess. Having chosen to oppose the Constitution, at least until such time as it was properly amended, Mason may have thought that he had to point to its every potential flaw, perhaps hoping that some that he did not consider that important might be sufficient to woe wavering delegates against ratification. Mason may also have become more critical the farther from Philadelphia he got and the more closely associated he became with the Anti-Federalist team. In a letter dated October 24, 1787, James Madison had observed that "Col. Mason left Philada. In an exceeding ill humour indeed. A number of little circumstances arising in part from the impatience which prevailed towards the close of the business, conspired to whet his acrimony. He returned to Virginia with a fixed disposition to prevent the adoption of the plan if possible" (*PGM*, III: 1007). After referencing Mason's concern about the absence of a bill of rights and some other matters, Madison observed that "Being now under the necessity of justifying his refusal to sign, he will of course, muster every possible one" (*PGM*, II: 1007).

Background

The Virginia Ratifying Convention met at the New Academy on Shockoe-Hill in Richmond, Virginia from June 3 to June 24, 1788. To put this time in context, The Federalist Papers were published from October 17, 1787 to May 28, 1788 and in book form in March and May, 1788. A total of 168 delegates attended. Richmond, which was more centrally located in the state than either Jamestown or Williamsburg, had become the capital on April 18, 1780. Fairfax County, which was the home of George Washington and favored ratification, had refused to send Mason who was chosen instead to represent Stafford County. Debates of this and other state ratifying conventions are now conveniently collected in *The Documentary History of the Ratification of the Constitution*, a multivolume work published by the Historical

Society of the University of Wisconsin, and hereafter referenced as *DH*.

Writing to his son John on July 21, 1788, Mason expressed concern that "The Debates are not Yet published; nor is there any Cause to expect that they will be authentic; the Short Hand Man who took them down, being a *federal* Partizan, they will probably be garbled, in some such Partial Manner as the Debates of the Pennsylvania Convention have been by Lloyd" (*PGM*, III: 1126)..A modern scholar would not, of course, expect the records to be a word-for-word transcript, nor could one ascertain with certainty whether all of Mason's speeches were recorded. Despite Mason's fears, in his case, at least, what he was reported to have said at the Ratifying Convention was remarkably consistent with what he had said in Philadelphia and elsewhere, and the arguments appear cogent.

On the first day of business, delegates voted to adopt the rules of the Virginia House of Delegates. Mason pointed out that the purpose of the meeting was that of "securing, as far as possible, to the latest generation, the happiness and liberty of the people" (*DH*, IX: 914). Believing that it was essential to discuss the document completely, he successfully proposed "That no question, general or particular, shall be propounded in this Convention, upon the proposed Constitution of Government for the United States, or upon any clause or article thereof, until the said Constitution shall have been discussed, clause by clause, through all its parts" (*DH*, IX: 914). Likely reflecting his experience at the concluding weeks of the Philadelphia Convention, Mason observed that "No man in this Convention is more averse to take up the time of the convention than I am; but I am equally against hurrying them precipitately into any measure" (*DH*, IX: 914).

Lance Banning believes that Mason introduced this motion in order to prevent a quick vote by Federalist supporters of the Constitution, in the event that they had a majority, but Banning notes both that the motion might have played to Madison's superior knowledge of the constitutional text and Madison's willingness to placate the opposition. Banning also observed that Anti-Federalists, particularly Patrick Henry, whose rhetoric was soaring, did not refrain from launching broadsides at the Constitution as a whole rather than examining it by article and section (1989, 275-276). Still, because the Convention was working with a proposed document and proceeded through it article by article and section by section, it is possible to examine Mason's objections through the debates fairly systematically.

CONSOLIDATED GOVERNMENT, DIRECT TAXES, AND OTHER MATTERS

Mason's first recorded speech on June 4 immediately followed Governor's Edmund Randolph's stunning announcement that because he considered himself to be "a friend to the Union" and eight states had already ratified, he was going to support the document (*DH,* IX: 936). The Convention began with a discussion of the Preamble and the first two sections of Article I, which deal with the legislative branch. Perhaps thinking that the opening words of the preamble called for some discussion of the nature of the government as a whole, Mason began with a critique that was far broader than the reasons he had provided at the Convention for deciding not to sign. Whereas advocates of the Constitution were calling themselves Federalists, Mason observed, in referencing to the power (not delineated until Article I, Section 8) of Congress to lay direct taxes, that the new government was properly designated as "a National Government" or as "one consolidated Government" rather than a "Confederation" (*DH,* IX: 936). Perhaps inflamed by an earlier speech of Patrick Henry, Mason further said that "The very idea of converting what was formerly a confederation, to a consolidated government, is totally subversive of every principle which has hitherto governed us" (*DH,* IX: 936). Mason feared that "This power is calculated to annihilate totally the State Governments," which would have to defer to the supremacy of the central government (*DH,* IX: 936-937).

Citing the arguments of the Baron de Montesquieu, which Madison had sought to refute in Federalist No. 10, Mason questioned the feasibility of a single republican government over such a large land area. He observed that "History also, supported by the opinions of the best writers, shew us, that monarchy may suit a large territory and despotic Government ever so extensive a country; but that popular Governments can only exist in small territories" (*DH,* IX: 937). Arguably situating himself among those who could support the Constitution, if properly amended," Mason said "that no man is a greater friend to a firm Union of the American States than I am" but followed with a rhetorical question: "But, Sir, if this great end can be obtained without hazarding the rights of the people, why should we recur to such dangerous principles?" (*DH,* IX: 937). Specifically focusing on the danger of direct taxes, Mason fleshed out his more diffuse criticisms of the House of Representatives in Philadelphia by observing that "Sixty-five members [the initial apportionment of that body] cannot possibly know the situation and circumstances of all the inhabitants of this immense continent" (*DH,* IX: 937).

Acknowledging "the inefficacy of the confederation" with respect to taxation, Mason believed that Congress should first give states the chance to meet tax quotas before laying direct taxes in the event of noncompliance (*DH*, IX: 938). Given the inadequate nature of representation within Congress, the Constitution should have granted its powers more sparingly. Rather than trust in "public virtue and confidence," and recognizing "the natural lust of power so inherent in man," Mason feared that "the thirst of power will prevail to oppress the people" (*DH*, IX, 939). Pointing out that the ratio of one representatives to every 30,000 people was a maximum rather than a minimum, Mason somewhat unrealistically feared that Congress might even reduce each state's representation to one delegate.

In listing his objections to the Constitution at the end of the Constitutional Convention, Mason had referred to the lack of a Constitutional Council as a "fatal defect" and allowing a simple majority (rather than a two-thirds majority) of states to adopt commercial and navigation laws as "an insuperable objection" (Farrand, II: 639, 640). Now referring to his fear that "the confederation is converted to one general consolidated Government" as his "principal objection," Mason indicated that "If such amendments be introduced as shall exclude danger, I shall most gladly put my hand to it" (*DH*, IX: 940). He further opined that "An indispensable amendment is this case, is, that Congress shall not exercise the power of raising direct taxes till the States shall have refused to comply with the requisitions of Congress" (*DH*, IX: 940). Mason further identified this change, as "a *sine qua non*, of its adoption" (*DH*, IX: 940).

Although Mason had thus both shifted and expanded his critique, Madison appeared to see hope in his comments. He thus observed that "It would give me great pleasure to concur with my honorable colleague in any conciliatory plan" (*DH,* IX: 940). Noting, however, that the provision relative to direct taxes was not immediately under discussion, he somewhat cagily postponed discussion of the amendment that Mason considered to be "indispensable."

MASON'S RESOLUTIONS

As the Virginia Ratifying Convention was meeting, New York Antifederalists sought information on amendments that they thought should be adopted prior to ratification. Perhaps because he was working with others on a response, or perhaps because of ill health, Mason gave no speeches from June 4 until June 11. There is, however, a manuscript written in his hand, that he is believed to have composed during this hiatus and that is remarkably consistent with many of the arguments that he made.

The document was preceded by four alternative resolutions recommending the addition of a number of amendments prior to constitutional ratification. Later versions actually begin with the language of Mason's own Declaration of Rights for Virginia and then follow with a number of proposals, most of which Mason addressed in later speeches. This initial version contains 13 proposals, some of which are relatively lengthy and which I will not therefore quote in full.

The first is a virtual quotation from Article II of the Articles of Confederation, securing each state's "sovereignty, freedom and independence, and every Power Jurisdiction and Right, which is not by this Constitution expressly delegated to the Congress of the United States" (*DH,* IX: 1055). The second calls for guaranteeing one representative in the U.S.

House of Representatives for every 30,000 persons, until it consists of 200 members or more.

The next two relate to congressional powers. The first of these would limit congressional power over elections to cases where state neglect or refused to do so. The second would forbid Congress from enacting direct taxes except in cases where it had first requisitioned states and they neglected or refused to pay it.

Mason also proposed preventing members of Congress from accepting any U.S. offices during the terms for which they were elected. His next proposal was the most complex. It would have provided for a constitutional council, whose head would act as vice-president. The council would assist the president in appointments and in treaty-making, with the latter subject to revision and ratification by both houses of Congress, with all commercial treaties requiring a two-thirds vote, and any dealing with territorial, fishing, or navigational rights requiring a three-fourths vote. The subsequent proposal would have required all navigation or commercial laws to be adopted by two-thirds of those present in both houses.

Proposals that followed called for a two-thirds vote of both houses to approve of a standing army or to authorize a president to take direct command of the troops. Other provisions would cap the enlistments of soldiers to four years or the duration of a war, limit mutiny acts to two years, suspend the president and other U.S. officers from their offices during impeachment proceedings, and prevent federal judges from holding other offices or receiving emoluments.

CORRUPTION, DIRECT TAXES, LACK OF A BILL OF RIGHTS, SLAVERY, AND CLEARER DELINEATIONS OF POWER

Mason gave his next recorded speech on June 11. Patrick Henry had been among those who continued to fire broadsides at the proposed constitution as a whole, but after Madison tried to redirect attention to specific provisions, Mason used his previous silence for indulgence to enter "at large into the subject" (*DH,* IX: 1154).

Once again, he redirected attention to the initial membership in the House of Representatives, now comparing its 65 initial representatives to the 550 members of the English House of Commons. Pointing out that the United States was much more geographically extensive than Great Britain, Mason believed that such a small number of representatives "cannot possibly be mingled with the different classes of the people, nor have a fellow-felling for them," and he again expressed fear that "They must form an Aristocracy, and will not regard the interest of the people" (*DH,* IX: 1155). He believed that it would be easier to bribe and corrupt a smaller number than a larger number and pointed out that the emoluments clause prohibited members from being appointed to other offices only during their terms of service.

Mason also renewed his concerns over congressional taxation, repeating his belief that Congress should only be able to enact direct taxes when states failed to meet their requisitions and adding a specific attack on poll taxes. Agreeing that such a tax "is simple and easily collected," he anticipated later advocates of progressive taxation by charging that the poll tax was "most grievous . . . . because it falls light on the rich, and heavy on the poor. It is most oppressive, for if the rich man is taxed, he can only retrench his superfluities; but the consequence to the poor man is, that it increases his miseries" (*DH*, IX: 1156). Further citing a proposal by Pennsylvania's Robert Morris for land taxes, Mason feared that it "will operate most unequally," and, as if anticipating the whiskey tax and the Rebellion that it would precipitate, feared that excise taxes "will carry the exciseman to every farmer's house who distills a little brandy, where he may search and ransack as he pleases" (*DH*, IX: 1157).

Tracking his arguments at the Philadelphia Convention, Mason observed that Virginians had "reserved certain great powers in the Bill of Rights," but that the laws of the United States would be paramount, and judges would have to heed them. Mason did not think it was sufficient to secure such rights "by implication' but "in a plain, direct, unequivocal manner" (*DH*, IX: 1158). If Virginians thought they had to secure their rights against 160 state legislators, Mason said that they should be even more vigilant against a body in which they only had 10 representatives who were most likely to be taken from "the wealthy" and "the well-born" (an apparent reference to John Adams's *Defence of the Constitutions*, which had just been published in 1787) who would attempt to govern like aristocrats (*DH*, IX: 1158).

Mason believed that a key purpose of government was to promote happiness. Responding to previous speeches by George Nicholas, Edmund Pendleton, and Edmund Randolph, Mason observed that "If this Government will endanger our liberties in its present state, its adoption will not promote our happiness at home" (*DH*, IX: 1159). Singling out their hopes that "if we be powerful and respectable abroad, we shall have liberty and happiness at home," Mason countered "Let us secure that liberty—that happiness first, and we shall then be respectable" (*DH*, IX: 1160). In one of his most colorful analogies, which seems to epitomize his overall view of human nature with respect to power, Mason said that some of the staunchest defenders of the new constitution reminded him of a cat who was transformed into a fine lady but who forgot her transformation and jumped from her chair to spring upon a rat.

Affirming that he supported national union, Mason thought that the purpose of such union was "the security of our liberty and happiness" (*DH*, IX: 1161). Returning to a familiar troupe that he had raised in Philadelphia, back at home in the South, Mason tried to appeal to those on both sides of the slavery issue. Arguing that the provision for continuing slave importation jeopardized the nation's safety, Mason simultaneously warned fellow planters that the Constitution provided no protection for slave property:

> Though this evil [the slave trade] is increasing, there is no clause in the Constitution that will prevent the Northern and Eastern States from meddling with our whole property of that kind. There is a clause to prohibit the importation of slaves after twenty years, but there is no provision made for secreting to the Southern States those they now possess. It is far from being a desirable property. But it will involve us in great difficulties and infelicity to be now deprived of them. There ought to be a clause in the Constitution to secure us that property, which we have acquired under our former laws, and the loss of which would bring ruin on a great many people. (*DH*, IX: 1161).

Mason seemed oblivious to the manner in which his argument on this point seemed at odds with his arguments for widespread liberty and happiness. Perhaps to blunt such criticisms, Mason raised the possibility that adoption of the

Constitution could lead to 20,000 families west of the Allegheny Mountains being driven from their lands by the Indiana Company (*DH*, IX: 1161).

Mason further discounted arguments that the new government would be in a better position to take care of debts than the old, and reasserted the necessity to amend the Constitution prior to adopting it. Mason once again expressed concern over outlining boundaries:

> We wish to give the Government sufficient energy, on real republican principles, but we wish to withhold such powers as are not absolutely necessary in themselves, but are extremely dangerous. We wish to shut the door against corruption in that place where it is most dangerous— To secure against the corruption of our own Representatives. We ask such amendments as will point out what powers are reserved to the State Governments and clearly discriminate between them, and those which are given to the General Government, so as to prevent future disputes and clashing of interests. Grant us amendments like these, and we will cheerfully with our hands and hearts unite with those who advocate it, and we will do every thing we can to support and carry it into execution. But in its present form we never can accede to it. (*DH*, IX: 1162).

CONTROL OF THE MILITIA, TREATY NEGOTIATIONS, SENATORIAL TERMS

Mason made his next recorded speeches on June 14th, as the Convention was discussing congressional powers as delineated in Article I, Section 8. Mason focused on the paragraph that provided that Congress could "provide for calling forth the Militia to execute the Laws of the Union, suppress Insurrections and repel Invasions," a provision to which he does not appear to have objected in Philadelphia. By contrast, he now feared that such power was "extremely unsafe, without some alterations" and might lead to "dreadful oppressions" (*DH*, X: 1269).

Arguing that Congress might call men from Georgia to quell disturbances in New Hampshire, Mason feared that the people might choose instead to "establish a standing army" (*DH*, X: 1269). With no reference to a corresponding provision in Article IV that provided that a president may send troops to protect states against domestic insurrection after receiving a request from the state legislature or the governor, Mason argued that state legislative consent should be required to send troops out of state. He also feared that Congress would have power both to declare and to carry out wars,[1] and that it might render the militia useless by disarming them. Arguing that "No man has a greater regard for the military" and expressing his admiration of "their intrepidity, perseverance, and valour," Mason observed that "when once a standing army is established, in any country, the people lose their liberty" (*DH*, X: 1271). Mason accordingly advocated a constitutional provision allowing "that in case the General Government should neglect to arm and discipline the militia, that there should be an express declaration, that the State Governments might arm and discipline them" (*DH*, X: 1271). Later that day, Mason,

---

[1] Mason was mistaken on this point. Although Congress can "declare" war, the president is commander-in-chief of the armed forces. At the Constitutional Convention in Philadelphia, Mason had expressed opposition against "giving the power of war to the Executive" or the Senate, but he had joined Madison and Gerry in altering the power of Congress to "make war" to that of declaring it (Farrand, II: 318-319).

perhaps thinking of his own militia experience, observed that if Congress exercised harsh discipline over militia members, they might quit, leaving it with no alternative but that of a standing army.

In this same speech Mason repeated the need to limit the powers of the new government to "such as were absolutely indispensable, and these to be most cautiously guarded" (*DH*, X: 1290). Professing to be no more suspicious than other men, Mason asked what would be done if a treaty were enacted through bribery or corruption. He thought that the impeachment mechanism would be inadequate in such contingencies and expressed fears that Congress would abuse its control over elections. Proceeding to a parade of horribles that suggested that he *was* more suspicious than the average delegate, Mason asked what would happen if Congress sought to require all the voters in Virginia to vote in Norfolk or all elections in America to be held in New York? Mason further worried that Congress might negotiate treaties in secret.

Even though he does not appear to have objected to a six-year term for senators at the Constitutional Convention, Mason now observed that, in contrast to the situation under the Articles of Confederation, U.S. Senators could not be recalled and were re-eligible for office. Under such conditions, and prescient of modern concerns about those who live and work "inside the beltway" or in the "swamp," Mason feared that it was probable "that those Gentlemen who will be elected Senators will fix themselves in the federal town, and become citizens of that town more than of our State" (*DH*, X: 1292). Anticipating that the Senate would be a more continuous body, Mason further feared that staying in the capital would not disadvantage them, and that they would therefore be able to wear down the House (*DH*, X: 1292).

THE NATION'S CAPITAL, IMPLIED POWERS, AND POWERS RESERVED TO THE STATES

Mason spoke a number of times on June 16. Renewing fears over a standing army, which resembled opposition to an all-volunteer force in the twentieth century, Mason feared that under a consolidated government, members of the militia might cease to represent the people as a whole and thus lose "fellow-feelings for the people" (*DH,* X: 1312). He also launched a new line of attack on the provision allowing Congress control over the nation's capital.[2]

Evoking the improbable possibility that Congress might allow this enclave to "become the sanctuary of the blackest crimes" (*DH,* X: 1317), he wondered whether jury trials would be permitted in civil cases that were tried in the District and whether felons might receive asylum there. Much like an attorney seeking to leave jurors with a memorable tag line, Mason cited the "incontrovertible axiom, that when the dangers that may arise from the *abuse,* are greater than the benefits that may result from the *use,* the power ought to be withheld" (*DH,* X: 1317, italics in original). Although he did not explicitly say so, Mason may have hoped that listeners would connect his fears to southern apprehensions that the capital might become an asylum for slave runaways.

Later in the day, Mason asked "Is there anything in this Constitution which secures to the States the powers which

---

[2] The primary concern with respect to the capital that Mason had expressed at the Constitutional Convention of 1787 was that it should not be located in any state capital. He feared that such a placement could lead to "disputes concerning jurisdiction" and might "give a provincial tincture to the Natl. deliberations" (Farrand, II: 933).

are said to be retained? Will powers remain to the States which are not expressly guarded and reserved?" (*DH*, X: 1325). Directing attention to congressional power to tax and spend and to the necessary and proper, or sweeping clause, Mason feared that the central government might trample the rights of a free press or trial by jury. Pointing out that Article II of the Articles of Confederation had provided that "Each state retains its sovereignty, freedom and Independence, and every power, jurisdiction, and right, which is not by this Confederation expressly delegates to the United States, in Congress assembled," Mason asked "why not then have a similar clause in this Constitution, in which it is the more indispensable necessary than in the Confederation, because of the great augmentation of power vested in the former?" (*DH*, X: 1326). Again noting how Virginians had protected themselves with a bill of rights, Mason warned that "Unless there were a Bill of Rights, implication might swallow up all our rights" (*DH*, X: 1328). He further corrected George Nicholas' assertion that the Virginia Bill had not prohibited torture (*DH*, X: 1334).

RENEWED CONCERN OVER SLAVE-RELATED ISSUES

On June 17, Mason now applied the term "fatal," which he had used in Philadelphia to describe the lack of a constitutional council, to the provision in Article I, Section 9 of the Constitution prohibiting Congress from interfering with slave importation for 20 years. Again, he sought both to criticize the continuation of slave trade, which he noted was further protected against amendment in Article V of the Constitution, and to criticize the lack of security for *property* in slaves. He thus observed that "though this infamous traffic be continued, we have no security for the property of that kind which we have already" (*DH*, X: 1238). Perhaps thinking that only reference to a higher power could exonerate him from such a contradiction, Mason quoted from the Book of Common Prayer by observing that "They have done what they ought not to have done, and have left undone what they ought to have done" (*DH*, X: 1338).

Commenting on other sections of Article I, Section 9, Mason thought that the provision limiting direct taxes according to the census "would be found to be no security whatsoever" (*DH*, X: 1343). He found little protection in the so-called fugitive-slave clause or in the prohibition against ex post facto laws, which he did not think would apply to the taxation of slave property (*DH*, X: 1343). He also believed that the prohibition against ex post facto laws would require the government to repay debts at face value, thus rewarding "rapacious speculators" (*DH*, X: 1355), and, as he had argued in Philadelphia (Farrand, II: 617), he wanted to amend the clause so that it explicitly applied only to criminal matters (X, 1363). Mason further objected to limitations on state inspection laws, specifically asking whether men in states with no tobacco were capable of regulating it (*DH*, X: 1363).

RE-ELIGIBILITY OF PRESIDENTS AND SENATORS, THE VICE-PRESIDENCY

That same day, the Convention began to discuss executive powers in Article II of the Constitution. When delegates at Philadelphia were considering allowing Congress to elect presidents to a six-year term, Mason had proposed limiting presidential terms to six of any twelve years (Farrand, I: 112). Similarly, in Richmond, Mason observed that "The President is elected without rotation" (*DH*, X:

1365). Rhetorically, he asked "Is there a single instance of a great man not being re-elected?" (*DH*, X: 1365). He further speculated that foreign nations, who could give presidents emoluments with congressional consent, would intervene to keep a friendly president in power, and feared that the nation would thus be stuck with "all the horrors and calamities of an elective Monarchy" (*DH*, X: 1365). Repeating a theme that he had expressed in favoring one-year terms for militia leaders, Mason observed that "Nothing is so essential to the preservation of a Republican Government, as a periodical rotation. Nothing so strongly impels a man to regard the interest of his constituents, as the certainty of returning to the general mass of the people, from whence he was taken; where he must participate [in] their burdens" (*DH*, X: 1366). Mason also thought that Senators should be prevented from running for re-election.

As he had done at the conclusion of deliberations in Philadelphia, Mason viewed the vice-presidency not only as "unnecessary" but potentially "dangerous" (*DH*, X: 1367). He thought it unfair to give an extra vote to a state (failing to mention that this only occurred in cases of a tie) when it was home to a vice-president. He also thought that the office improperly mixed legislative and executive powers. Acknowledging that he may be mistaken (although he wasn't), Mason also thought that having a vice-president might prevent the speedy election of a new one in case of the death or removal of the president (*DH*, X: 1368).

Electoral College, Presidential Powers of Command and Pardon, Treaty Making

In Philadelphia, Mason had expressed fears that the electoral college would send most elections to Congress and had successfully argued that the power to choose a president in such circumstances should be switched from the Senate, which represented states as states, to the House of Representatives, whose members were directly elected by the people (Farrand, II: 527). In debates on June 18, in Richmond, rather than focusing on this victory, Mason chose to describe the Electoral College as "a mere deception" making the people believe that they were choosing the president, when on most occasions such elections would be settled in the House. He further argued that the House should choose from the top two, rather than from among the top five, candidates (in 1804 the Twelfth Amendment limited the choice to the top three).

Given Mason's belief that both the presidency and the Senate would be aristocratic institutions, it is hardly surprising that he objected that the Constitution "has made them man and wife" (*DH*, X: 1376). Harkening back to one of his disappointments in Philadelphia, Mason argued that the delegates could have prevented this by the adoption of a constitutional council. Mason thought that senators would align with any presidents they were called upon to impeach and lamented that a president would remain in office during his trial. If natural affinity with the Senate did not protect the president, Mason raised the possibility that he could call out troops to protect himself.

Mason also expressed concern that the president might command the army in person. Although their differing positions on ratification would disrupt their long, if never particularly intimate, friendship (Gawalt, 2012), Mason praised George Washington's disinterestedness but feared others who were more ambitious and thought that majorities in both houses of Congress should have to approve such direct command. He reiterated his objection to the omission of an Executive Counsel and objected to the presidential pardon power "because he may frequently pardon crimes which were advised by himself" (*DH,* X: 1379). He further identified as a "weighty objection" the fact that "If he has the power of granting pardons before indictment, or conviction, may he not stop inquiry and prevent detection?" (*DH,* X: 1379).

In discussing treaty-making power, Mason focused on the fact that the Constitution had not required two-thirds of the states (nine had been required to approve treaties under the Articles of Confederation) to approve treaties, but only two-thirds of a quorum to do so (*DH,* X: 1380). He further hypothesized that the president might seek to call for ratification when delegates from states likely to oppose would be absent or that the president might even conspire with senators to give away parts of the nation.

COMMON LAW AND JUDICIAL JURISDICTION

On June 19, the Convention turned to its discussion of Article III of the Constitution. At long last, Mason returned to one of the more exotic claims that he had made in Philadelphia. Whereas most Founders lauded the security of written over unwritten constitutions, like that of Great Britain, Mason observed that the British Constitution "is founded on a number of maxims, which by long time are rendered sacred and inviolable" and "which have secured their persons and properties and prevented a dismemberment of their country" (*DH,* X: 1390). Attributing this protection to the common law, Mason opined that the Constitution did not secure this law in America.

Observing that "The indiscriminate admission of all foreigners to the first rights of citizenship, without any permanent security for their attachment to the country, is repugnant to every principle of prudence and good policy," Mason argued that further security was required to prevent treaties that might effect this (*DH*, X: 1391). Any such move, like any attempts at dismemberment of the nation, should require a three-fourths vote of both houses of Congress.

Mason also expressed great concern about the continuing viability of state courts under the new system. Examining the grants of power to federal courts in Article III, Mason said "There is no limitation. It goes to everything. The inferior Courts are to be as numerous as Congress may think proper. They are to be of whatever nature they please" (*DH*, X: 1401). In what may have been a veiled reference to slavery, Mason feared that federal courts might threaten "private property" (*DH*, X: 1402). Suspecting, without being able to verify, that the convention in Philadelphia had conspired to undermine state powers, he responded to an interruption by Madison, whose continuing friendship might well have depended on his answer, to admit that he had never heard him express such sentiments.

As he continued, Mason's arguments got more passionate. Pointing to the difficulty of getting justice even in local courts, he asked, "If any of the Federal officers should be guilty of the greatest oppressions, or behave with the most insolent and wanton brutality to a man's wife or daughter, where is this man to go to get relief?" (*DH*, X: 1404). He further wondered how poor men could go hundreds of miles to seek relief in federal appellate courts. Mason also wanted appellate federal jurisdiction to extend in common law matters only to issue of law and not issues of fact, which he thought juries could better decide (*DH*, X: 1404).

Further delving into the jurisdiction of federal courts, Mason expressed particular concern over cases that would bring states to court, especially those involving western land claims. He asked "Is not this disgraceful?—Is this State to be brought to the bar of justice like a delinquent individual?—Is the sovereignty of the State to be arraigned like a culprit, or private offender?—Will the States undergo this morti-fication?" (*DH,* X: 1406). Doubting that federal judges could call states to heel, Mason observed that "A power which cannot be executed, ought not to be granted" (*DH,* X: 1406), a position later adopted with the ratification of the Eleventh Amendment.

Again referencing the Virginia Declaration of Rights and its protection for jury trials, Mason observed that "This great palladium of national safety, which is secured to us by our own Government, will be taken from us in those Courts; or if it be reserved, it will be but in name, and not in substance" (*DH,* X: 1407). Mason further indicated that he feared a case involving his own interests in the Northern Neck of Virginia as well as west of the mountains. He accordingly proposed an amendment specifying "That the Judicial power shall extend to no case where the cause of action shall have originated before the ratification of this Constitution, except in suits for debts due to the United States, disputes between States about their territory, and disputes between persons claiming lands under the grants of different States" (*DH,* X: 1409). He further objected to concurrent jurisdiction by state and federal authorities.

FULL FAITH AND CREDIT CLAUSE AND COMMERCE AND NAVIGATION

On June 23, Mason said that he did not understand the full faith and credit clause in Article IV of the Constitution. Madison, who had done the most at the Virginia Ratifying Convention to defend the Constitution clause by clause and was rarely caught off guard, observed that he had not previously heard any objections to the clause and that he had "not employed a thought on the subject" (*DH*, X: 1471), and Mason appears to have dropped the argument.

As the Convention wound down, Mason repeated his apprehension that the fugitive slave clause would provide little security for property in slaves. His chief concerns remained "the insecurity of our rights and privileges," which he thought were too dependent "on vague, indefinite, and ambiguous implications" (*DH*, X: 1471). He feared that "the adoption of a system so replete with defects . . . could not but be productive of the most alarming consequences," which might even include "popular resistance to its operation" (*DH*, X: 1471).

The next day, Mason further drew upon his knowledge as a participant at the Constitutional Convention in responding to Edmund Randolph's argument that the regulation of commerce and navigation had been "a *sine qua non* of the Union" (*DH*, X: 1488). Saying that such a sine qua non did not exist, Mason recollected that eight of twelve states had accepted the necessity of a two-thirds majority until the compromise that permitted the continuing importation of slaves for 20 years in exchange for reducing this vote to a majority. Mason further believed that Eastern states had agreed to a two-thirds majority to ratify treaties in part to protect "Newfoundland fisheries" (*DH*, X: 1488).

POST CONVENTION MEETING

As the Virginia Ratifying Convention had progressed, Mason's already voluminous objections appear to have multiplied. By the end of the meeting, Mason remained unhappy. He had called for a meeting of the Antifederalists on the evening of June 17, only to have a document that he had drafted rejected as being too inflammatory (*DH*, X: 1560). Similarly, Mason failed in an attempt to reprimand Governor Randolph for failing to inform the Convention in a timely fashion of a letter that he had received from New York Antifederalist Governor George Clinton.

Mason would have to wait to see if any of his suggestions for a bill of rights, or for other constitutional amendments, would be adopted now that a sufficient number of states had ratified the Constitution. He had fought a good fight, but neither he nor the other delegates knew for sure how the new government would operate.

REFERENCES

Banning, Lance. 1989. "Sectionalism and the General Good," *Ratifying the Constitution*, ed. Michael Allen Gillespie and Michael Lienesch. Lawrence: University Press of Kansas, 261-299.

The Documentary History of the Ratification of the Constitution, ed. John P. Kaminski and Gaspare J. Saladino. Madison: State Historical Society of Wisconsin. Vols. VIII-X cover Virginia and were published from 1990-1993. Cited as *DH*, volume number, and page number.

Farrand, Max, ed. 1966. *The Records of the Federal Convention of 1787*. 4 vols. New Haven, CT: Yale University Press.

Gewalt, Gerard W. 2012. *George Mason and George Mason: The Power of Principle*. North Charleston, SC: CreateSpace.

Heideking, Jurgen. 2012. *The Constitution Before the Judgment Seat: The Prehistory and Ratification of the American Constitution, 1787-*

1792, ed. John P. Kaminski and Richard Leffler. Charlottesville: University of Virginia Press.

Johnston, F. Claiborne, Jr. 1988. "Federalist, Doubtful, and Antifederalist: A Note on the Virginia Convention of 1788," *The Virginia Magazine of History and Biography* 96 (July): 333-344.

Kaminski, John P. and Gaspare J. Saladino, eds. 1988, 1990, 1993. *The Documentary History of the Ratification of the Constitution, Ratification of the Constitution by the States, Virginia.* Volumes VIII-X. [Documentary History].

Kukla, Jon. 1988. "A Spectrum of Sentiments: Virginia's Federalists, Antifederalists, and 'Federalists Who Are for Amendments,' 1787-1788." *The Virginia Magazine of History and Biography* 96 (July): 276-296.

Maier, Pauline. 2011. *Ratification: The People Debate the Constitution, 1787-1788.* New York: Simon & Schuster.

Smith, Robert W. 2014. "Foreign Affairs and the Ratification of the Constitution in Virginia." *The Virginia Magazine of History and Biography* 112: 40-67.

Storing, Herbert J., ed. 1981. *George Mason and George Washington: What the Anti-Federalists Were For.* Vol. 1 of *The Complete Anti-Federalist.* Chicago: The University of Chicago Press.

8

George Mason, Late Life Views of Representation and Evaluation

One reason that Mason is not as well-known as other founding fathers was his age. Unlike Washington, Adams, Jefferson, and Madison, Mason did not go on to become a president, nor like Alexander Hamilton did he secure a cabinet post. He did have the opportunity, which he rejected, of serving as one of two U.S. Senators from Virginia, but he died in 1792, prior to the end of the nation's first presidential administration.

Although he left the Virginia Ratifying Convention in a distemper that left him at permanent loggerheads with his neighbor George Washington, Mason took some comfort in the proposal of the Bill of Rights. Thus in a letter to Samuel Griffin, a Virginia lawyer who was serving in the U.S. House of Representatives, dated September 8, 1789, Mason observed that: "I have received much Satisfaction from the Amendments to the federal Constitution, which have lately passed the House of Representatives; I hope they will also pass the Senate" (*PGM,* III: 1172). Perhaps having been so accustomed to drafting such documents on his own, Mason observed that "With two or three further Amendments . . . I cou'd cheerfully put my Hand & Heart to the new Government" (*PGM,* III: 1172). Showing that he actually hoped for more, however, he then listed four amendments that he favored. They consisted of "confining the federal Judiciary to Admiralty & Maritime Jurisdiction, and to Subjects merely federal—fixing the Mode of Elections either in the Constitution itself (which I think wou'd be preferable) or securing the Regulation of them to the respective States—Requiring more than a bare Majority to make Navigation & Commercial Laws, and appointing a constitutional amenable Council to the President, & lodging with them most of the Executive Powers now vested in the Senate" (*PGM,* III: 1172).

Apart from two initial amendments, the former dealing with representation, which the states rejected, and the second dealing with congressional pay raises, which states later ratified as the Twenty-Seventh Amendment, the amendments included in the federal bill of rights all related to civil rights and liberties, with the last (today's Tenth Amendment) focusing on rights reserved to the states. Although Mason thus appeared satisfied on that score (Congress had protected far more of these than he had requested), he was still not comfortable either with the U.S. Senate or the federal judiciary, both of which he feared would be aristocratic. He also remained concerned over possible federal control over state elections, and with what he perceived to be the lack of security for southern states on matters of navigation.

On a more personal note, Mason remained on friendly terms with Thomas Jefferson who had hoped that remaining states might delay their confirmation of the Constitution until the adoption of the bill of rights. Mason also sought to sooth any ill feelings with James Madison that Mason might have generated at the Virginia Ratifying Convention. Mason thus sent a letter to Jefferson in which he wrote:

> I beg the Favour of you to present my best Respects to our Friend Mr. Madison. He is one of the Few Men, whom from a pretty thorough Acquaintance, I really esteem; tho' I have been apprehensive some late Difference (and it has only been a late one) on political Questions has caused a Coolness between us. I am sure it has not on my Part; for if I know my own Heart, I have more Liberality than to think the worse of a Friend for a Disagreement on any theoretical Opinions; and I well know that the iniquitous Attempts, too frequently made in our Assembly, were almost enough to shake any Man's democratical principles. (*PGM*, III: 1218).

As indicated in the previous chapter, just a week before his death, Mason further told Jefferson, who was visiting Gunston Hall, that he could have had "set his hand & heart to" the Constitution, within a "fortnight" of the Philadelphia Convention's adjournment prior to what he considered to be compromises between the New England states and the deep southern states, that traded deleting the supermajority requirements on navigation matters for the right to import slaves for an additional 20 years (*PGM*, III: 1275). According to Jefferson's recollection, Mason had also expressed objections to the lack of presidential term limits and the possibility of the reelection of senators, both of which Mason probably associated with his fears of either monarchy or aristocracy.

MASON AND REPRESENTATION

One of the themes that emerged fairly prominently from Mason's speeches at both the Constitutional Convention of 1787 and the Virginia Ratifying Convention of 1788 was his emphasis on the importance of representation. Some of his most trenchant criticism of the Constitution centered on the difficulty that he thought ten representatives from Virginia and 65 members of the U.S. House of Representatives would have in representing the interests of Virginia and 13 diverse states. Indeed, one of the amendments that he favored was to increase this representation.

Although Mason did not accept national office, he continued to remain active on the state and local levels. At least three of his actions, one just after the U.S. Constitutional Convention, and the other two after states ratified the Constitution, point to the manner in which Mason remained concerned not only for the forms but also for the substantive elements of republican government.

PETITION COMPLAINING ABOUT OVERSEERS OF THE POOR

On November 24, 1787, Mason authored a petition to the state General Assembly complaining about overseers of the poor. Often finding himself at odds with the town of Alexandria, Mason was concerned that when the legislature divided Fairfax County into two districts (city and county) to oversee the poor, the latter representatives refused to serve, and, as a consequence, the needs of county residents received short shrift. This situation was exacerbated when the former commissioners insisted on keeping the poor-house within the city limits rather than "near the Middle of the County," where Mason believed that it could more easily have served residents of both (*PGM*, III: 1013).

Mason argued that lodging in the town was more expensive than in the country, and that lodging residents there deprived them of grounds for gardens where they could provide for some of their own support. In arguably exaggerated terms, which would be familiar to those who study modern opponents of welfare programs, Mason charged that the poor were "maintained in such Idleness, Ease and Plenty, as cannot fail continually to increase their Number" (*PGM*, III: 1014). This had resulted in the imposition of oppressive taxes on county residents. Perhaps recalling the situation that had led to independence from Britain, Mason observed that:

> the Inhabitants of the Town generally having very few Tytheables, they participate little in the Burdens they lay upon others; and have not that common Interest and fellow-feeling with the People of the County, so indispensably necessary to produce Attention, Moderation, and Frugality in Public Expenses; so that 'what is Sport to them may be Death to us' and the other People of the County; who are so grievously oppressed with the necessary public Taxes, and the Unnecessary Expenditure and charges of the County" (*PGM*, III: 1014).

Further addressing the administration of projects, Mason argued that "the Custom of uniting different & distinct Offices of Power and Authority in the same Men tends to create an undue Influence in particular Individuals, naturally subversive of Liberty, and productive of Oppression; incompatible with the Genius of Republican Government, and consistent with the Principles of our own Laws and Constitution" (*PGM*, III: 1015). More specifically, Mason, who had expressed similar concerns about federal courts, wanted to limit the jurisdiction of Corporation Courts to citizens of the town rather than extending such jurisdiction to members of the county as well.

Mason indicated that he did not oppose the creation of a special district for members of the town of Alexandria but did not think that they should also be able to vote in county elections. According to Robert Rutland, the editor of Mason's papers, the legislature acted on Mason's suggestions and provided for separate houses for those who resided in the towns rather than the surrounding county (*PGM*, III: 1016).

Petition Seeking Removal of the Fairfax County Courthouse from Alexandria

On November 3, 1789, Mason authored a petition, signed by 558 individuals, to members of the Virginia General Assembly. It sought to remove the Fairfax County Courthouse from the town of Alexandria to a more centralized location within the county. This petition shows not only that Mason continued to value politics at the local level but also demonstrated his continuing concern over accessibility to the courts to members of all classes.

The petition began with arguments that the current courthouse was in such a state of disrepair that it would almost cost as much to repair it as to build a new one, but Mason's chief argument had to do with accessibility and convenience. Noting that the existing courthouse was "Situate on the extream Edge of the County, and within Two hundred Yards of the Boundaries of the State of Virginia," Mason observed that this:

> is extreamly inconvenient to the bulk of the Inhabitants of the County; who are obliged to attend Court, at more than double the distance they would have occasion to do, if the Court house was fixed (as of Right it ought to be) near the Center of the County; from Whence the greater part of the Inhabitants, when obliged to Attend Court, could conveniently Return to their own homes, every

> night; and thereby Save the charge of putting up in Taverns and publick houses; an expence grievous to them all, and ruinous to many of the poorer Sort of People" (*PGM,* III: 1182-1183).

Mason believed that the distance and expense deterred county justices from attending court and "Country Gentlemen, and Reputable Farmers and planters" from serving on juries (*PGM,* III: 1183). He feared that "the notorious unfitness, and partiality of Town Jurys, has already begun to create a prejudice in the minds of many good Citizens, in different parts of the Country, against Jury Trials; Which if not timely Removed, by proper Regulations, may gradually undermine, and finally abolish this inestimable Privilege, and Security of the People" (*PGM,* III: 1183). Moreover, a corporation court already took cases from citizens of the town, thus preventing a change in location of the county court from inconveniencing them.

In answering arguments that locating the county court in the town of Alexandria promoted trade and commerce, Mason somewhat moralistically responded that "altho' Trade and Commerce are objects of great Importance, and Justly entitled to the Attention of a wise Legislature, and all proper encouragements; Yet any Trade so circumstanced, as to require Support from the Increase of idleness and Extravagance; and compelling the People to Spend their money and their time in Tipling houses, and Taverns, is not worth encouraging" (*PGM,* III: 1184). He further observed that justice has been delayed in counties that insisted on holding court in similarly-situated towns where "the Justices generally employ that time in doing their own private business, which ought to be Devoted to the Publick" (*PGM,* III: 1184).

Although town residents sent a counter petition with 104 signatures, the legislature again heeded Mason's petition. It adopted an act in December 1789 for moving the court, which was not, however, finished until 1801 (*PGM,* III: n. 1185).

PROTEST AGAINST THE CREATION OF A FAIRFAX-LOUDOUN CONGRESSIONAL DISTRICT

On January 24, 1791, Mason expressed concerns over what later became known as gerrymandering, and returned to some of his more familiar political themes. Mason appears to have been mistaken about the creation of the district he was opposing, and it remains unclear whether his work was intended to be a letter or a newspaper article. In either case, it addressed fundamental issues that continue into modern times.

In language quite similar to the Second of the Fairfax Resolves, to which he had contributed, Mason began by observing that "the essential Difference" between freedom and despotism, Freemen and slaves, rested on the ability of the former to "chuse the Men who are to make Laws for them, and are therefore governed by no Laws, but such [as] are made by Men of their own chusing in whom they can confide, who are amenable to them; and if they abuse their Trust, can be turned out, at the next Election" (*PGM,* III: 1219-1220). By contrast, "Subjects of arbitrary Governments, having no such Right of Suffrage, in electing their own Law-makers, are governed by Laws made by Men, whom they do not chuse, who therefore are not amenable to them, over whom they have no Controul, in whom they have no Confidence, with whom they have no common Interest, or fellow-felling; and whose Interest and Views may be, and frequently will be, in direct Contrast and Opposition to the Rights and Interest of the Bulk of the

People" (*PGM,* III: 1219). From these statements, Mason drew the conclusion that "this Right of Suffrage, in the Choice of their own Law-makers, is the Foundations and Support of all the other Rights and Privileges of Freemen. And whenever they shall be deprived of it, all their other Rights and Privileges must soon moulder away, and tumble to the Ground" (*PGM,* III: 1291).

Prioritizing the right to vote is fascinating for at least two reasons. First, Mason's analysis is much more specific than any that he offered in his speeches at the Constitutional Convention of 1787, or in his proposals to amend the Constitution—the closest he came in this respect was his critique of the House of Representatives as being too small to represent the interests of the American people—at the Virginia Ratifying Convention. Second, although the U.S. Supreme Court has declared voting to be a "fundamental right," to this day, neither the first ten amendments nor any of the subsequent amendments to the Constitution affirmatively grant this right, although the Fifteenth, Nineteenth, and Twenty-sixth Amendments prohibit discrimination on the basis of race, sex, or age above 18.

Mason observed, however, that if the right to vote is fundamental, then "Whenever it shall be impaired or weakened, all the other Rights and Privileges of a free People will be impaired or weakened, in the same Proportion" (*PGM,* III: 1791). In such cases the people whose votes have been so impaired "will possess only the Name and Shadow of Liberty; which without the Substance, is not worth preserving" (*PGM,* III: 1791).

Although bills and declaration typically focus on rights, scholars generally argue that rights have correlative duties. Mason believed that Freemen had a duty not only to themselves but to their posterity "To watch over, and guard this sacred and inestimable Right of Suffrage; and with manly Firmness, to resist the smallest Attempt of Invasion, or Encroachment on it; for every Encroachment will grow into a Precedent for some other Encroachment" (*PGM*, III: 1220).

Mason's articulation of this fundamental right was more illuminating than its application to the case at hand. Noting that as a result of the last census, Virginia's representatives would change from 10 to 21 members (excluding Kentucky) and believing that the counties of Stafford, Prince William, Fairfax, Loudoun, and Fauquier, which were formerly together, would be split into two districts, with those in Fairfax and Loudoun now combined in a district in which the population of the latter being three times that of the former, Mason feared for voters in Fairfax County. He thus observed that "a Candidate in Fairfax (let him be ever so good a Man) will have no chance of succeeding against one in Loudoun: the comparative Merits of the candidates will be sacrificed to local Attachment; and the People in Fairfax will, in Reality, have little more Hand in electing their nominal Representatives in Congress, than they have in electing the Representatives of Maryland, or Pennsylvania" (*PGM*, III: 1221).[1] Reminiscent of fears that he had expressed at the Virginia Ratifying Convention, Mason further anticipated that this situation would be aggravated when part of Fairfax County was incorporated into the Federal District.

---

[1] This analysis differs considerably from James Madison's analysis in Federalist No. 10 (Hamilton, Madison and Jay 1961) in which he argued that expanding to sphere of republican government would make it more likely that voters would choose men of merit. By contrast, Mason suggests that preferences for local candidates might well trump preferences for better men.

Mason observed that when the Virginia government had been formed in 1776, special efforts had been made to keep districts equal. He thought the reasons for providing equality in the choice of members of Congress were even stronger. His ultimate hope was that in any redistricting, "it is of the utmost Consequence, that they shou'd be fairly and justly made; and not with a view of serving any temporary, local Party-Job whatever" (*PGM*, III: 1223). Although Mason was clearly concerned about his own district, he recognized that it tied to larger concerns.

ANALYSIS OF MASON'S FINAL YEARS

In opining about legislative districts, Mason distinguished between shadow and substance. His stance on the location of a poor house or a county court, or on how districts should be combined for purposes of creating legislative districts, were hardly as consequential and were not nearly as likely to capture the same attention as his plea for a declaration of rights. Still, the whole purpose of this book is to show that Mason's philosophy cannot be reduced to that single concern, no matter how important it proved to be.

It is possible for a system to work on paper and result in unfairness just as critics might argue that it is possible to put critiques of constitutions to paper that never materialize. It is striking that, despite Mason's objection to the Constitution, he still managed to retain the confidence of many of the fellow citizens who knew him best. They apparently recognized that, however his own social and economic situation might distinguish him from his fellows, he retained a deep concern that republican government not be undercut by the inability of its poorest and most isolated citizens to access justice.

ANALYSIS OF MASON'S LIFE WORK

Surveying Mason's life work as a whole, it is important to recognize that individual founding fathers tend to fall in and out of favor depending on the mood of the times. Scholars have long noted, and some have lamented, that Mason has not generated nearly the attention of Washington, Adams, Jefferson, Franklin, Madison, or Hamilton. Moreover, there are times when Founders in general are considered suspect. After I gave a recent speech to a local civic group on the Declaration of Independence, one of the members asked if I were celebrating Thomas Jefferson and other Founders knowing that they were slave holders. I replied that I was celebrating them not *because* they owned slaves but *in spite of* this. I further said that I did so because they articulated principles that led fairly quickly to American independence from Britain, to the establishment of republican government, and eventually to the destruction of slavery and other institutions and beliefs that had interfered with the security of their lives, liberties, and their pursuit of happiness.

Mason's earliest political writings reveal that he was firmly committed to the principles that he associated with the British constitution and colonial charters, and particularly with the principle of no taxation without representation. He believed that the colonists had brought their freedoms with them to the New World and that they had secured the continent against hostile forces through their own efforts. Mason worked while he could to vindicate colonial rights short of war, but he eventually came to believe that revolution was the only way to avert tyranny and to avoid the corruption that he associated with the British system.

Sadly, Mason was among those, who, while often lauded for opposing slavery, actually had a far more limited agenda in opposing its spread through further importation. Fortunately, this was not his only political goal. As this book reveals, he was deeply committed to constitutionalism, which included the articulation of a declaration, or bill, of rights and a written constitution that provided for bicameralism, separation of powers, and an executive council. Although the declaration that Mason authored for Virginia, differed significantly from the Bill of Rights that James Madison would introduce in part as a result of Anti-Federalist criticisms of the U.S. Constitution, Mason's Declaration began a list of rights that included religious liberty, freedom of the press, and rights for criminal defendants, to which other statesmen added as they gained better understanding of the prerequisites for republican government. So too, the Virginia Constitution provided a model for other states.

Mason continued to work consistently for religious freedom, especially within his own state, and he stood guard over undue exercises of executive power, even in times of emergency. He believed strongly in the need for fiscal accountability, in the need for citizen participation and control over their local militia, and in civilian control over military power. Like later leaders of the Democratic-Republican Party, he often favored state over national power and preferred the adoption of constitutional amendments to expansive constitutional constructions that might serve as precedents for future incursions on liberty. Opposing such construction while realizing the weaknesses of the Articles of Confederation, he joined those who thought that the Confederation needed to be amended to secure republican government, which he thought the specter of monarchy and aristocracy constantly threatened.

Mason accordingly took a leading role in the U.S. Constitutional Convention. Although he succeeded on numerous occasions on bending the Constitution to his republican vision, he was ultimately unconvinced that it should be adopted without further amendments, in part because he feared that the document did not provide adequate protection for his own region. Hence, he could oppose both the Constitution's permissiveness involving the continuation of the slave trade and its failure to protect slavery itself. Although these and other positions sometimes gave a regional tincture to his arguments (which would not have been inconsistent with his service as a delegate from Virginia), at least one of his proposals (a two-thirds requirement for congress to adopt trade measures) might have prevented future regional controversies.

Although Mason enlarged his critiques as the debates over the Constitution continued in the Virginia Ratifying Convention and elsewhere, he still recognized the deficiencies of the existing Articles of Confederation and worked for improvements. He expressed at least some satisfaction over the adoption of the first ten amendments and managed to sustain his friendship with Jefferson and Madison. As leaders of the Democratic-Republican Party, they would in time come to wonder whether they were witnessing the fulfilment of some of the concerns that he had expressed over monarchical and aristocratic trends.

Although other delegates at the Convention went on to higher office, Mason was content to sit under his own vine and eat from his own fruit trees at Gunston Hall while participating in state and local politics. As this final chapter reveals, Mason continued to distinguish between what he considered to be political shadow and substance. He recognized that conflicts between cities and counties over such mundane matters as the location of poor houses and court houses and between counties and their neighbors over the apportionment of legislative districts could have major implications for republicanism.

There are elements of Mason's republicanism, like his support for sumptuary legislation, which can appear quaint. There are others, such as his insistence on reliance upon state militia rather than a standing army, which may today appear fairly impractical. Although I believe that Mason's thought is fascinating in its own right, I also think that his political writings have continuing political relevance. At a time when Americans remain increasingly concerned that the nation's capital has become a "swamp," in which private interests often use their money and power to dominate over others, Mason reminds us that even if we are fortunate enough to inhabit the top 1% (as he himself undoubtedly did), our children and their children may not be so blessed. Government does not exist for the exclusive benefit of the few but for the safety and happiness of the many. True governments are directed to the common weal, which can be undermined not only by lack of formal constitutional structures and guarantees but also by corruption, public inattention, and by the temptation to vest strong men (or women) with inordinate power to solve immediate problems while sowing seeds for an imperial executive or judiciary.

There are times when Mason seemed almost excessively preoccupied by the threat of monarchy and aristocracy, and less confident that he might have been in protections like separation of powers and periodic elections. Still, Mason recognized that these mechanisms will not work if people are so kowtowed by current exigencies that they cede their power to others.

Despite this book, Mason will probably always be remembered for his observation that "There is no Declaration of Rights" (Farrand, II: 637), but this critique was but part of Mason's larger vision. As he indicated in his first draft of the Virginia Declaration of Rights, Mason envisioned a republican government that recognized "That all Men are born equally free and independent, and have certain inherent natural Rights, of which they can not by any Compact, deprive or divest their Posterity; among which are the Enjoyment of Life and Liberty, with the Means of acquiring and possessing Property, and pursuing and obtaining Happiness and Safety" (*PGM*, I: 277). He recognized that such government required continuing citizen vigilance against any attempts to subvert their liberties, which had been dearly gained and that remain essential to their continuing happiness.

REFERENCES

Farrand, Max, ed. 1966. *The Records of the Federal Convention of 1787.* 4 vols. New Haven, CT: Yale University Press.

Hamilton, Alexander, James Madison, and John Jay. 1961. *The Federalist Papers.* New York: New American Library.

Mason, George 1970. *The Papers of George Mason, 1725-1792.* 3 vols. Ed. Robert A. Rutland. Chapel Hill: The University of North Carolina Press.

BIBLIOGRAPHY

Adair, Douglass. 1945. "James Madison's Autobiography." *The William and Mary Quarterly* 2 (April): 191-2.

Adair, Douglass. 1952. "Rumbold's Dying Speech, 1685, and Jefferson's Last Words on Democracy, 1826," *The William and Mary Quarterly* 9 (October): 521-531.

Adams, John. April 1776. Thoughts on Government. From The Papers of John Adams, Vol. IV. Posted at https://www.masshist.org/publications/apde2/view?&id=PJA04dg2.

Adams, John. 1969. *The Works of John Adams, Second President of the United States,* ed. by Charles Francis Adams. Freeport, NY: Books for Libraries Press.

Adams, Willi Paul. 2001. *The First American Constitutions: Republican Ideology and the Making of the State Constitutions in the Revolutionary Era,* trans. By Rita and Robert Kimber. Lanham: Rowman & Littlefield.

Ammerman, David. 1974. *In the Common Cause: American Response to the Coercive Acts of 1775.* Charlottesville: University Press of Virginia.

Aristotle. 1954. *The Politics of Aristotle,* ed. Ernest Barker. New York: Oxford University Press.

Armitage, David. 2007. *The Declaration of Independence: A Global History.* Cambridge, MA: Harvard University Press.

Asper, Lewis D. 1969. "The Long and Unhappy History of Loyalty Testing in Maryland." *The American Journal of Legal History* 13 (April): 97-109.

"*A Letter from the Committee of Merchants in* London, *trading* to North America, *directed to the merchants in* New York, *dated Feb. 28, 1766.*" *Virginia Gazette* (Purdie) 16 May 1766, p. 2 of 4. Found at http://research.history/org/CWDLImages/VA_GAZETImages/PD/1766/0043hi.jpg.

Bailyn, Bernard, ed. 1993. *The Debate on the Constitution: Federalist and Antifederalist Speeches, Articles, and Letters During the Struggle Over Ratification.* N.p.; The Library of America. 2 vols.

Banning, Lance. 1989. "Sectionalism and the General Good," *Ratifying the Constitution,* ed. Michael Allen Gillespie and Michael Lienesch. Lawrence: University Press of Kansas, 261-299.

Billings, Warren M. 1992. "'That all Men Are Born Equally Free and Independent' Virginians and the Origins of the Bill of Rights." *The Bill of Rights and the States: the Colonial and Revolutionary Origins of American Liberties,* ed. Patrick T. Conley and John P. Kaminski. Madison, WI: Madison House, 335-369.

_____. 2004. *A Little Parliament: The Virginia General Assembly in the Seventeenth Century.* Richmond: Library of Virginia.

Bodah, Andrew T. 2018. "The Road to 'Due Process': Evolving Constitutional Language from 1776 to 1789." *Thomas Jefferson Law Review* 40 (Spring): 102-169.

Bogen, David S. 1983. "The Origins of Freedom of Speech and Press." *Maryland Law Review* 42 (Spring): 429-465.

Boyd, Julian P. 1976. "On the Need for 'Frequent Recurrence to Fundamental Principles." *Virginia Law Review* 62 (June): 859-871.

Brant, Irving. 1941. *James Madison: The Virginia Revolutionist, 1751-1780.* New York: Bobbs-Merrill.

Braxton, Carter. "An Address to the Convention of the Colony and Ancient Dominion of Virginia on the Subject of Government in General, and Recommending a Particular Form to Their Attention." 1983 [1776]. *American Political Writing During the Founding Era, 1760—1805,* vol. I of 2, ed. by Donald S. Lutz and Charles S. Hyneman. Indianapolis: Liberty Fund.

Breen, T.H. 1997. "Ideology and Nationalism on the Eve of the American Revolution: Revisions Once More in Need of Revising." *The Journal of American History* 84 (June): 13-39.

Bresler, Kenneth. 1991. "Rediscovering the Right to Instruct Legislators." *New England Law Review* 26 (Winger): 335-394.

Broadwater, Jeff. 2006. *George Mason: Forgotten Founder.* Chapel Hill: The University of North Carolina Press.

Broadwater, J. March 6, 2014. "George Mason (1725-1792)." Encyclopedia Virginia. Retrieved from http://www.EncyclopediaVirginia.org/Mason_George_1724-1792.

Broadwater, Jeff. 2017. "George Mason, James Madison, and the Evolution of the Bill of Rights," *Georgetown Journal of Law & Public Policy.*" 15 (Summer): 547-568.

Brown, Bennie. 2017. "John Mercer: Merchant, Lawyer, Author, Book Collector," in *"Esteemed Bookes of Law" and the Legal Culture of early Virginia,* ed. Warren M. Billings, and Brent Tarter. Charlottesville: University of Virginia Press.

Calabresi, Steven G. Sarah E. Agudo, and Kathryn L. Dore. 2012. "State Bills of Rights in 1787 and 1791: What Individual Rights Are Really Deeply Rooted in American History and Tradition?" *Southern California Law Review* 85 (September): 1451-1550.

Cash, Arthur H. 2006. *John Wilkes: The Scandalous Father of Civil Liberty.* New Haven: Yale University Press.

Chaffin, Robert J. 1974. "The Declaration Act of 1766: A Reappraisal." *The Historian* 37 (November): 5-25.

Chester, Edward W. 1989. "George Mason— Influence Beyond the United States." *George Mason and the Legacy of Constitutional Liberty,* ed. Donald J. Senese. Fairfax County History Commission, 128-146.

Cogliano, Francis D. 2013. "'The Whole Object of the Present Controversy': The Early Constitutionalism of Paine and Jefferson." *Paine and Jefferson in the Age of Revolutions,* ed. Simon P. Newman and Peter S. Onuf. Charlottesville, VA: University of Virginia Press, 26-48.

"Constitutional Convention, 1787." 1861. *The Historical Magazine* 2st ser. V (January): 18.

Cornell, Saul. 2004. "Beyond the Myth of Consensus: The Struggle to Define the Right to Bear Arms in the Early Republic," *Beyond the Frontiers: New Approaches to the Political History of the Early American Republic,* ed. Jeffrey L. Pasley, Andrew W. Robertson, and David Waldstreicher, Chapel Hill: University of North Carolina Press.

Copeland, Pamela C. and Richard K. MacMaster. 2016. *The Five George Masons.* Charlottesville: University of Virginia Press.

Curtis, Christopher Michael. 2012. *Jefferson's Freeholders and the Politics of Ownership in the Old Dominion.* New York: Cambridge University Press.

"Declaration on Taking Arms," July 6, 1775, as found in *The Declaration of Independence in Historical Context: American State Papers, Petitions, Proclamations, & Letters of the Delegates to the first National Congresses,* compiled, edited by Barry Alan Shain. Indianapolis, IN: Liberty Fund, 2014, pp. 277-282.

Dill, Alonzo. 1983. *Carter Braxton, Virginia Signer: A Conservative in Revolt.* Lanham, MD. University Press of America.

Dinan, John J. 2006. *The American State Constitutional Tradition.* Lawrence: University Press of Kansas.

The Documentary History of the Ratification of the Constitution, ed. John P. Kaminski and Gaspare J. Saladino. Madison: State Historical Society of Wisconsin. Vols. VIII-X cover Virginia and were published from 1990-1993. Cited as *DH,* volume number, and page number.

Donohue, Laura K. 2016. "The Original Fourth Amendment." *The University of Chicago Law Review* 83 (Summer): 1181-1328.

Dougherty, Keith L. 2001. *Collective Action under the Articles of Confederation.* Cambridge: Cambridge University Press.

Douma, Michael J. 2017. "How the First Ten Amendments Became the Bill of Rights." *Georgetown Journal of Law & Public Policy* 15 (Summer): 593-614.

Dreisbach, Daniel L. 2000. "George Mason's Pursuit of Religious Liberty in Revolutionary Virginia." *The Virginia Magazine of History and Biography* 108: 2+5-44.

Dunaway, W.F., Jr. 1904. "The Virginia Conventions of the Revolution." *The Virginia Law Register* 10 (November): 567-586.

Farr, James. 2008. "Locke, Natural Law, and New World Slavery." *Political Theory* 36 (August): 495-522.

Farrand, Max, ed. 1966. *The Records of the Federal Convention of 1787.* 4 vols. New Haven, CT: Yale University Press.

Fleming, Thomas. 1997. *Liberty! The American Revolution.* Viking: New York.

Ford, Paul Leicester, ed. 1892. *Essays on the Constitution of the United States Published During its Discussion by the People, 1787-1788.* Brooklyn, NY: Historical Printing Company.

Friedman, Dan. 2002. "Tracing the Lineage: Textual and Conceptual Similarities in the Revolutionary-Era State Declarations of Rights of Virginia, Maryland, and Delaware." *Rutgers Law Journal* 33 (Summer): 929-1028.

Ganter, Herbert Lawrence. 1937. "The Machiavellianism of George Mason." *The William and Mary Quarterly* 17 (April): 239-264.

Gates, George Marion. 1930. *The Influence of George Mason on the Framing and Adoption of the Constitution.* A thesis presented to the Department of History University of Southern California for Master of Arts degree.

Gewalt, Gerard W. 2012. *George Mason and George Mason: The Power of Principle.* North Charleston, SC: CreateSpace.

Goldwin, Robert A. 1997. *From Parchment to Power: How James Madison Used the Bill of Rights to Save the Constitution.* Washington, DC: AEI Press.

Gould, Philip. 1993. "Virtue, Ideology, and the American Revolution: The Legacy of the Republican Synthesis." *American Literary History* 5 (Autumn): 564-577.

Grigsby, Hugh Blair. 1855. *The Virginia Convention of 1855.* Richmond, VA: J.W. Randolph.

Haffenden, Philip S. 1958. "The Crown and the Colonial Charters, 1675-1788: Part I." *The William and Mary Quarterly* 15 (July): 297-311.

_____. 1958. "The Crown and the Colonial Charters, 1675-1688: Part II." *The William and Mary Quarterly* 15 (October): 452-466.

Hamilton, Alexander, James Madison, and James Monroe. 1961 [1787-1788]. *The Federalist Papers.* New York: New American Library.

Hartz, Louis. 1955. *The Liberal Tradition in America: An Interpretation of American Political Thought Since the Revolution.* New York: Harcourt, Brace & World.

Heideking, Jurgen. 2012. *The Constitution Before the Judgment Seat: The Prehistory and Ratification of the American Constitution, 1787-1792,* ed. John P. Kaminski and Richard Leffler. Charlottesville: University of Virginia Press.

Henriques, Peter R. 1989. "An Uneven Friendship: The Relationship between George Washington and George Mason." *The Virginia Magazine of History and Biography.* 97. (April): 185-204.

Heymsfeld, Carla R. and Joan W. Lewis. 1991. *George Mason, Father of the Bill of Rights.* Alexandria, VA: Patriotic Education Incorporated.

Hilldrup, Robert Leroy. 1935. *The Virginia Convention of 1776: A Study in Revolutionary Politics.* Dissertation for Ph.D., University of Virginia.

Hoffert, Robert W. 1992. *A Politics of Tensions: The Articles of Confederation and American Political Ideals.* Niwot, CO: University Press of Colorado.

Horrell, Joseph. 1983. "George Mason and the Fairfax Court." *The Virginia Magazine of History and Biography.* 92 (October): 418-439.

Howard, A.E. 1968. "'For the Common Benefit': Constitutional History in Virginia as a Casebook for the Modern Constitution-Maker." *Virginia Law Review* 54 (June): 816-902.

Hyland, William G., Jr. 2019. *George Mason: The Founding Father Who Gave Us the Bill of Rights.* New York: Regnery History.

Hudson, James H. ed. 1987. *Supplement to Max Farrand's The Records of the Federal Convention of 1787.* New Haven, CT: Yale University Press.

Hunt, Gaillard. 1917. "The Virginia Declaration of Rights and Cardinal Bellarmine." *The Catholic Historical Review* 3 (October): 276-289.

Jameson, John Alexander. 1887. *A Treatise on Constitutional Conventions; Their History, Powers, and Modes of Proceeding.* 4th ed., Intro. by John R. Vile. Clark, NJ: The Lawbook Exchange, 2014.

Jefferson, Thomas. "From Thomas Jefferson to Henry Lee, 8 May 1825." Founders Online. https://founders.archives.gov/documents/Jefferson/98-01-02-5212.

Jefferson, Thomas. [1781] 1964. *Notes on the State of Virginia.* New York: Harper & Row.

Jefferson, Thomas. June 24, 1826. "Letter to Roger C. Weightman." Teaching American History.org. http://teachingamericanhistory.org/library/document/letter-to-roger-c-weightman/.

Jefferson, Thomas. 1950. *The Papers of Thomas Jefferson,* Vol. I, 1760-1776. Ed. Julian P. Boyd. Princeton, NJ: Princeton University Press.

Jefferson, Thomas. 1905. *The Works of Thomas Jefferson,* ed. Paul Leicester Ford. New York: G.P. Putnam's Sons, Knickerbocker Press.

Jellinke, Georg. 1902. *The Declaration of the Rights of Man and of Citizens: A Contribution to Modern Constitutional History,* trans. By Max Farrand. New York: Henry Holt and Company.

Jensen, Merrill. 1966. *The Articles of Confederation.* Madison: University of Wisconsin Press.

Johnston, F. Claiborne, Jr. 1988. "Federalist, Doubtful, and Antifederalist: A Note on the Virginia Convention of 1788," *The Virginia Magazine of History and Biography* 96 (July): 333-344.

Kaminski, John P. and Gaspare J. Saladino, eds. 1988, 1990, 1993. *The Documentary History of the Ratification of the Constitution, Ratification of the Constitution by the States, Virginia.* Volumes VIII-X. [Documentary History].

Kammen, Michael. 1970. "The Meaning of Colonization in American Revolutionary Thought." *Journal of the History of Ideas* 31 (July-September): 337-358.

Kendall, Willmoore, and George W. Carey. 1970. *The Basic Symbols of the American Political Tradition.* Baton Rouge: Louisiana State University Press.

Kukla, Jon. 1988. "A Spectrum of Sentiments: Virginia's Federalists, Antifederalists, and 'Federalists Who Are for

Amendments, 1787-1788." *The Virginia Magazine of History and Biography* 96 (July): 276-296.

Kurland, Philip B. and Ralph Lerner, eds. *The Founders' Constitution.* 5 vols. Chicago: The University of Chicago Press.

Labunski, Richard. 2006. *James Madison and the Struggle for the Bill of Rights.* New York: Oxford University Press.

Levy, Leonard W. 1999. *Origins of the Bill of Rights.* New Haven, CT: Yale University Press.

Liddle, William D. 1979. "'A Patriot King or None': Lord Bolingbroke and the American Renunciation of George III." *The Journal of American History* 65 (March): 951-970.

[Lind, John]. 1776. *An Answer to the Declaration of the American Congress.* London: J. Walter, Charingcross and T. Sewell.

Locke, John. 1955. *Of Civil Government: Second Treatise.* Chicago: Henry Regnery Company.

Looney, J. Jefferson. 2004. "Thomas Jefferson's Last Letter." *The Virginia Magazine of History and Biography* 112:178-184.

Lutz, Donald S. 1992. *A Preface to American Political Theory.* Lawrence: University Press of Kansas.

McCarthy, Finbarr. 1995. "Participatory Government and Community Property: Two Radical Concepts in the Virginia Charter of 1606." *University of Richmond Law Review* 29 (March): 327-380.

McDonnell, Michael A. 1998. "Popular Mobilization and Political Culture in Revolutionary Virginia: The Failure of the Minutemen and the Revolution from Below." *The Journal of American History* 85 (December): 946-981.

McGill, Kathy O. 2017. "A Meteor and a Generous Mind: The Revolutionary Political Thought of Thomson Mason," *The Virginia Magazine of History and Biography* 125: 98-137.

McLaughlin, Andrew C. 1962 [1905]. *The Confederation and the Constitution, 1783-1789.* New York: Collier Books.

Madison, James. 1962. *The Papers of James Madison,* ed. by William T. Hutchinson, et al. 17 vols. Chicago: University of Chicago Press; Charlottesville: University Press of Virginia.

Maier, Pauline. 1997. *American Scripture: Making the Declaration of Independence.* New York: Alfred A. Knopf.

Maier, Pauline. 2011. *Ratification: The People Debate the Constitution, 1787-1788.* New York: Simon & Schuster.

Maier, Pauline. 1999. "John Randolph Tucker Lecture: The Strange History of 'All Men Are Created Equal,'" *Washington & Lee Law Review* 56 (Summer): 873-888.

Marshall, Peter. 1965. "Lord Hillsborough, Samuel Wharton and the Ohio Grant, 1769-1775." *The English Historical Review* 80 (October): 717-739.

Martin, Thomas S. 1986. "The Long and the Short of It: A Newspaper Exchange on the Massachusetts Charters, 1772." *The William and Mary Quarterly* 43 (January): 99-110.

Mason, George. *The Papers of George Mason, 1725-1792,* ed. Robert A. Rutland. 3 vols. Chapel Hill: The University of North Carolina Press, 1970), pp. 65-72. [Cited throughout this book as *PGM*].

Mason, John. 2004, *The Recollections of John Mason: George Mason's Son Remembers His Father and Life at Gunston Hall.* Ed. Terry K. Dunn. Epm Publishers.

Meyers, Marvin, ed. 1973. *The Mind of the Founder: Sources of the Political Thought of James Madison.* Indianapolis: The Bobbs-Merrill Company, Inc.

Meyerson, Michael I. 2012. *Endowed by Our Creator: The Birth of Religious Freedom in America.* New Haven: Yale University Press.

Morris, Richard B. 1985. "The Mount Vernon Conference: First Step Toward Philadelphia." *this Constitution,* no. 6 (Spring): 38-49.

Munves, James. 1978. *Thomas Jefferson and the Declaration of Independence: The writing and editing of the document that marked the birth of the United States of America.* New York: Charles Scribner's Sons.

O'Connor, John F. 1995. "The Emoluments Clause: An Anti-Federalist Intruder in a Federalist Constitution." *Hofstra Law Review* 24 (Fall): 89-178.

Oliver, George Brown. 1959. *A Constitutional History of Virginia 1776-1860.* Diss. for Doctorate of Philosophy in Department of History in the Graduate School of Arts and Sciences at Duke University.

Olson, Alison G. 1982. "The London Mercantile Lobby and the Coming of the American Revolution." *The Journal of American History* 69 (June): 21-41.

_____. 1983. "The Virginia Merchants of London: A Study in Eighteenth-Century Interest-Group Politics." *The William and Mary Quarterly* 40 (July): 363-388.

Paine, Thomas. 1958. *Common Sense and Other Political Writings.* New York: The Liberal Arts Press.

Paine, Thomas. *Common Sense* [1776]. *Classics of American Political & Constitutional Thought,* vol. 1, *Origins through the Civil War,* ed. By Scott J. Hammond, Kevin R. Hardwick and Howard L. Lubert. Indianapolis, IN: Hackett Publishing Company, Inc., 2007), pp. 267-280.

Parkinson, Robert G. 2016. *The Common Cause: Creating Race and Nation in the American Revolution.* Chapel Hill: University of North Carolina Press.

Pendleton, Edmund. 1967. *The Letters and Papers of Edmund Pendleton 1734-1803,* ed. by David John Mays. Charlottesville: The University Press of Virginia.

Pittman, R. Carter. 1960. "Review of Sources of Our Liberties by Richard L. Perry." *The Virginia Magazine of History and Biography* 68 (January): 109-112.

Randolph, Edmund. 1936. "Edmund Randolph's Essay on the Revolutionary History of Virginia 1774-1781 (Continued)." *The Virginia Magazine of History and Biography* 44 (January): 35-50.

"Report on Address to the States by Congress." April 25, 1983. Founders Online. https://founders.archives.gov/documents/Madison/01-06-02-0180.

Revolutionary Virginia, The Road to Independence. 1983. ,Vol VII, Part One *Independence and the Fifth Convention, 1776,* ed. Brent Tarter. Charlottesville: University Press of Virginia.

Rowland, Kate Mason. 1892. *The Life of George Mason, 1725-1792.* 2 vols. New York: Russell & Russell, Inc.

Rowland, Kate Mason. 1893. "The Ohio Company." *The William and Mary Quarterly* 2 (April): 197-203.

Rutland, Robert A. 1961. *George Mason: Reluctant Statesman.* Williamsburg, VA: Colonial Williamsburg.

Rutland, Robert A. 1976. *George Mason and the War for Independence.* Williamsburg, VA: Virginia Independence Bicentennial Commission.

Sainsbury, John. 1978. "The Pro-Americans of London. 1769 to 1782." *The William and Mary Quarterly* 35 (July): 423-454.

Schlesinger, Arthur M. 1935. "The Colonial Newspapers and the Stamp Act." *The New England Quarterly* 8 (March): 63-83.

Schlesinger, Arthur M. 1964. "The Lost Meaning of 'The Pursuit of Happiness,'" *The William and Mary Quarterly* 21 (July): 325-327.

Selby, John E. 1976. "Richard Henry Lee, John Adams, and the Virginia Constitution of 1776." *The Virginia Magazine of History and Biography* 84 (October): 387-400.

Senese, Donald J. 1989. *George Mason and the Legacy of Constitutional Liberty: An Examination of The Influence of George Mason on the American Bill of Rights.* Fairfax, County, VA: Fairfax County Historical Commission.

Shakespeare, William. 1986. *The Complete Works.* Ed. Stanley Wells and Gary Taylor. Oxford: Clarendon Press.

Smith, Robert W. 2014. "Foreign Affairs and the Ratification of the Constitution in Virginia." *The Virginia Magazine of History and Biography* 112: 40-67.

Storing, Herbert J., ed. 1981. *George Mason and George Washington: What the Anti-Federalists Were For.* Vol. 1 of *The Complete Anti-Federalist.* Chicago: The University of Chicago Press.

Sweig, Donald M. 1983. "A New-Found Washington Letter of 1774 and the Fairfax Resolves." *The William and Mary Quarterly* 40 (April): 283-291.

Taylor, Alan. 2016. *American Revolutions: A Continental History, 1750-1804.* New York: W.W. Norton & Company.

Trenchard, John and Thomas Gordon. *Cato's Letters: or, Essays on Liberty Civil and Religious, and other Important Subjects.* Four volumes in two. Ed. Ronald Hamowy. Indianapolis: Liberty Fund. 1995.

Tucker, St. George. 2013. *St. George Tucker's Law Reports and Selected Papers 1782-1825,* 3 vols. Ed. Charles F. Hobson. Chapel Hill: University of North Carolina Press.

Varga, Nicholas. 1954. "The English Parliament's Authority over Virginia before the Restoration." *The Virginia Magazine of History and Biography* 62 (July): 281-288.

Vile, John R. 2016. *The Constitutional Convention of 1787: A Comprehensive Encyclopedia of America's Founding.* Rev. 2nd edition. 2 vols. Clark, NJ: Talbot Publishing.

Vile, John R. 2016. *Conventional Wisdom: The Alternate Article V Mechanism for Proposing Amendments to the U.S. Constitution.* Athens: The University of Georgia Press.

_____. 1992. *The Constitutional Amending Process in American Political Thought.* New York: Praeger.

_____. 2015b. *Encyclopedia of Constitutional Amendments, Proposed Amendments, and Amending Issues, 1789-2015.* 4th ed. 2 vols. Santa Barbara, CA: ABC-CLIO.

_____. 2015c. *Founding Documents of America: Documents Decoded.* Santa Barbara, CA: ABC-CLIO.

_____. 2015d. *The Wisest Council in the World: Restoring the Character Sketches by William Pierce of Georgia of the Delegates to the Constitutional Convention of 1787.* Athens: The University of Georgia Press.

Wallenstein, Peter. 1994. "Flawed Keepers of the Flame: The Interpreters of George Mason," *The Virginia Magazine of History and Biography* 102 (April): 229-260.

Washington, Henry Augustine. 1852. *The Virginia Constitution of 1776: A Discourse Delivered Before the Virginia Historical Society at their Annual Meeting.* Richmond: MacFarlane & Fergusson.

Index

ABOUT THE AUTHOR

JOHN R. VILE (Ph.D. in Government, UVA) is Dean of the University Honors College at Middle Tennessee State University. In addition to other books on the U.S. Constitution, the constitutional amending process, civil rights and liberties, and related subjects, his books related to American Founding Fathers include the following: *A Constellation of Great Men: Exploring the Character Sketches by Dr. Benjamin Rush of Pennsylvania of the Signers of the Declaration of Independence* (2019); *The Declaration of Independence: America's First Founding Document in U.S. History and Culture* (2018); *The Constitutional Convention of 1787: A Comprehensive Encyclopedia of America's Founding*, rev. 2nd ed. 2 vols. (2016); *The Wisest Council in the World": Restoring the Character Sketches by William Pierce of Georgia of the Delegates to the Constitutional Convention of 1787* (2015); *The Men Who Made the Constitution: Lives of the Delegates to the Constitutional Convention of 1787* (2013); and *The Making and Ratification of the U.S. Constitution: Practical Virtue in Action* (2012). Vile has also edited a series of four books collecting and decoding documents from America's founding period through the Civil War and Reconstruction periods (2015-2018).

www.ingramcontent.com/pod-product-compliance
Lightning Source LLC
LaVergne TN
LVHW091526200926
848483LV00002B/318
* 9 7 8 1 6 1 6 1 9 6 3 1 8 *